336 (catalog number)
Caravaggio head on
fake wood panel
20 August 1973
Oil on canvas, 14½″ x 11½″

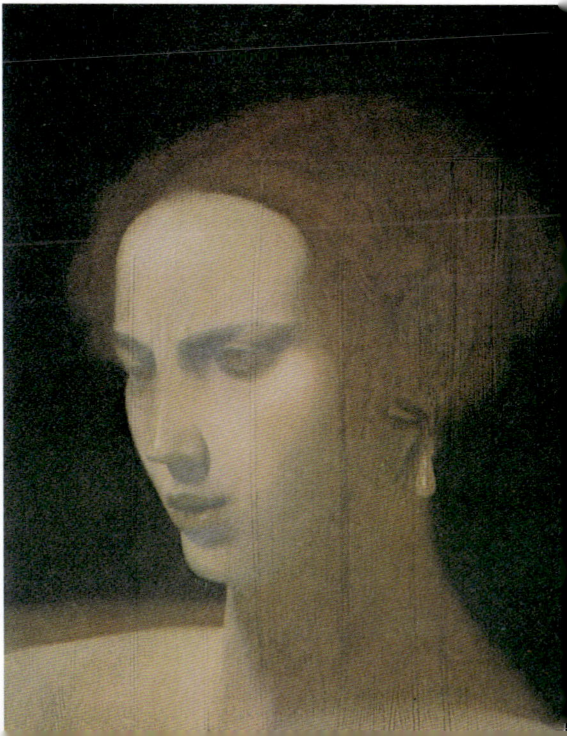

335
Day-Glo poster
6 August 1973
Photo print and acrylic
27"x 18"

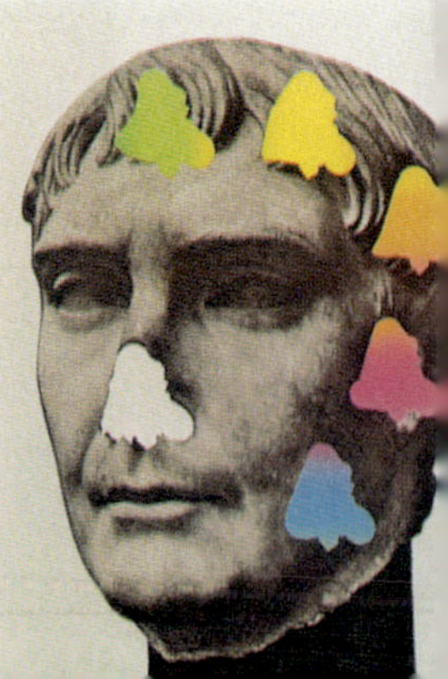

334
Leonard's Landscape
6 August 1973
Oil on canvas, 38½″x 59″

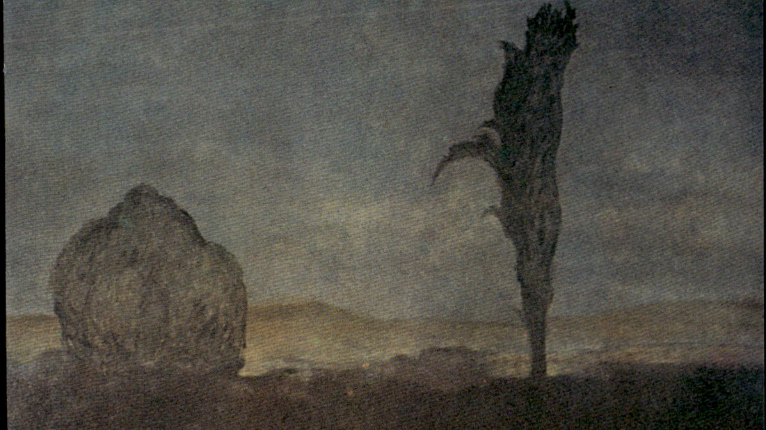

333
Princess restoration
c. 1850 anon.
19 July 1973
Oil on canvas, 18″x 15″

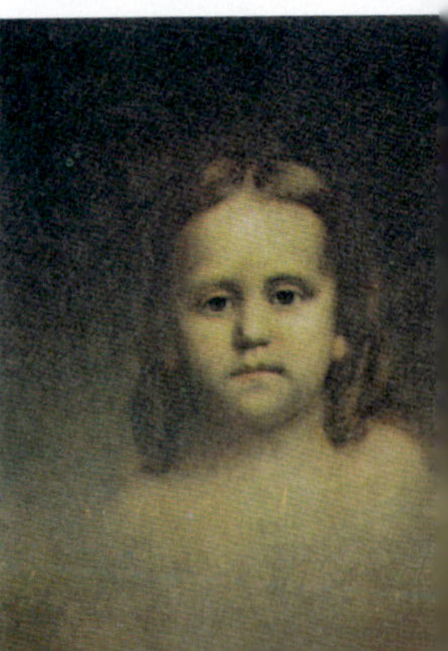

332
Studebaker Crotch
29 July 1973
Oil on canvas
13¾″ x 17½″

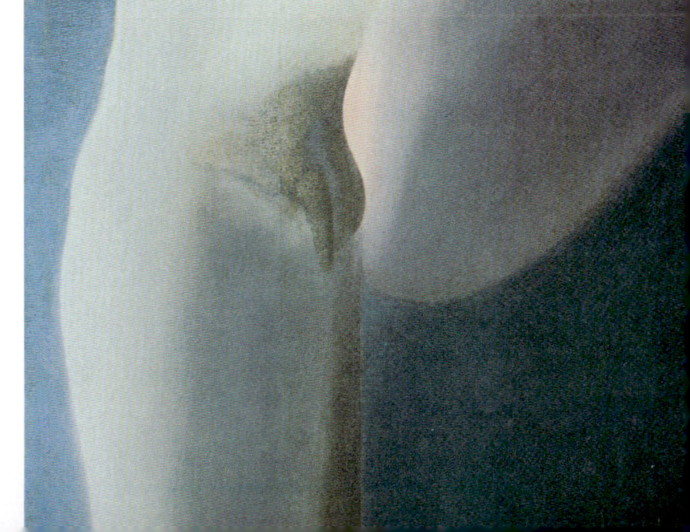

331
White wall with drawing
27 July 1973
Oil on canvas, 25″x 38″

330
Blue door wall
13 May 1973
Oil on canvas
18″x 26″

329
Brick & Blue Wall
13 May 1973
Oil on canvas, 18″x 22½″

328
Door Stop
3 May 1973
Milk chocolate
1¼″x 1¼″x 4″
Edition of 6

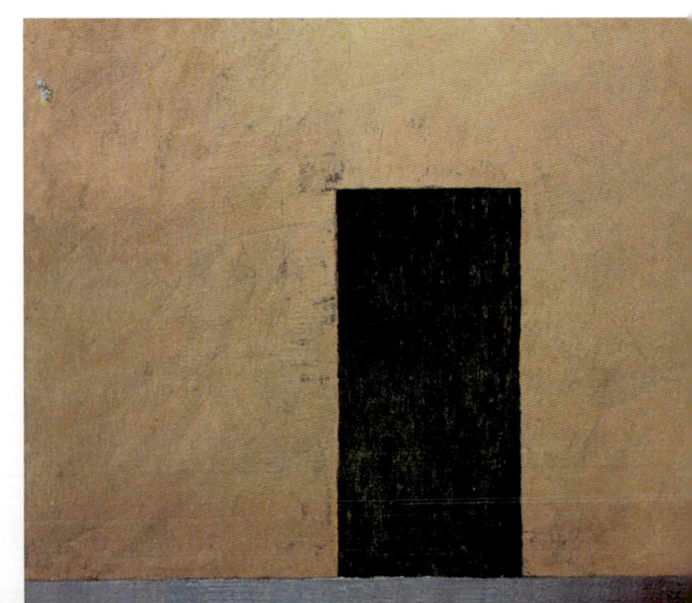

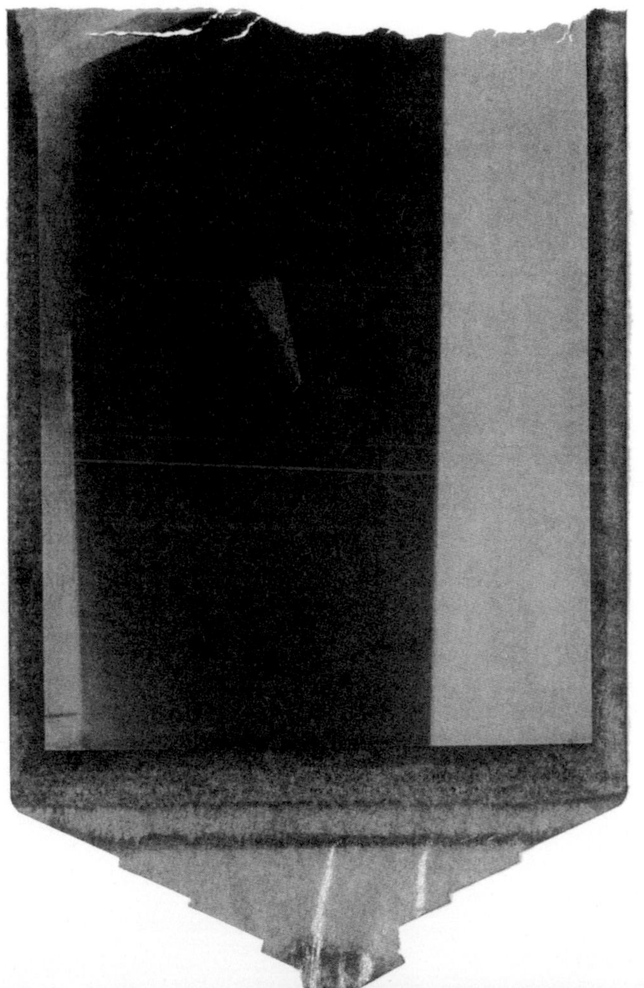

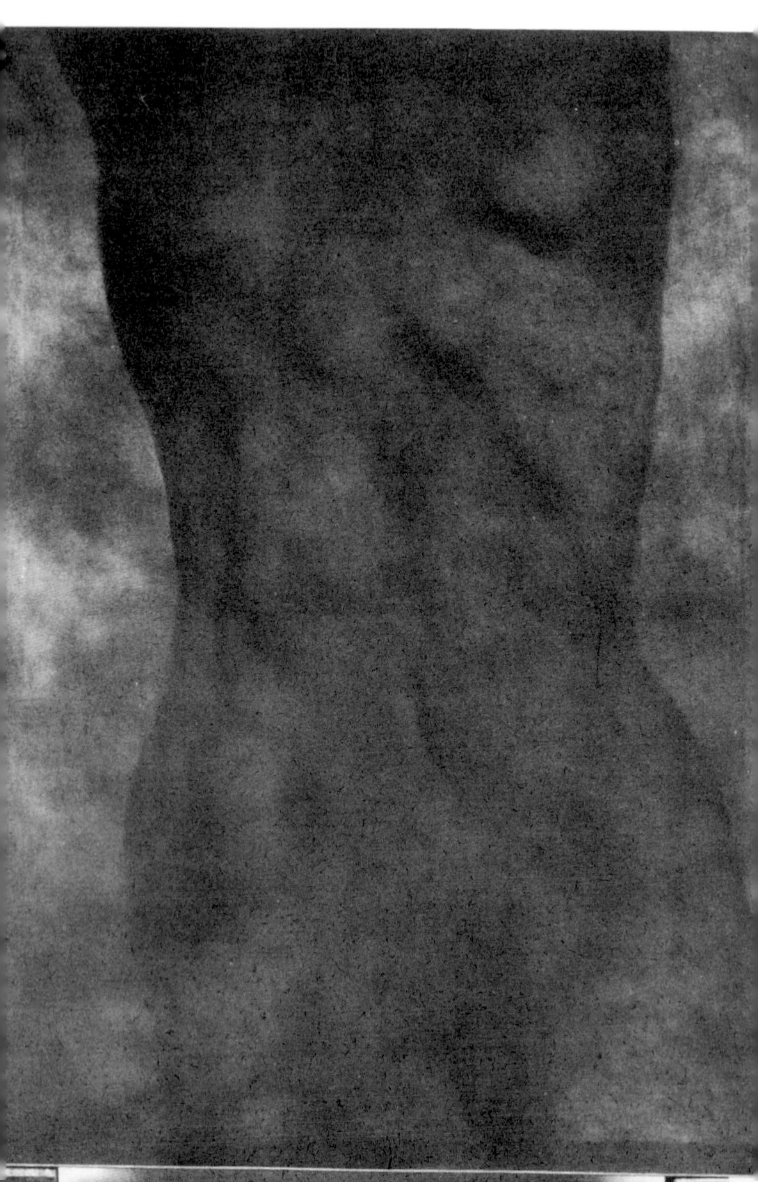

327
Vertical torso with grey edge
1 May 1973
Oil on canvas, 84″ x 60″

326
Big Bertha Torso
30 April 1973
Oil on canvas, 72″ x 60″

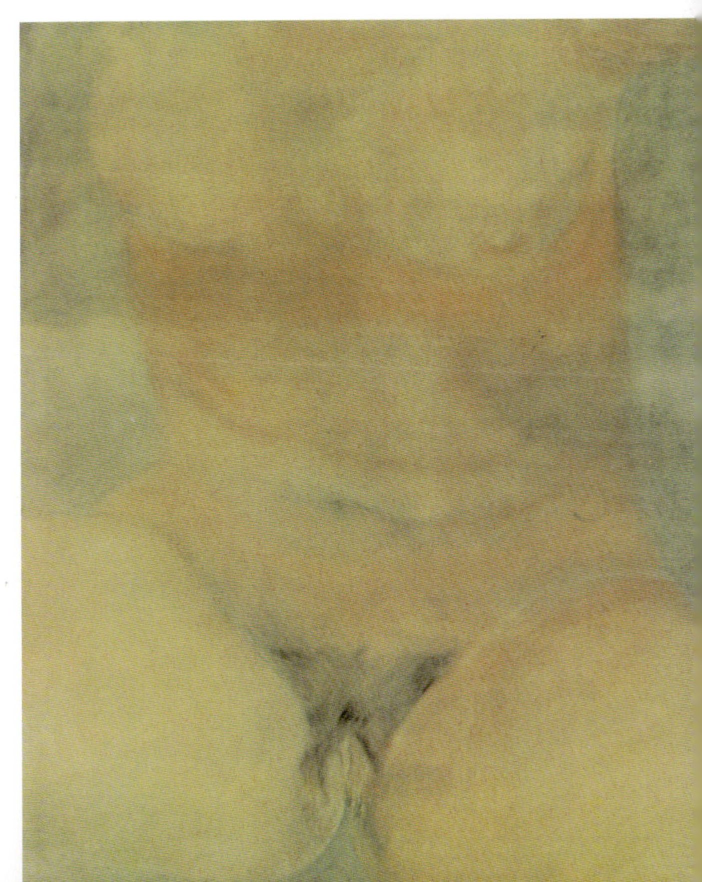

325
Torso with struts
28 April 1973
Oil on canvas, 72″x 96″

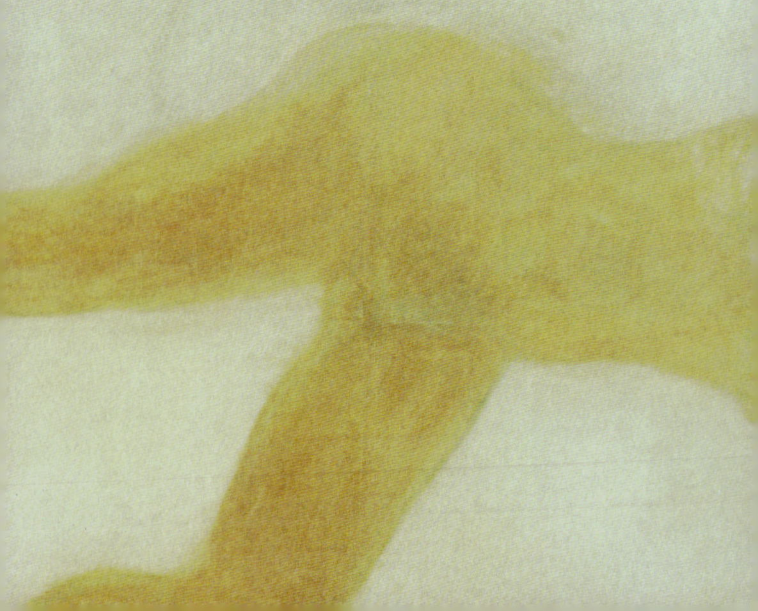

324
Orange and blue torso
23 April 1973
Oil on canvas, 18⅛″ x 18⅛″

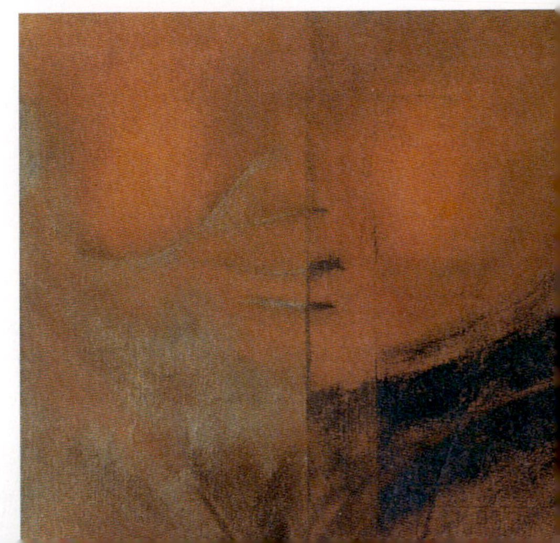

323
Portrait of Bobbi Roberts
15 April 1973
Oil on canvas, 14½″ x 13½″

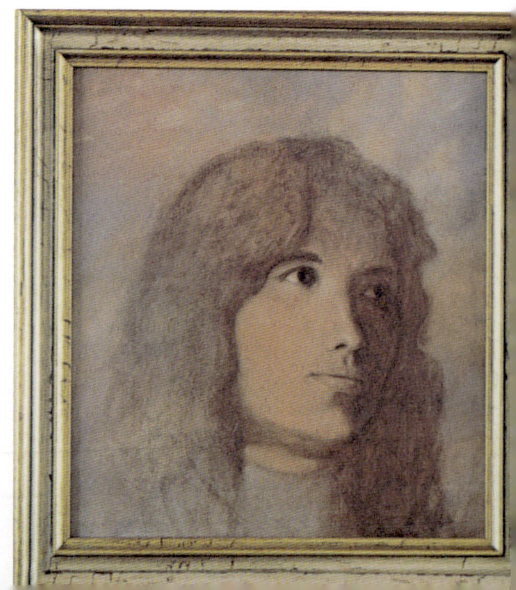

322
Double Head
29 March 1973
Pen on paper
2⅜″ x 2⅛″

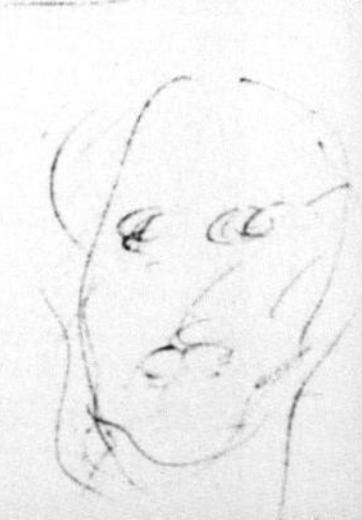

321
Torso with rust edge
25 March 1973
Oil on canvas, 12⅛″x 12¾″

320
Kill a Roach
22 March 1973
Serigraph
23¾″x 32¾″
Issue of 18

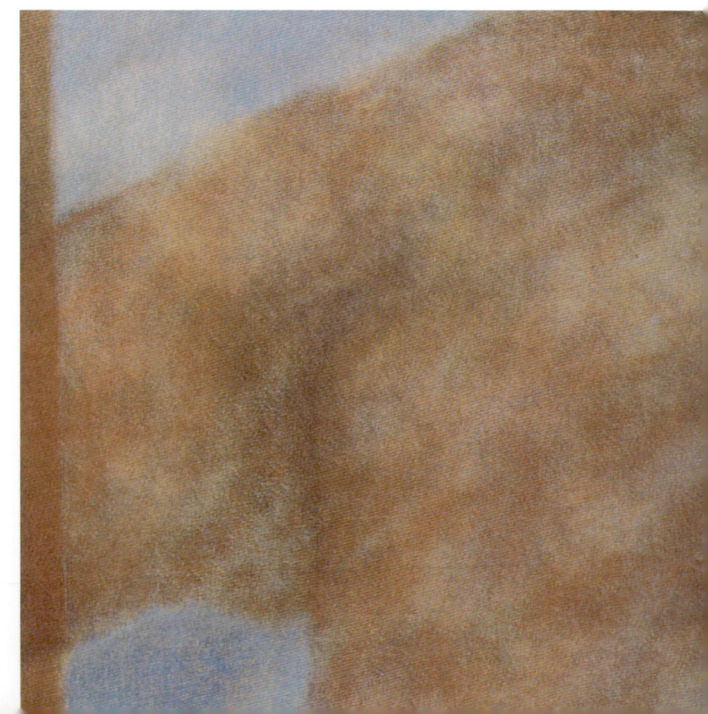

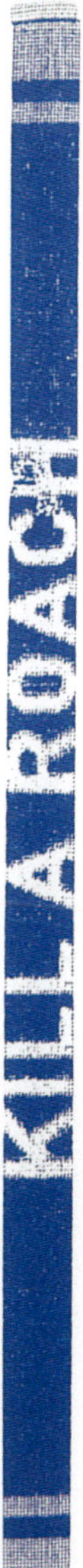

KILL A ROACH

319
TV test pattern
16 February 1973
Latex rubber, 13¼″x 15¾″
Prop for Stretch Video piece

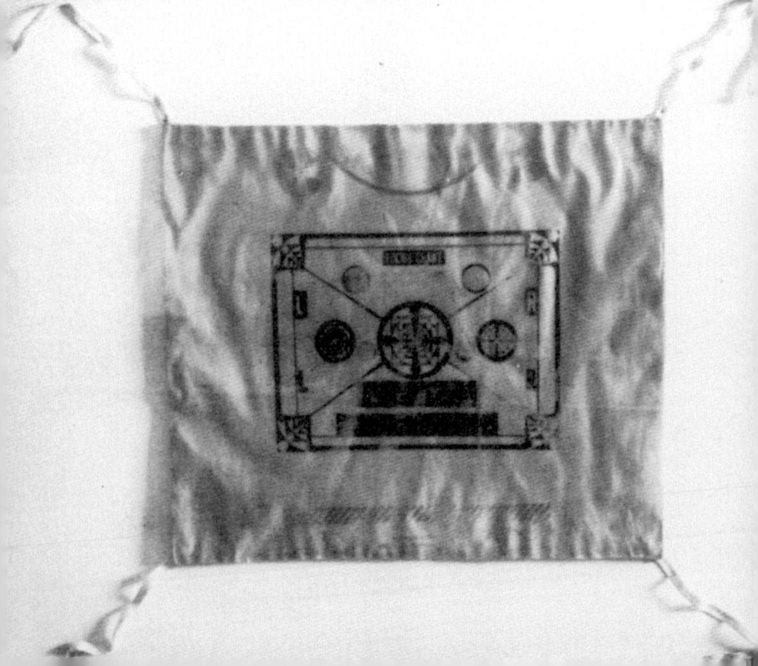

318
Two Faces Head
16 February 1973
Oil on canvas
14¼″ x 11″

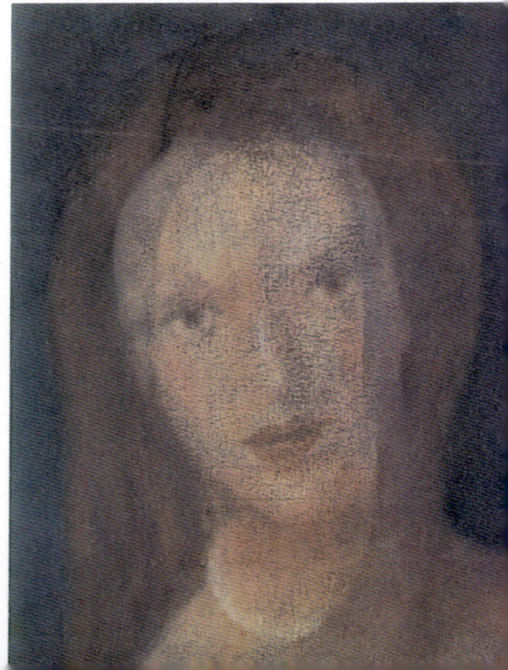

317
Warhol Head
15 February 1973
Oil on canvas
20″ x 16″

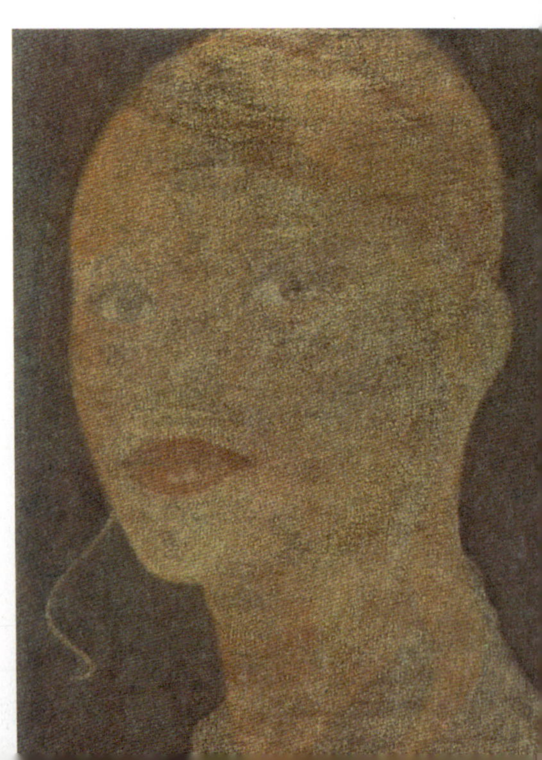

316
Two Rocks
13 February 1973
Oil on canvas
14″x 18″

315
St. Serapion's Collar
12 February 1973
Oil on canvas, 7″x 9″

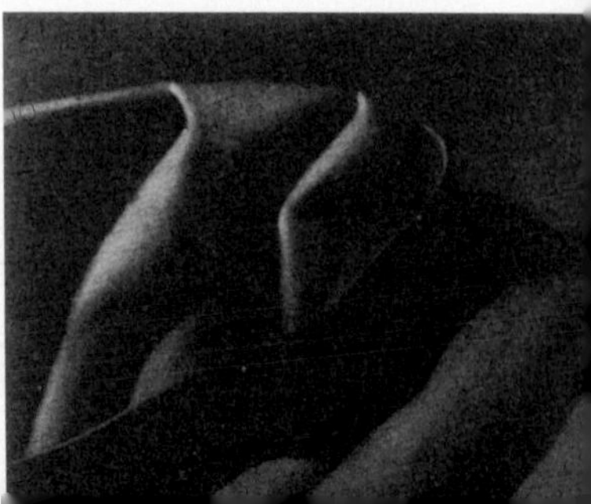

314
Castle Cloud
12 February 1973
Oil on canvas, 14″x 18″

313
Cauliflower Clouds
10 February 1973
Oil on canvas, 14″ x 18″

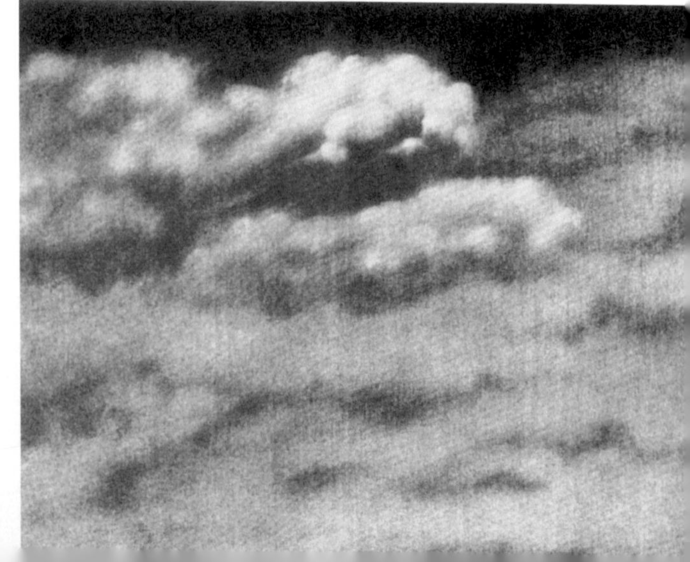

312
Lotto head on test panel
10 February 1973
Oil on canvas, 11½″ x 9½″

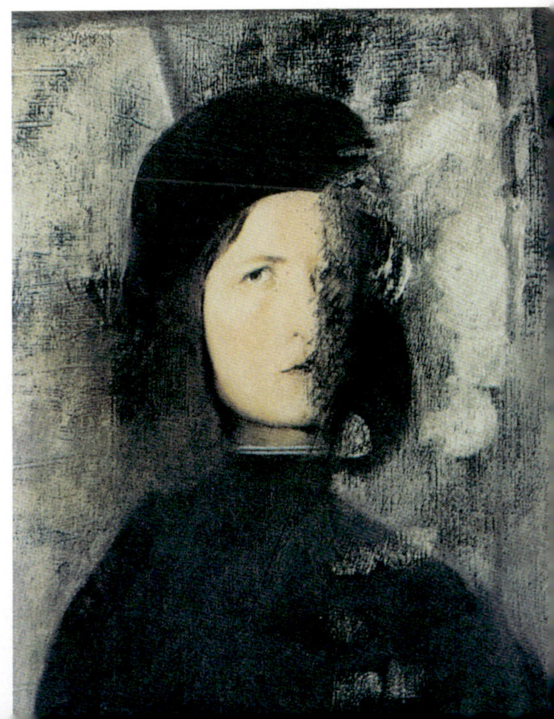

311
Cotan still life
on fake wood panel
5 February 1973
Oil on canvas, 11″x 14½″

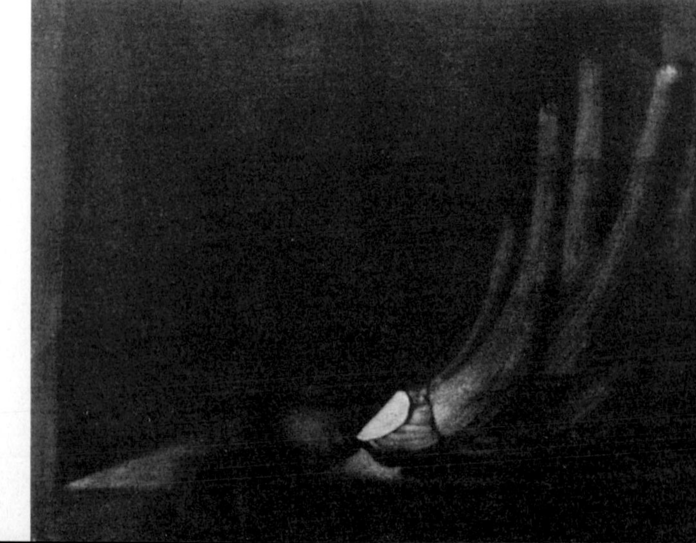

310
Jordaens head on
fake wood panel
20 January 1973
Oil on canvas, 12½″x 11″

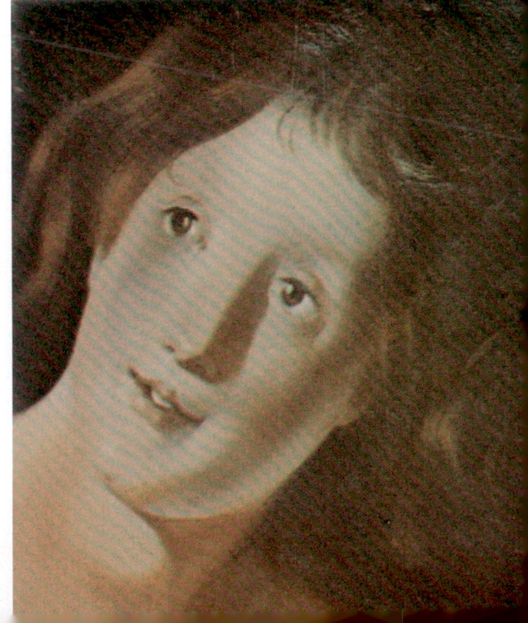

309
Mt. Rainier Navel
17 January 1973
Latex rubber, wood
and copper wire
12⅞″x 13⅝″

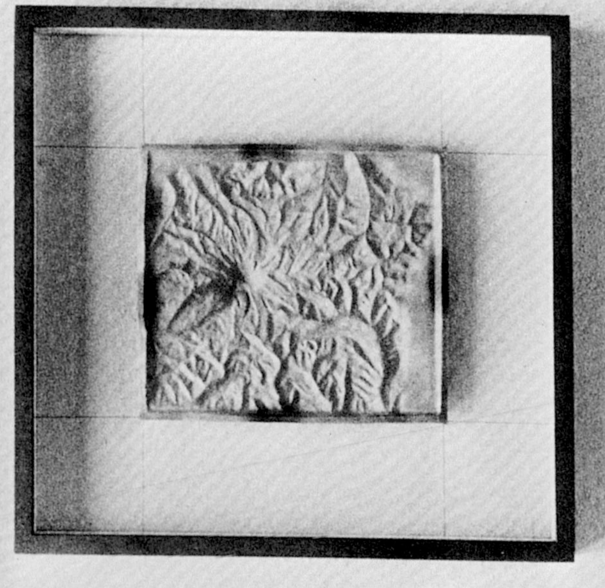

308
Dürer head on
fake wood panel
15 January 1973
Oil on canvas, 14″x 11″

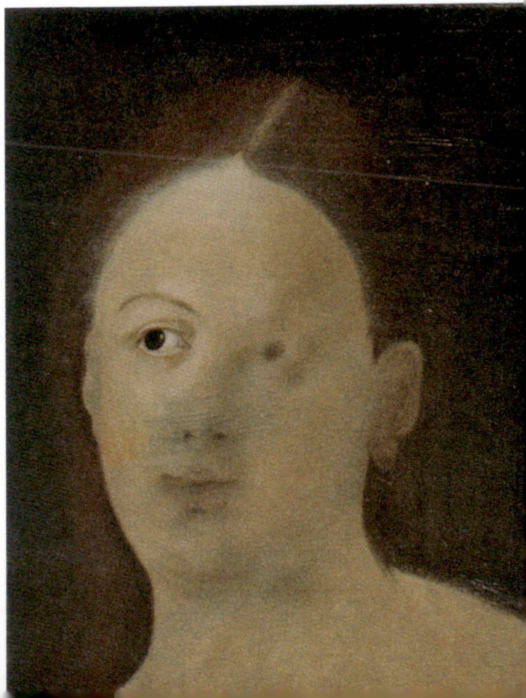

307 (not illustrated)
Wall rubbing No. 2
14 January 1973
Chalk on plaster wall
40″x 53″
Destroyed 15 Sept. 1973

306
Two Tangerines
1 January 1973
Oil on canvas
4¾"x 6"

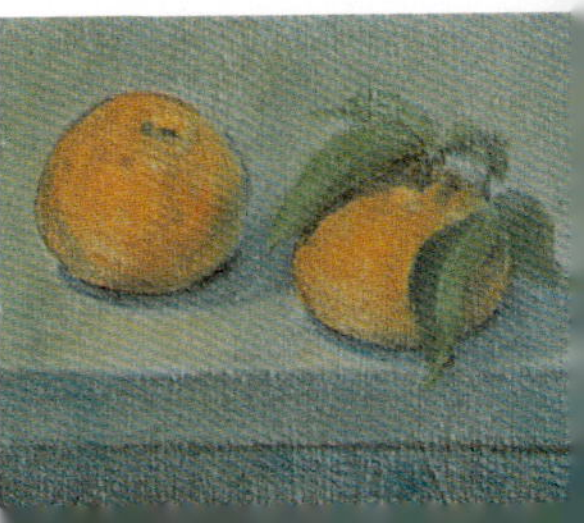

305
One Tangerine
1 January 1973
Oil on canvas
4¼″ x 6¼″

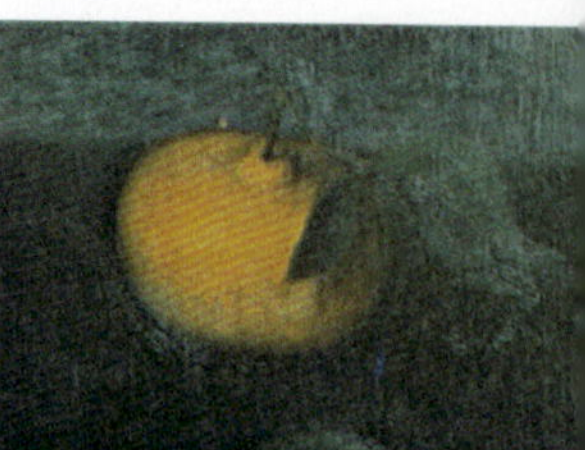

304
Fuzzy Rock
30 December 1972
Oil on canvas
11¾″x 14″

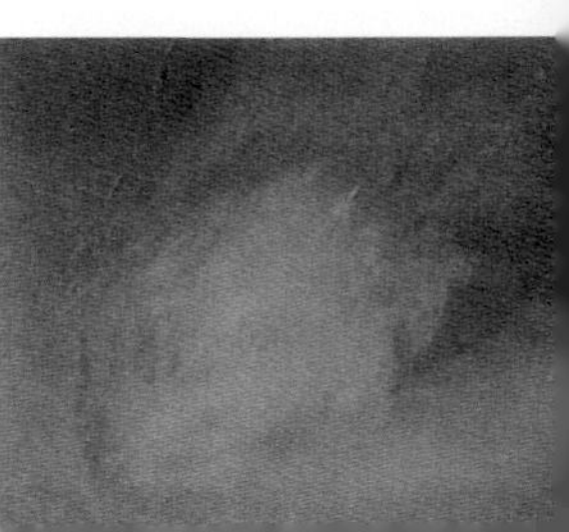

303
Blue Woman
30 December 1972
Oil on canvas, 6″ x 5″

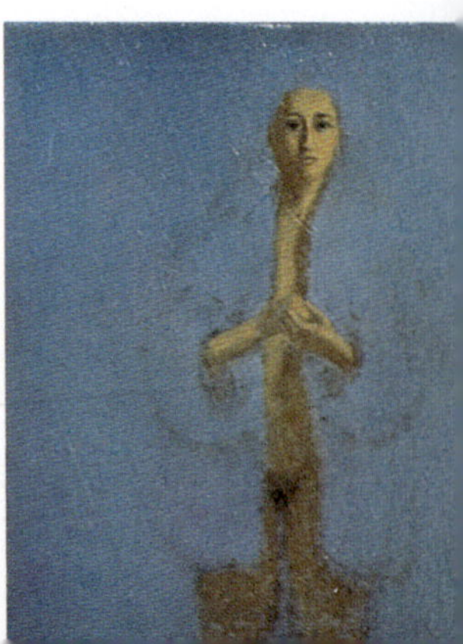

302
Square Tangerines
30 December 1972
Oil on canvas, 4″ x 5¾″

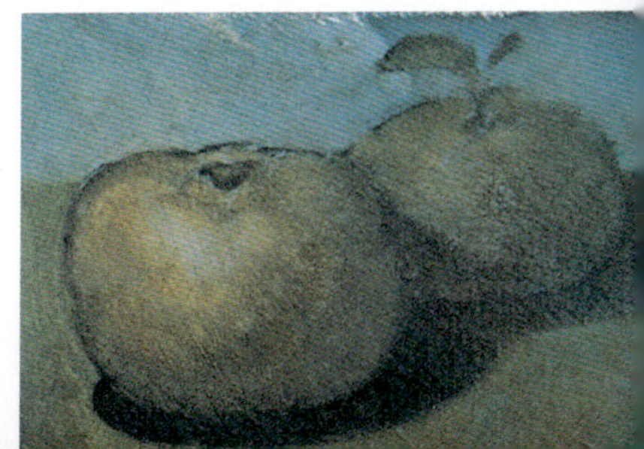

301
Old Man Head
30 December 1972
Oil on canvas, 15″ x 13¼″

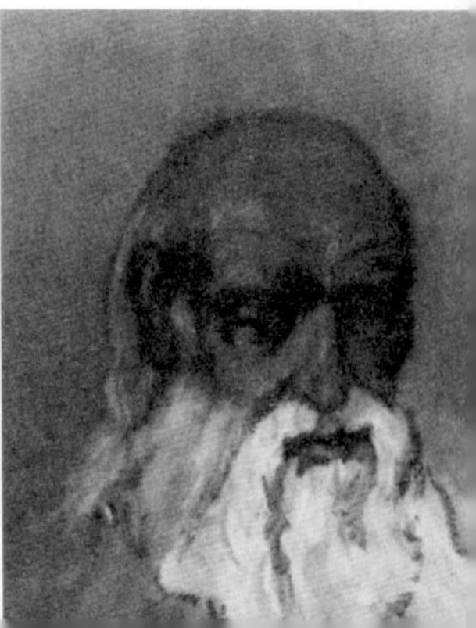

300
Single Cloud
29 December 1972
Oil on canvas, 5″x 6″

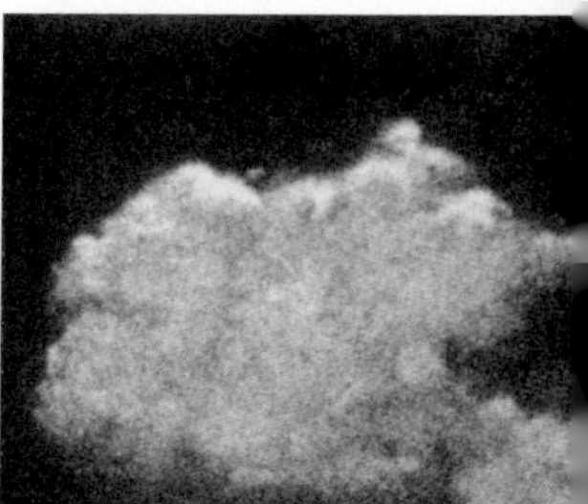

299
Sky Plane
28 December 1972
Oil on canvas
14¼"x 18"

298
4-Square Scrap
28 December 1972
Canvas and latex rubber
71¾″x 70½″

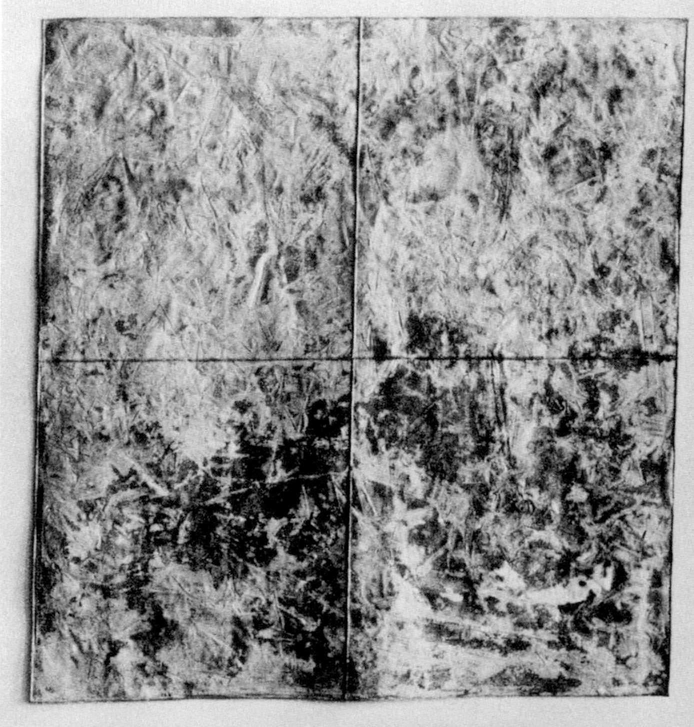

297
Random Scrap
28 December 1972
Canvas and latex rubber
36"x 36"

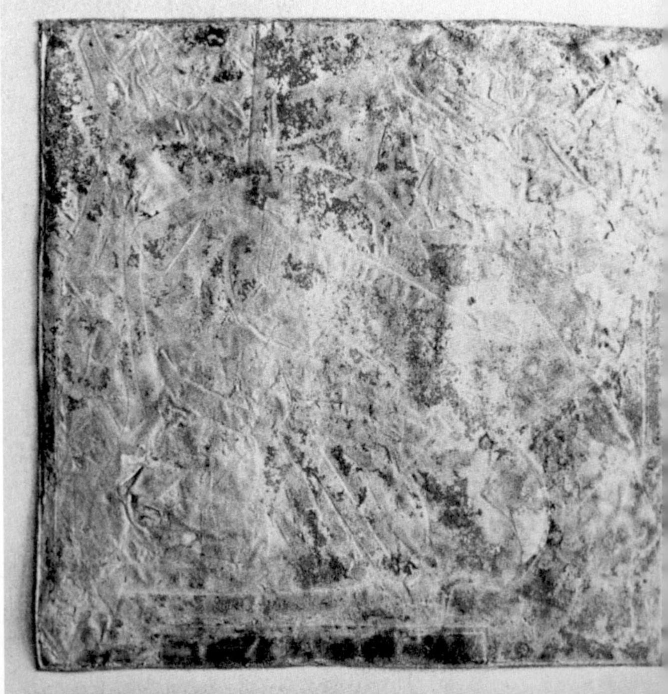

296
Square Scrap
28 December 1972
Canvas and latex rubber
35"x 36"

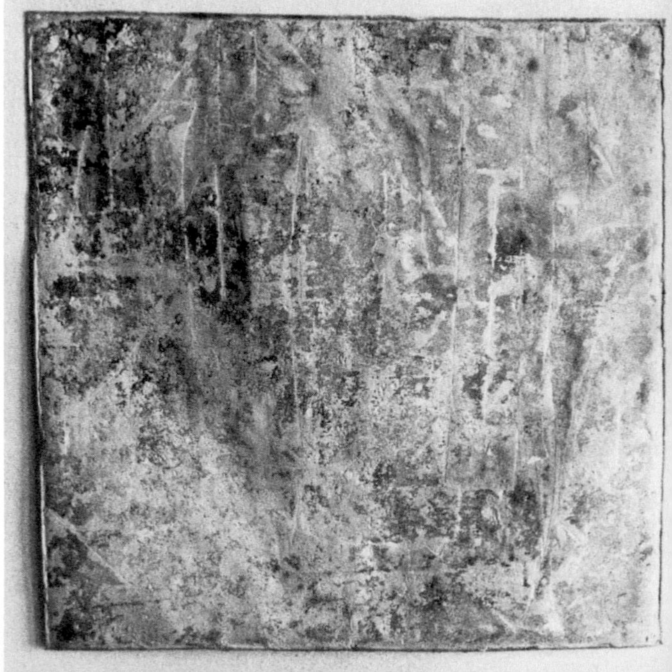

295
Judy's Teeth No. 2
24 December 1972
Oil on canvas, 5¼″ x 5½″

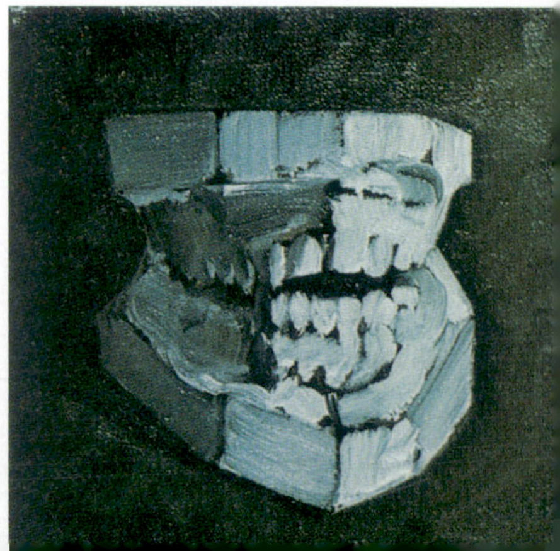

294
Green Tangerine
24 December 1972
Oil on canvas, 7″x 9″

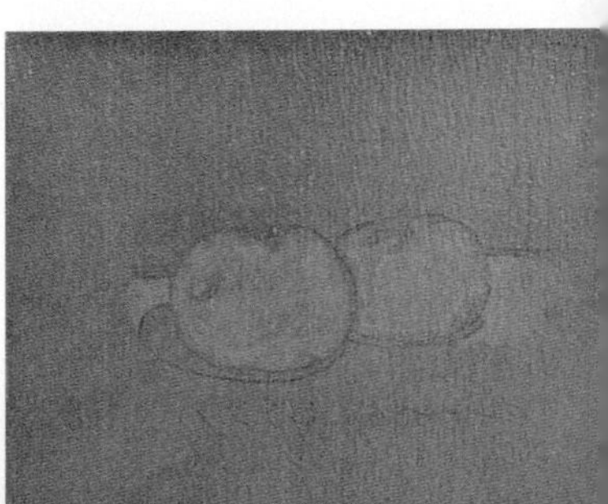

293 (detail)

293
Over the Hill
24 December 1972
Oil on canvas
4¼″ x 5″

292
Roman Tangerine
24 December 1972
Oil on canvas
2¾″ x 4″

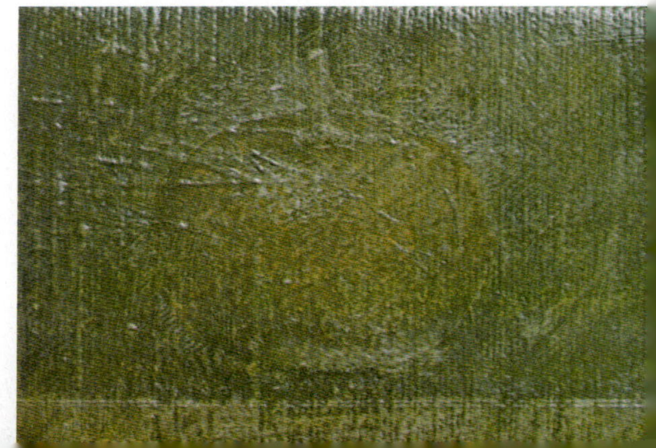

291
Matisse Tangerine
24 December 1972
Oil on canvas, 5″x 4″

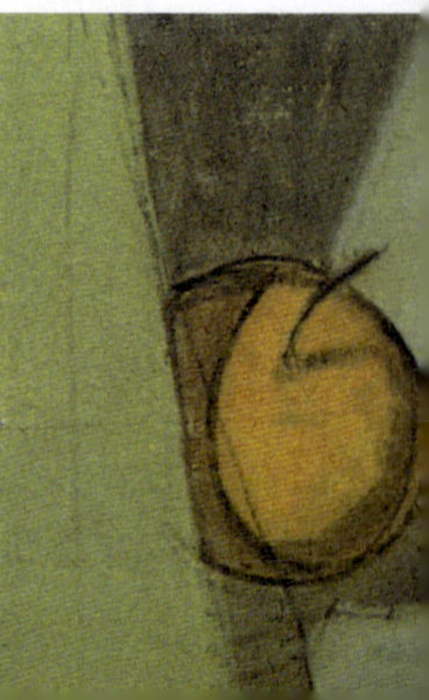

290
Portrait of Jack Ellis
12 December 1972
Oil on canvas, 34″x 28½″

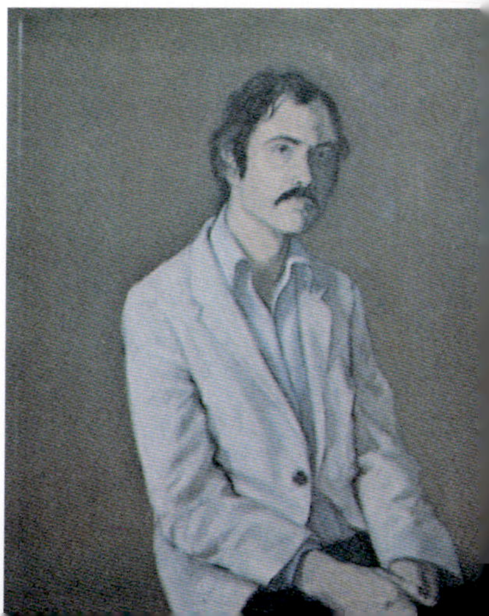

289
Portrait of Bobbi Roberts
10 December 1972
Oil on paper, 23″x 18″

288
Red Wall
6 December 1972
Oil on canvas
17¼″x 27¾″

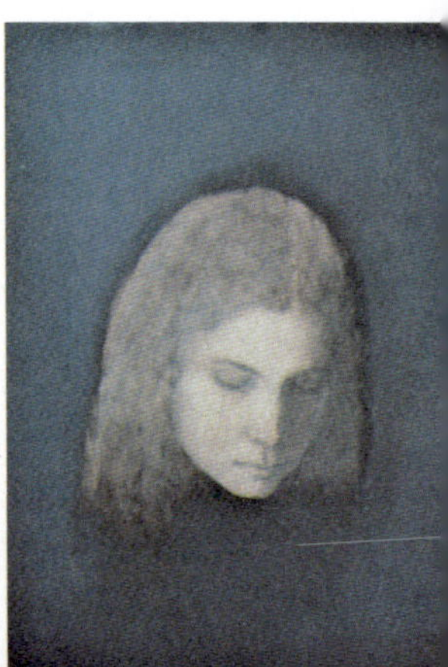

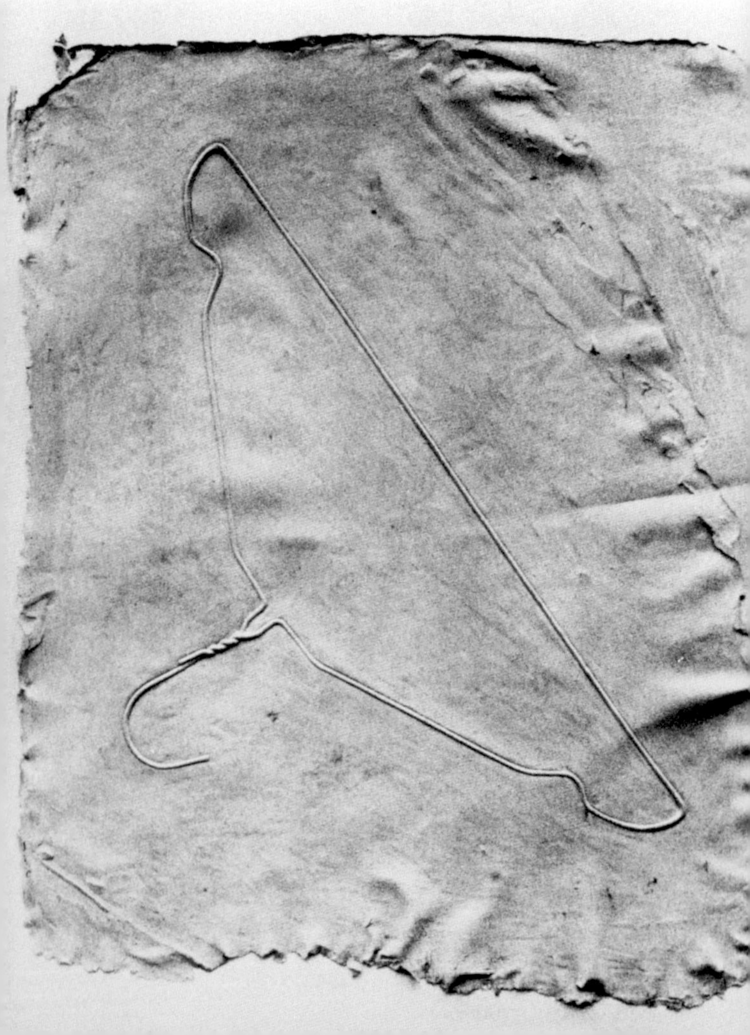

286
Roomscape
4 December 1972
Oil on canvas
24½″x 18″

285
Tit Rock
2 December 1972
Oil on canvas
18″x 22″

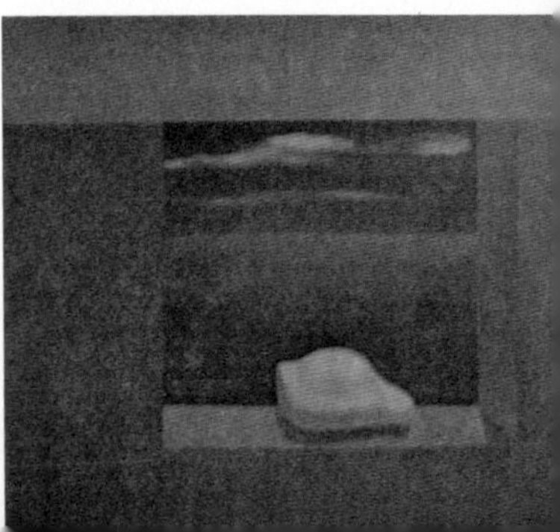

284
Rothko's Kerchief
2 December 1972
Oil on canvas
28″x 28″

283
Dent
2 December 1972
Oil on canvas
18″x 24″

282
Judy's Teeth No. 1
1 December 1972
Oil on canvas, 20″ x 16″
Destroyed 24 Dec. 1972

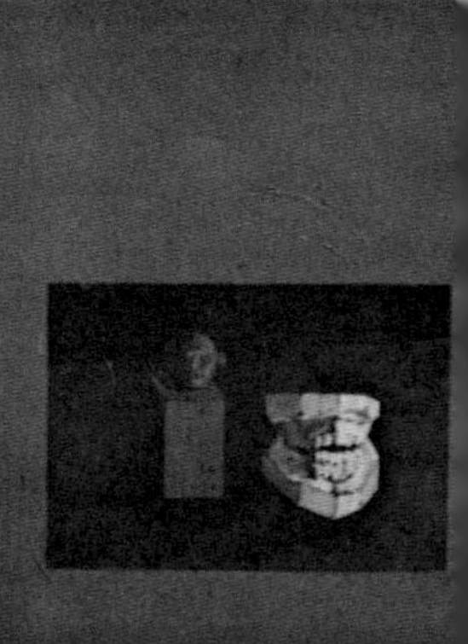

281
Clean Window
28 November 1972
Oil on canvas, 10″ x 16″

280
Portrait of Paul uncorrected before Singapore
22 November 1972
Acrylic and oil on paper, 22¼″x 17½″

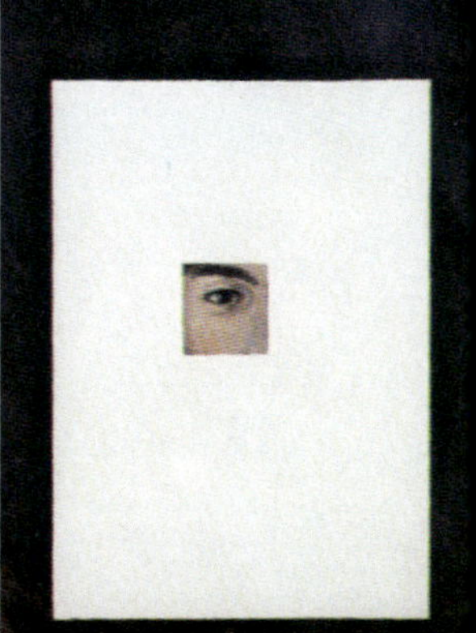

279
Dark Landscape
17 November 1972
Gouache on paper
17"x 23"

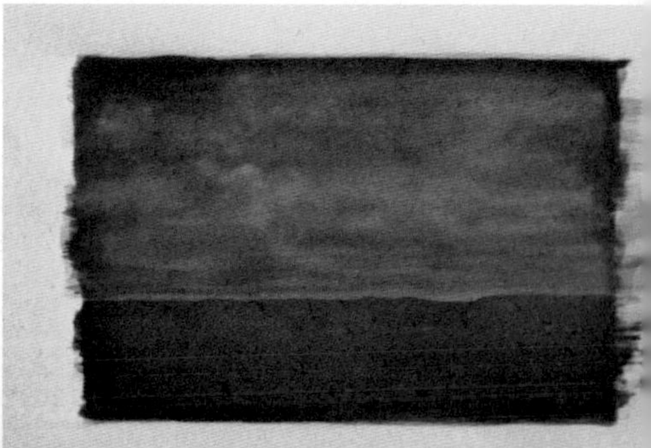

278
B&B Brick Horizon
14 November 1972
Oil on canvas
13¼″x 18¼″

277
Portrait of Paul
8 November 1972
Charcoal on paper
22"x 17"

276
N.Y. color rubbings
5-15 October 1972
Chalk on paper
Series of 14

Bobbi's color rubbing
40"x 27"

Red and green rubbing
27"x 40"

Red and turquoise
vertical rubbing
40"x 27"

Orange and blue
Vertical rubbing
40"x 27"

Orange and blue rubbing
27"x 40"

Red and blue rubbing
27"x 40"

Brown and black rubbings
(2) 23½"x 34½"
(3) 24"x 38"
(4) 24"x 36½"

Brown rubbings
(1) 27"x 40" small drawing
(5) 27"x 40"

B&w color rubbings
(6) 27"x 40"
(7) 27"x 40" for Weber

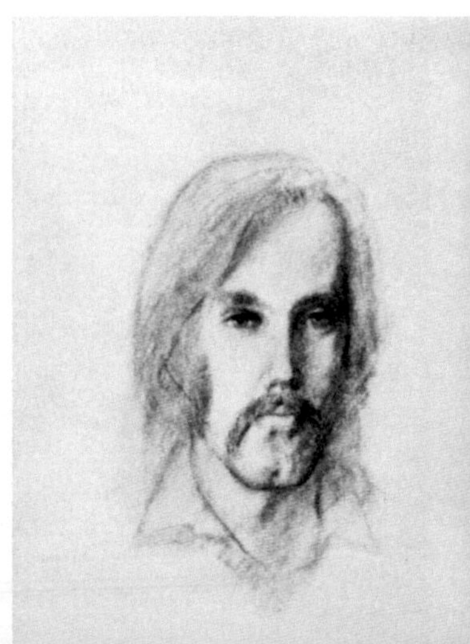

275
N.Y. b&w rubbings
1-11 October 1972
Chalk on paper
Series of 6

First b&w rubbing
27¼"x 51½"

Second b&w rubbing
31"x 54"
Kitchen wall No. 1
63¼"x 30¼"

Living room wall
74"x 28¾"

274
Pink and green door map
5 September 1972
Canvas, 76"x 57¼"

Kitchen wall No. 2
63¼"x 30¼"

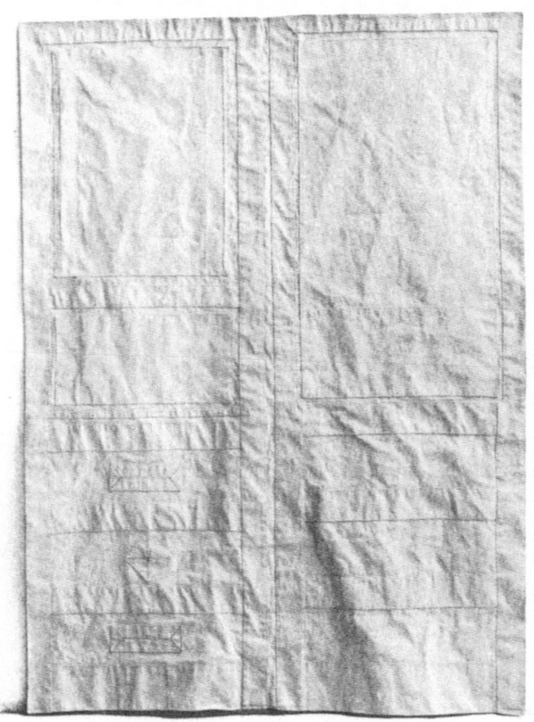

273
School door map
5 September 1972
Canvas
80¼″ x 36¾″

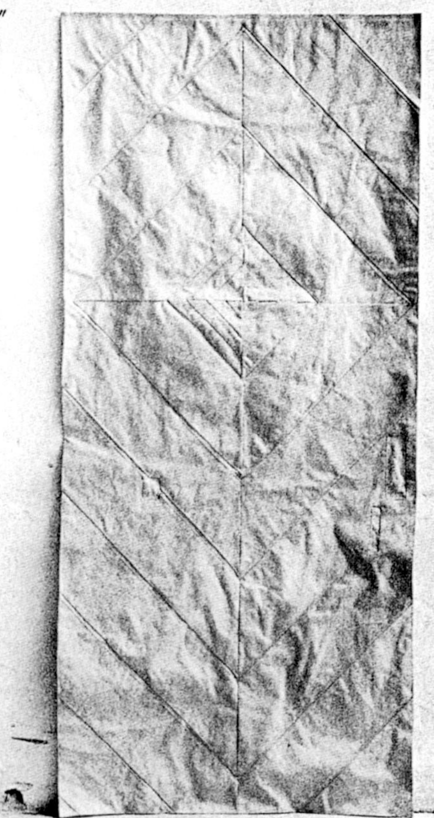

272
Grey wall map
5 September 1972
Canvas

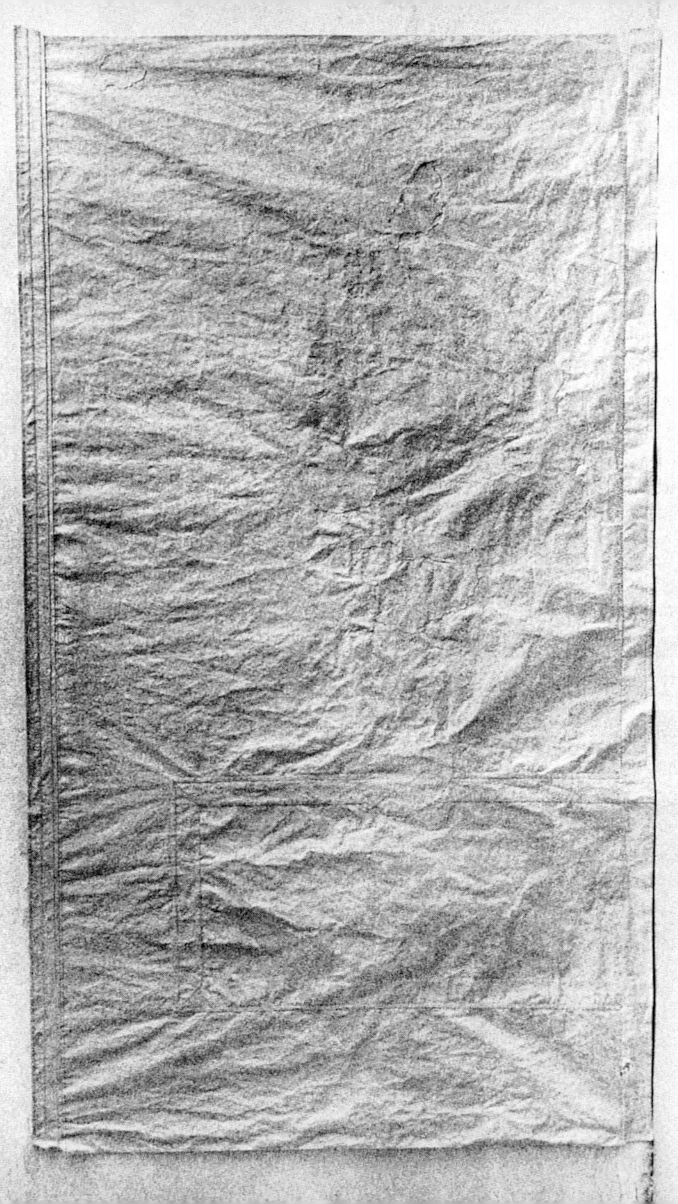

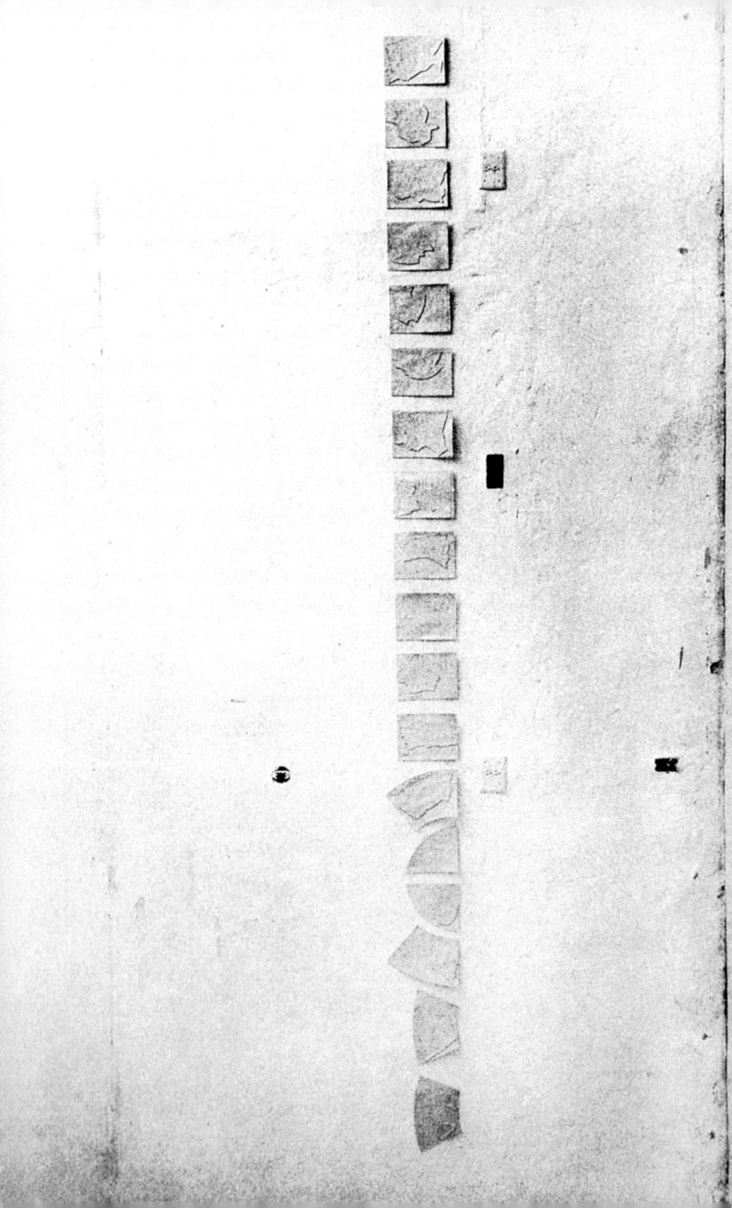

271
Broken window maps
4 September 1972
Canvas
2 panels 9″x 8″
2 panels 13½″x 8½″
2 panels 12″x 9″
12 panels 10½″x 7¾″

270
L.A. window map
2 September 1972
Canvas, 49¼″x 21″

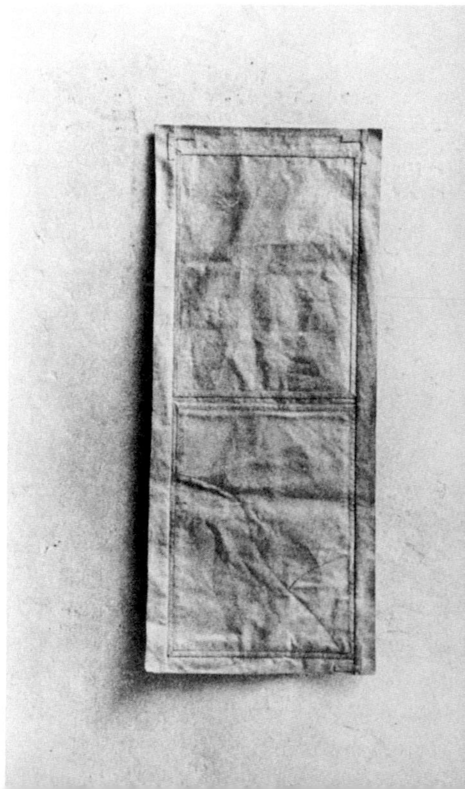

269
Tone-bar room map
30 August 1972
Canvas, 107″ x 116″

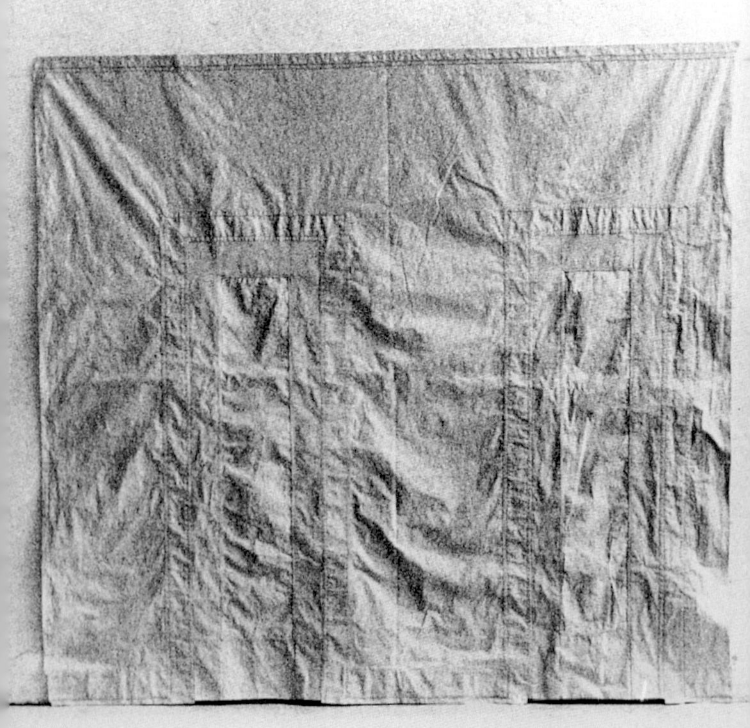

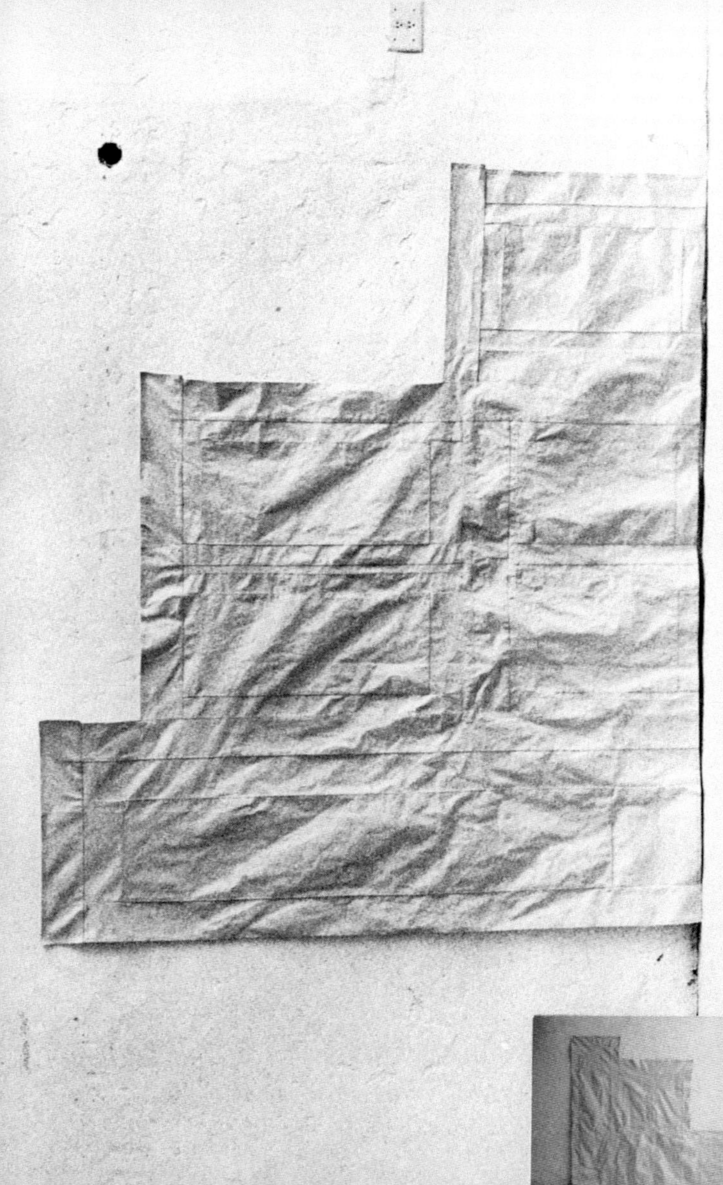

267
Blue screen door map
23 August 1972
Canvas, 74¾″x 31″

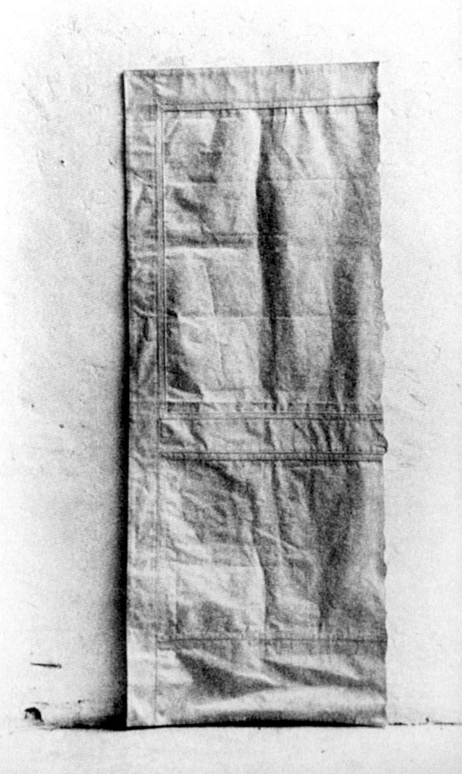

266
Tone-bar door map
21 August 1972
Canvas, 78″x 30″

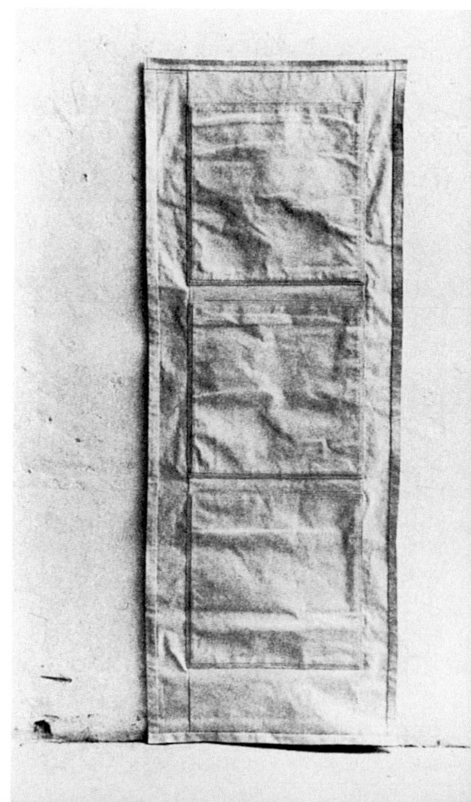

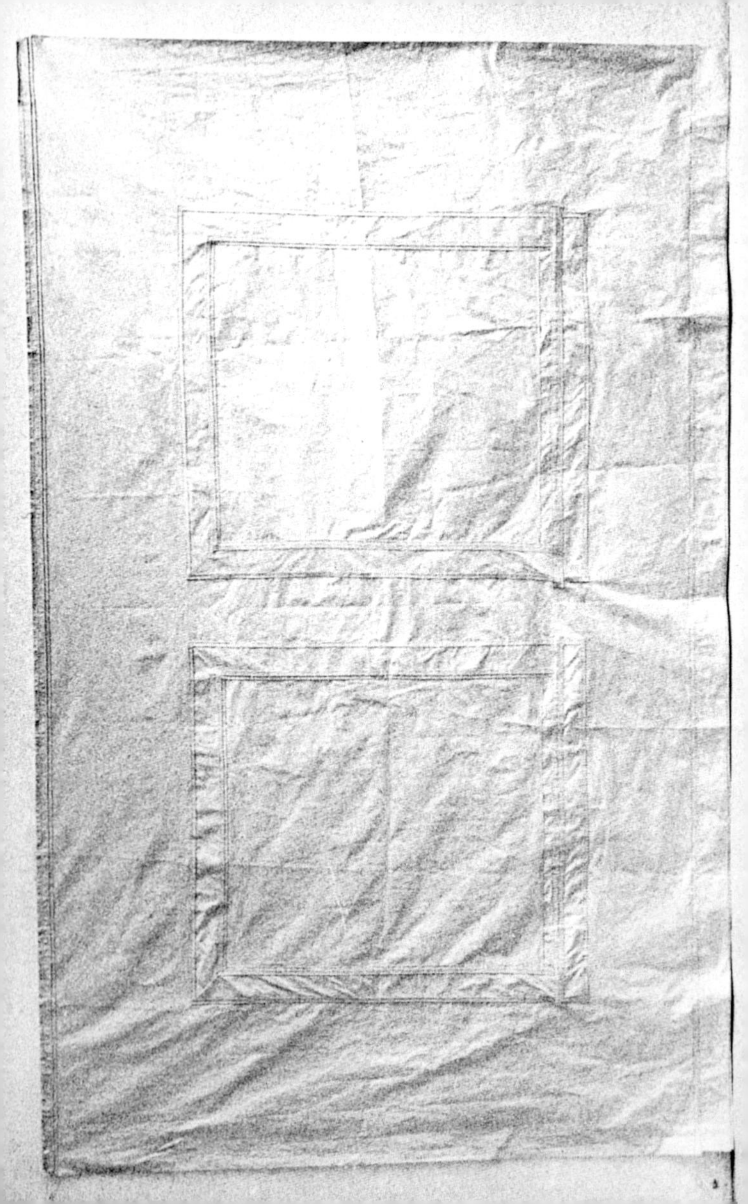

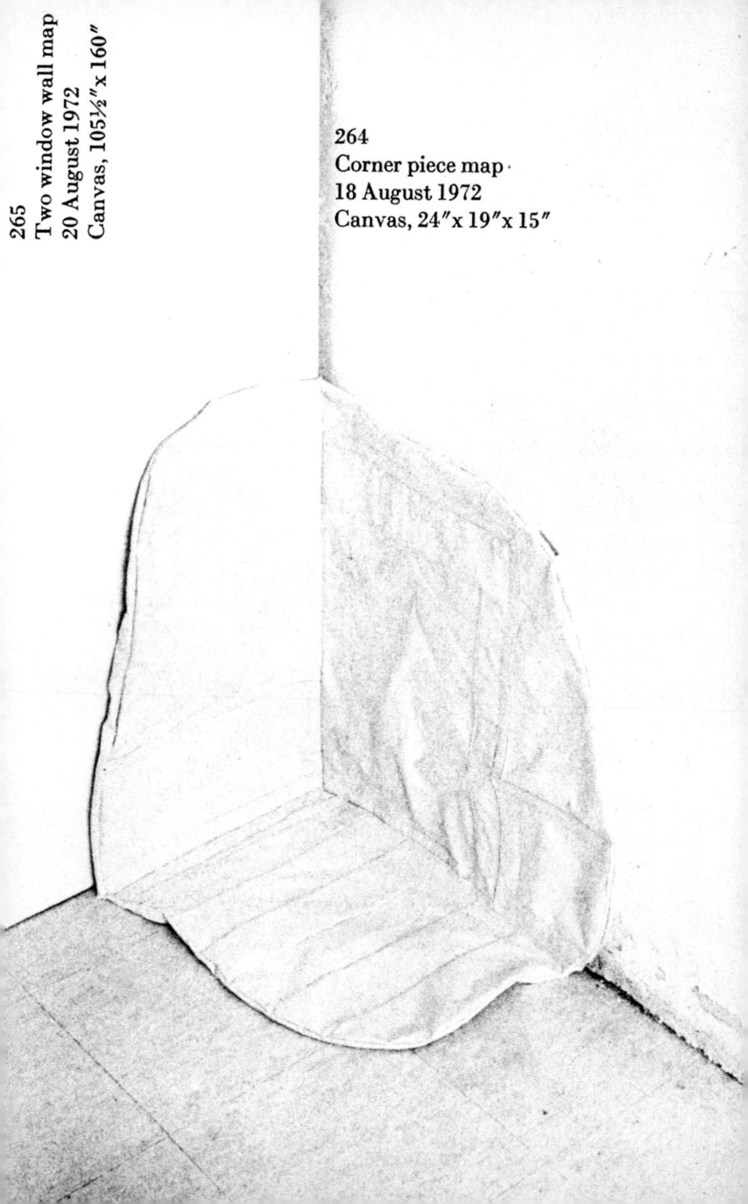

265
Two window wall map
20 August 1972
Canvas, 105½"x 160"

264
Corner piece map
18 August 1972
Canvas, 24"x 19"x 15"

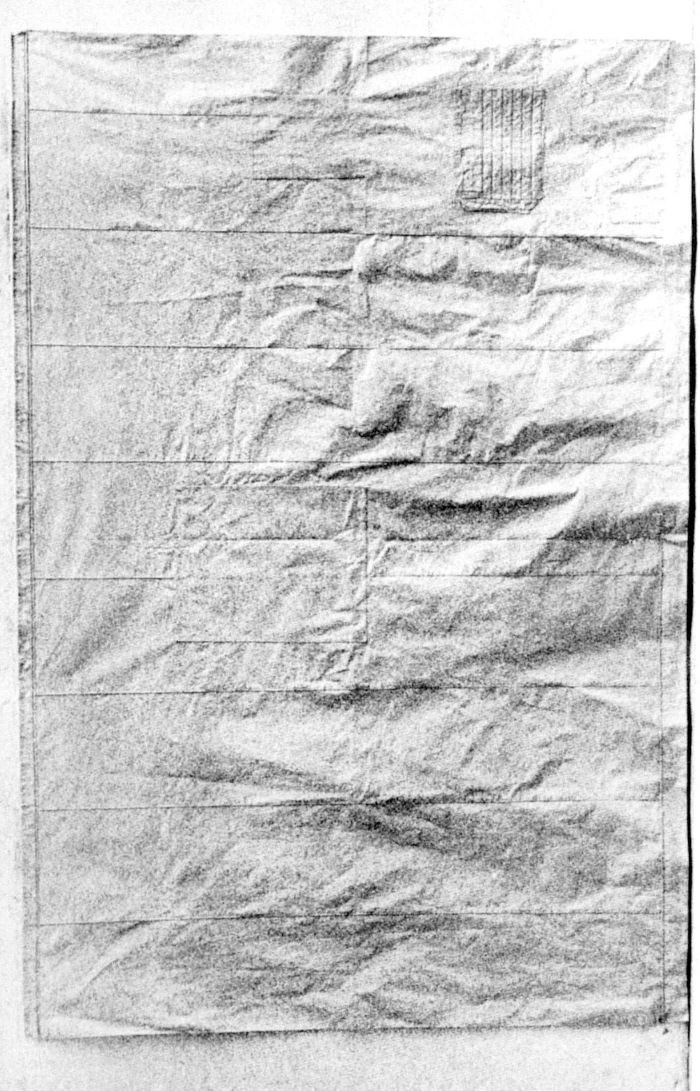

263
Color room wall map
6 August 1972
Canvas, 102½″x 145½″

262
Six brick panels
13 July 1972
Latex rubber

1. 84½″x 77½″
2. 85″x 65¼″
3. 85″x 65″
4. 85½″x 66½″
5. 86½″x 66″
6. 86¼″x 74″

261
Pink and green door
12 July 1972
Latex rubber, 78½″x 61″

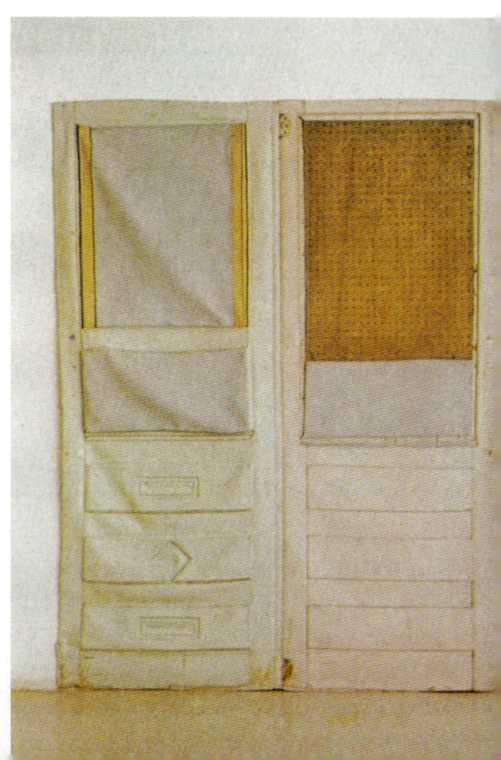

260
Miller's Wall
12 July 1972
Latex rubber
67″ x 80¼″

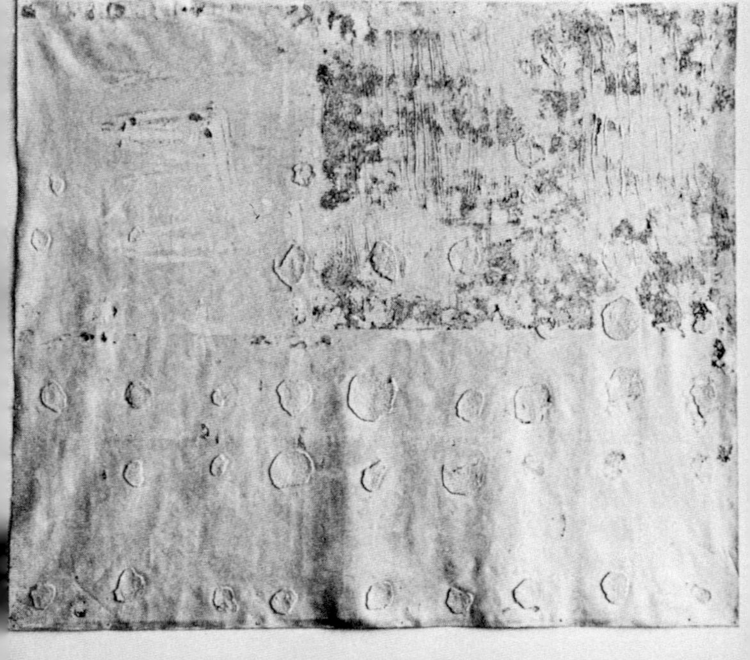

259
Painting with 4 photos
12 July 1972
Latex rubber and photos
23″x 28¼″

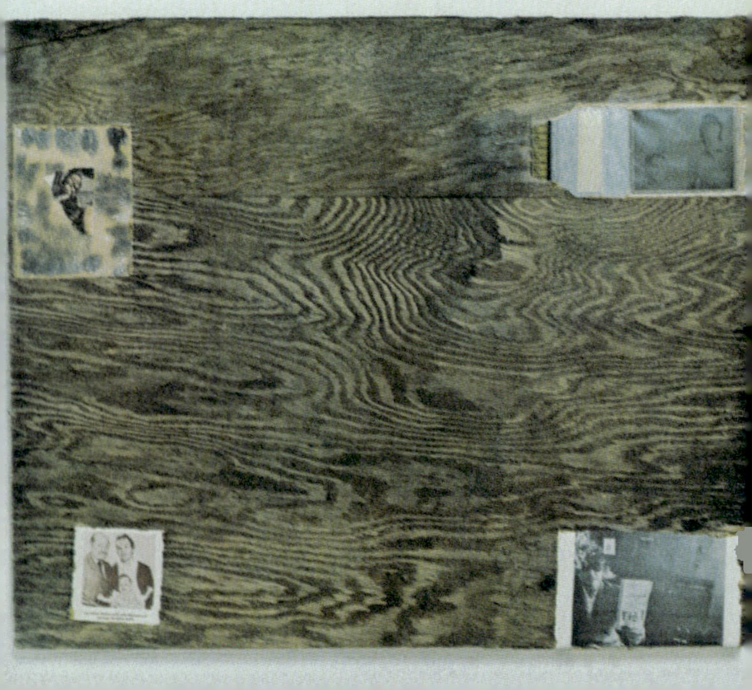

258
Door edges
12 July 1972
Latex rubber

1. 82¾″ x 1½″
2. 83¾″ x 1½″
3. 45½″ x 1½″
4. 45½″ x 1½″

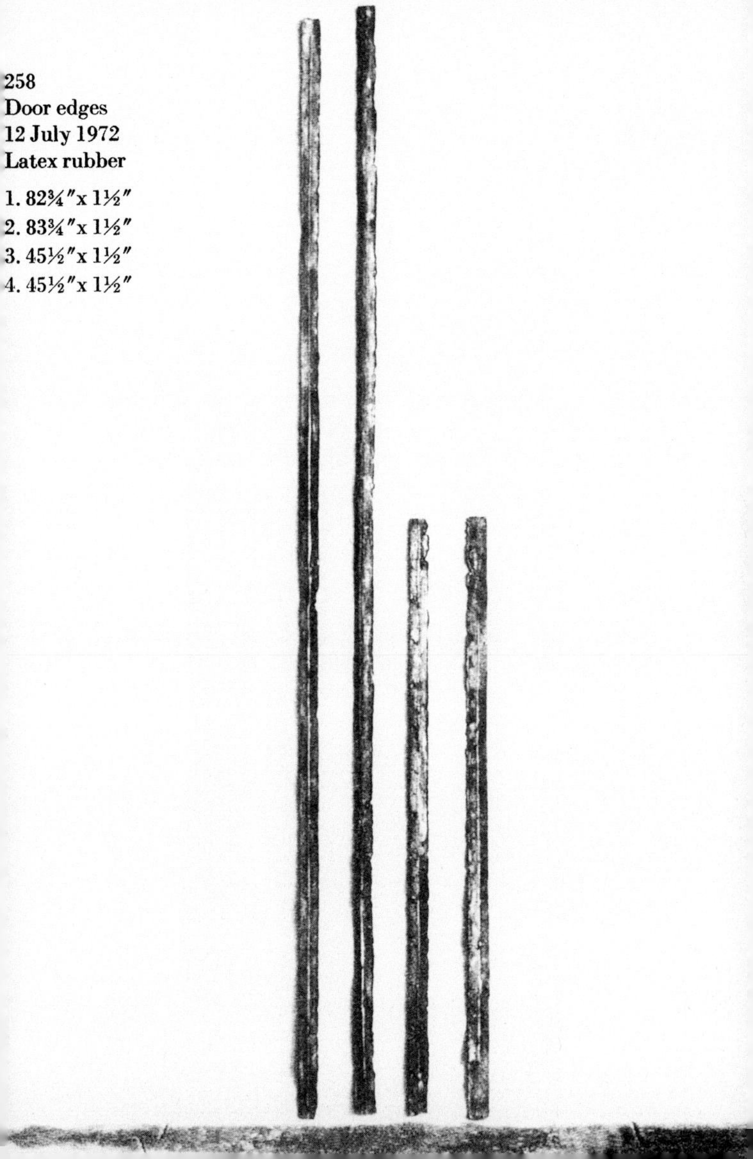

257
Grey slatted door
12 July 1972
Latex rubber, 78¼″ x 23¾″

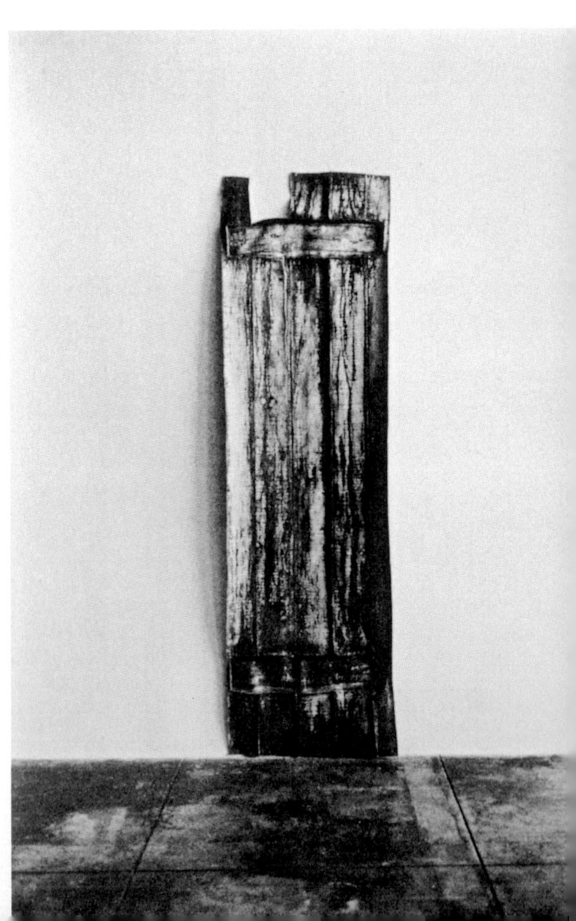

256
Green door with small window
11 July 1972
Latex rubber, 80¾″ x 56″

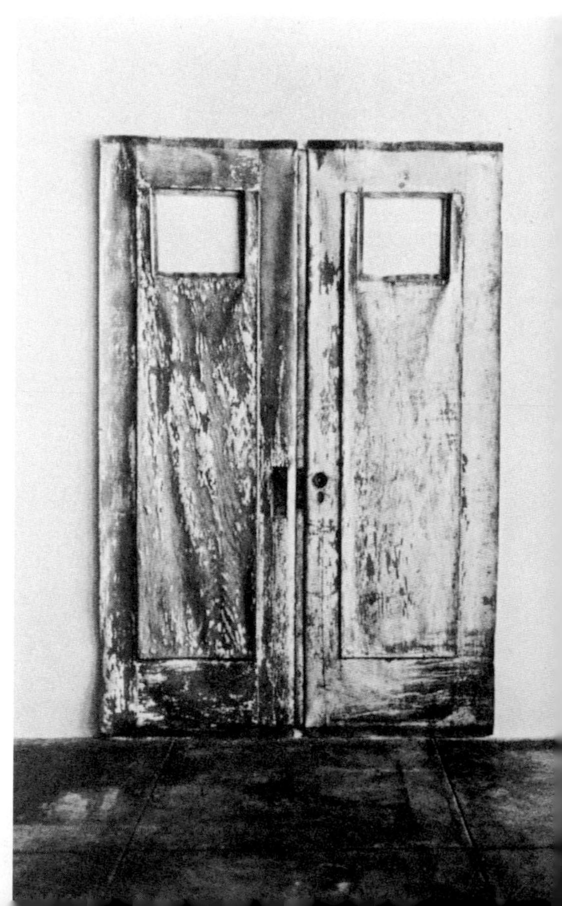

255
L.A. window with Venice bird shit
10 July 1972
Latex rubber and bird shit
50½″ x 21¾″

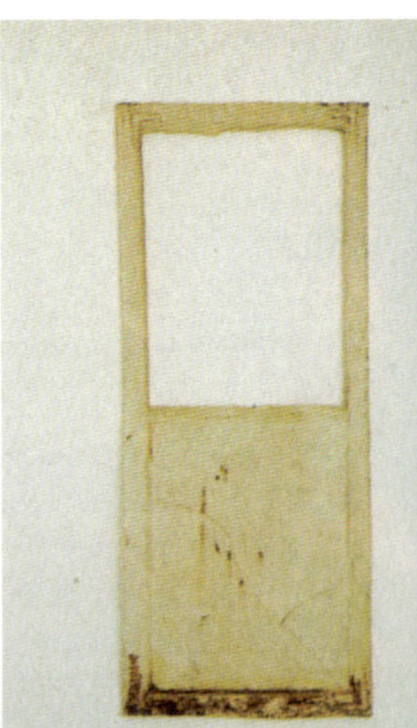

254
Green screen door
10 July 1972
Latex rubber with
metal handle and hinge
80″x 29¾″

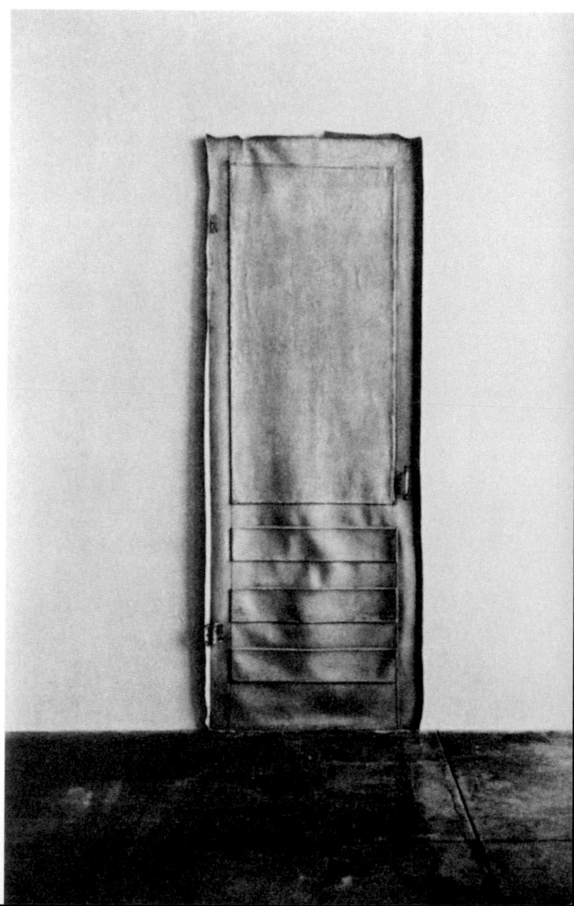

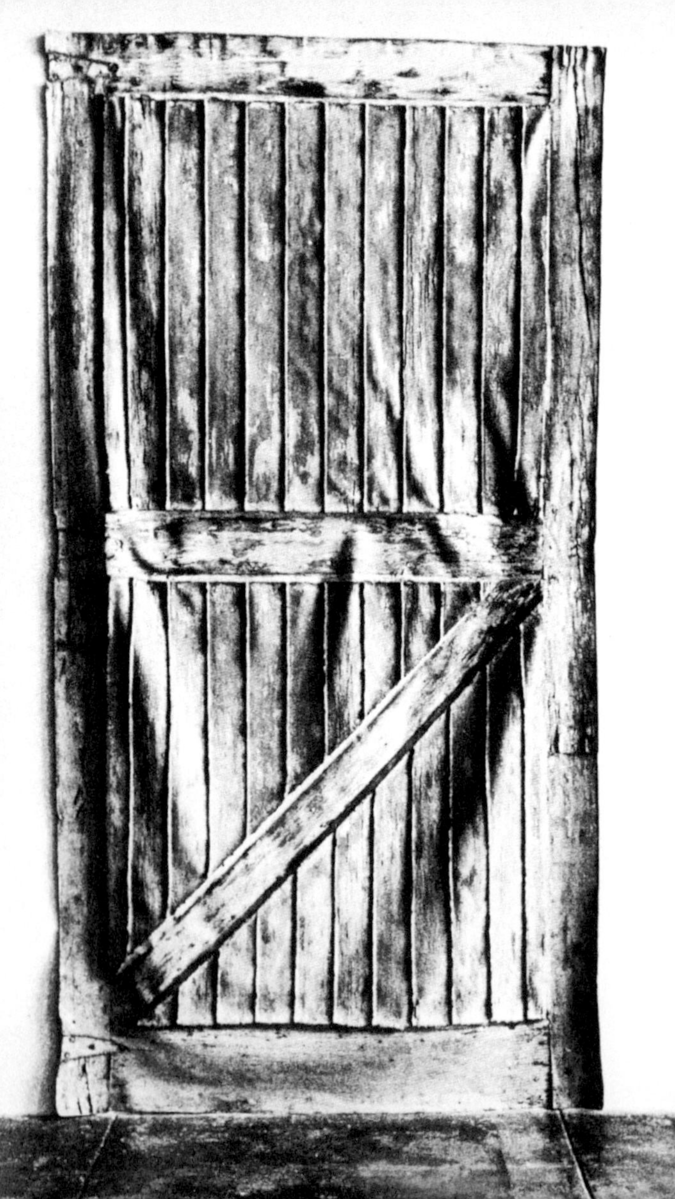

253
Garage Door 2
10 July 1972
Latex rubber
84¼″ x 44¾″

252
Back of Garage Door
10 July 1972
Latex rubber
84¼″ x 44¾″

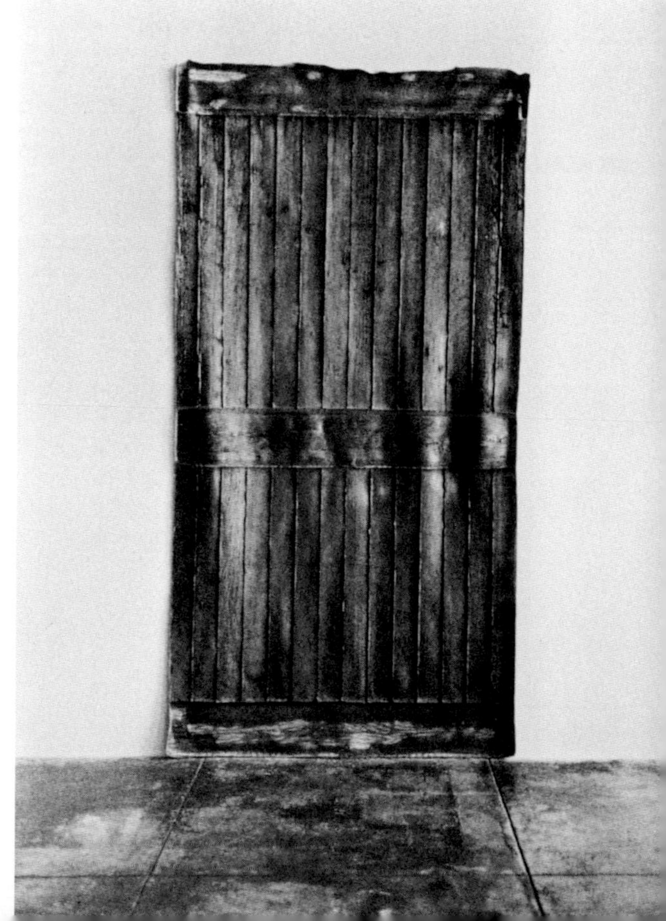

251
Grey school door
10 July 1972
Latex rubber
81½″x 39″

250
Maroon narrow screen door
9 July 1972
Latex rubber, 80½″x 11¾″

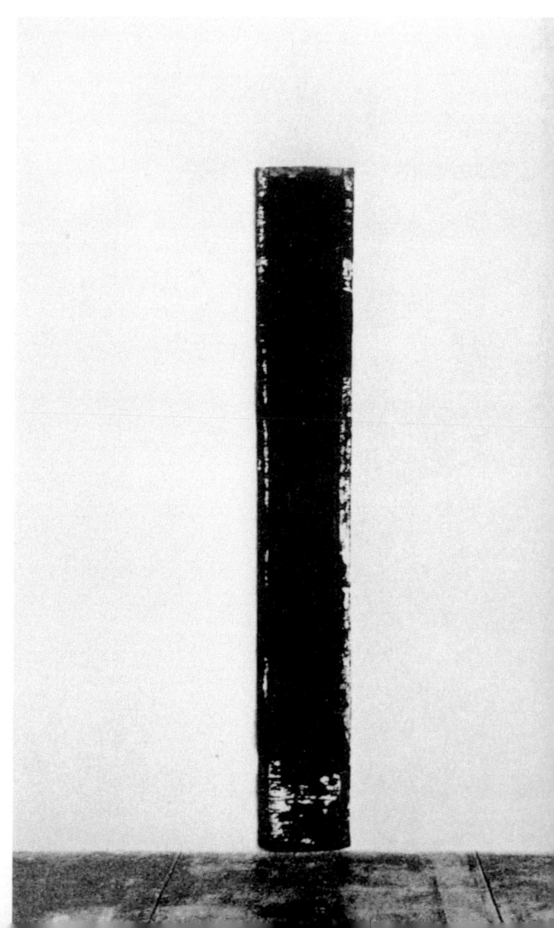

249
Stripped narrow screen door
9 July 1972
Latex rubber, 80½″x 11¾″

248 (two illustrated)
Three plywood sheets
9 July 1972
Latex rubber, all 47″x 66″

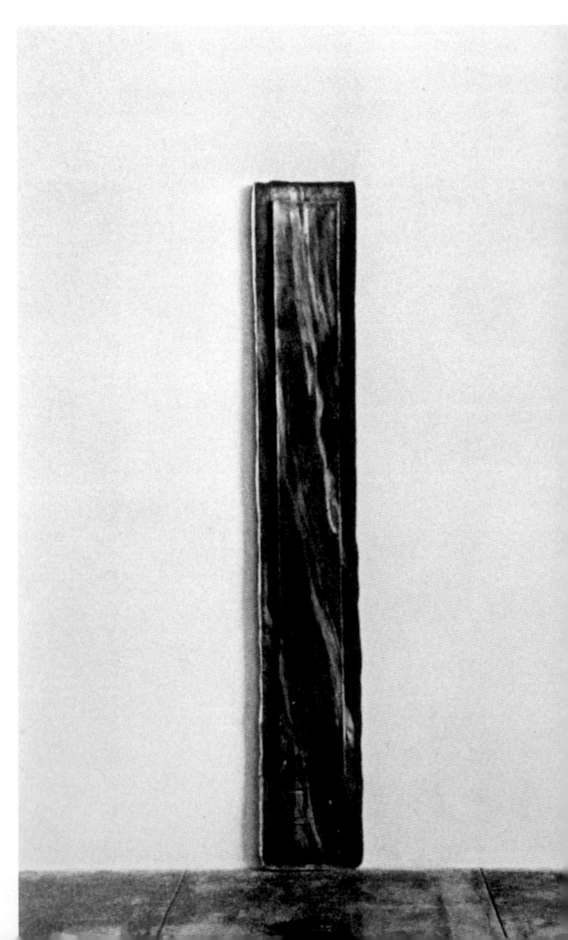

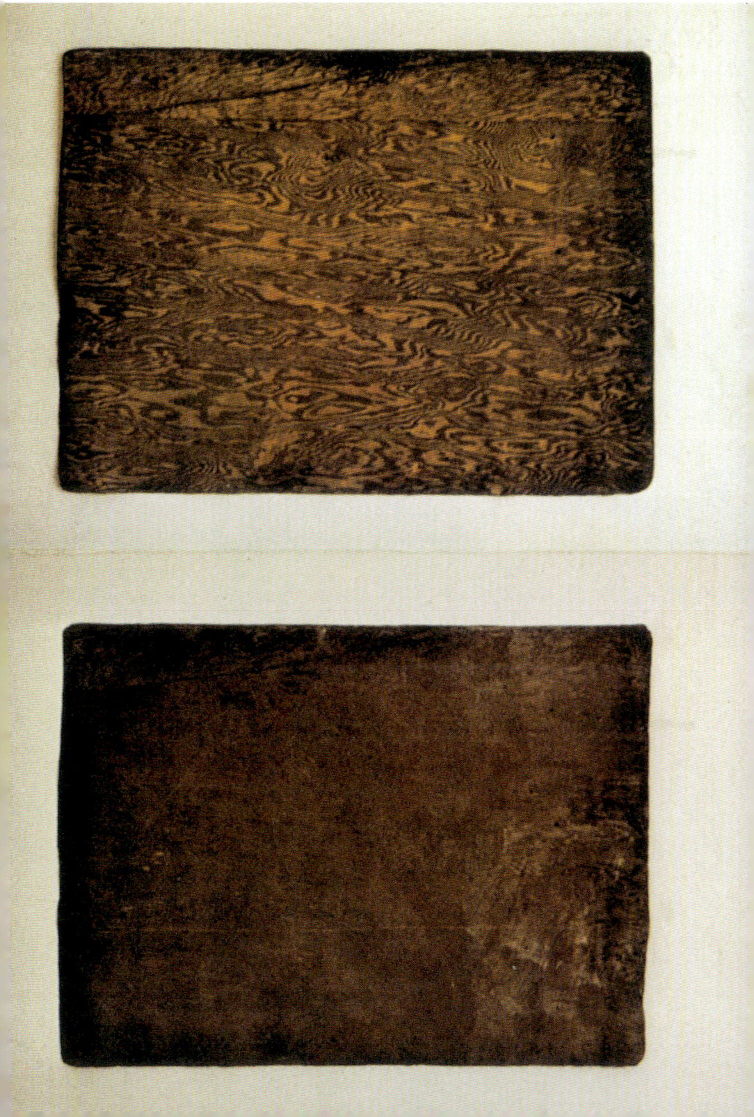

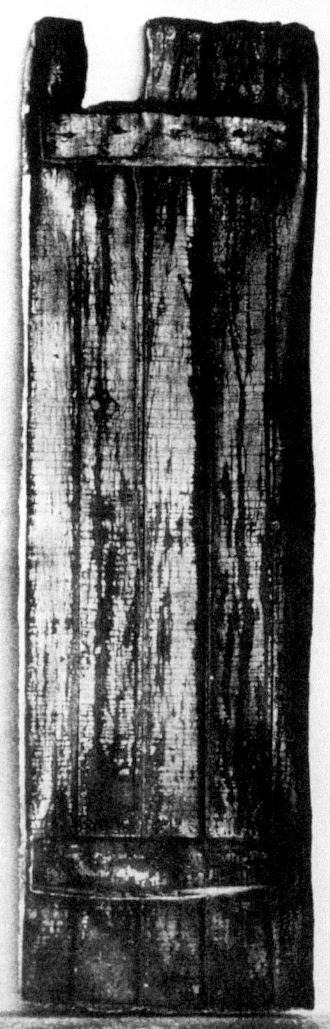

247
Blue slatted door
6 July 1972
Latex rubber
78¼" x 23¾"

246
Corner piece
unlimited multiple
15 June 1973
Latex rubber
28" x 24" x 16" appr

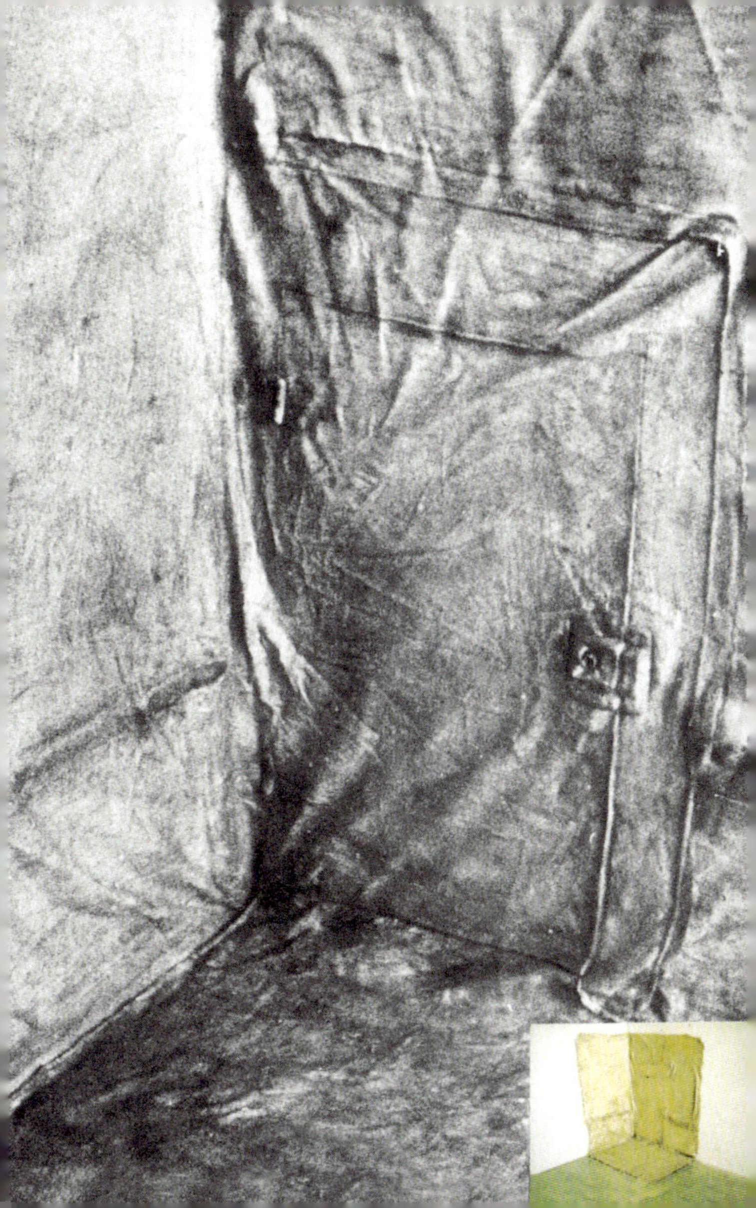

245
Yellow door with bumps
15 June 1972
Latex rubber, 79½″x 43″

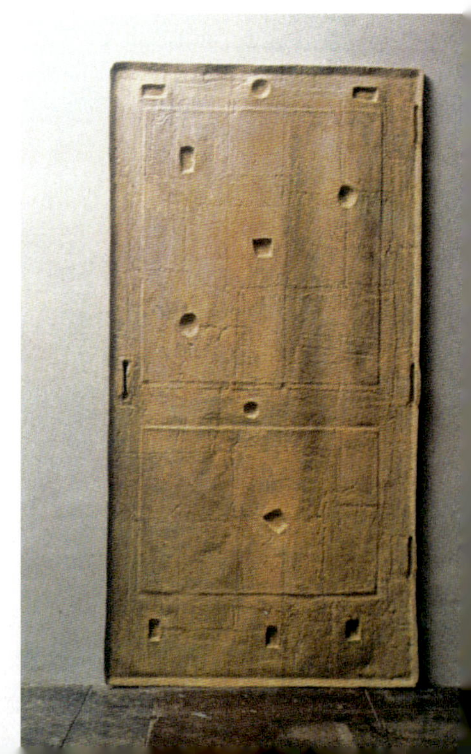

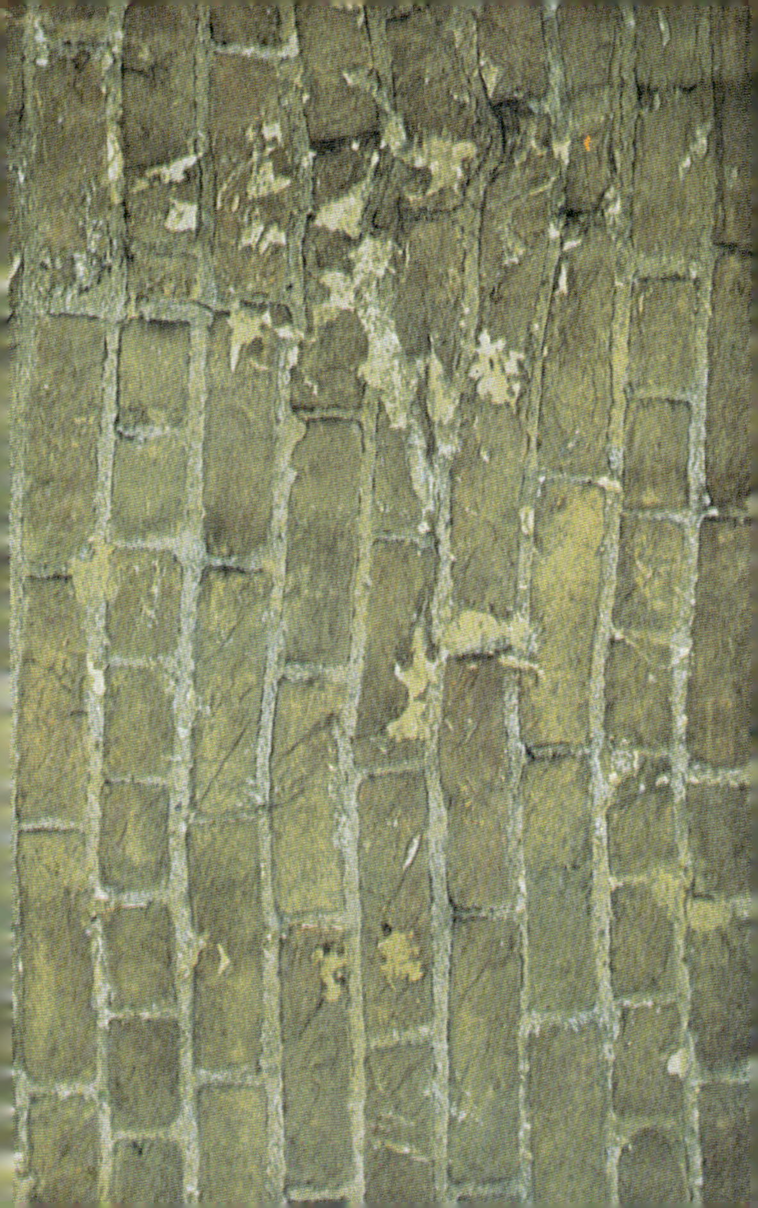

243
Brick painting small
12 June 1972
Latex rubber, 17¼″ x 25½″

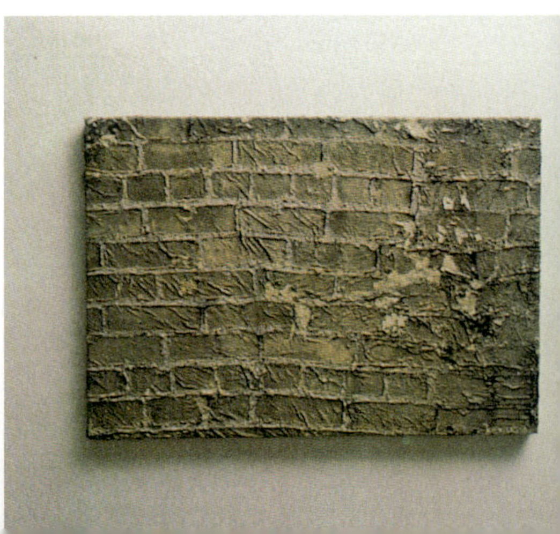

242
Ochre school door
1 June 1972
Latex rubber, 81½″ x 39″

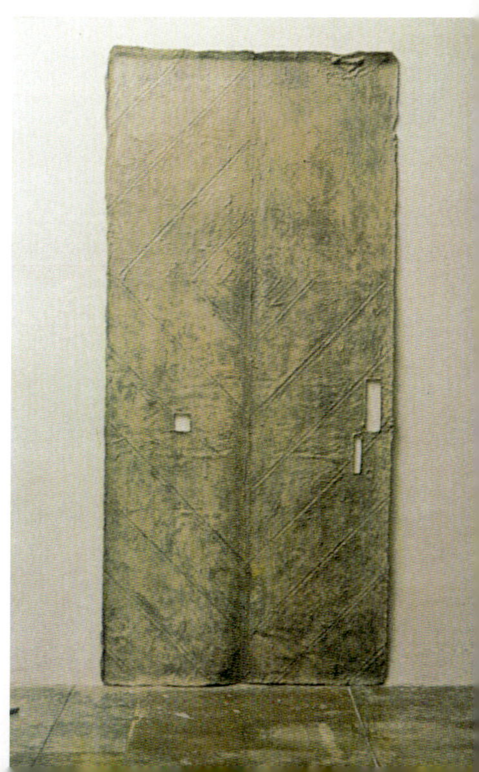

241
Fish
24 May 1972
Latex rubber, 3⅜″ x 5¼″

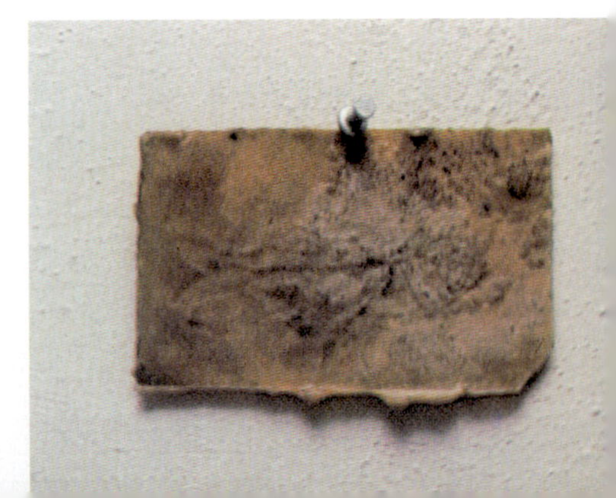

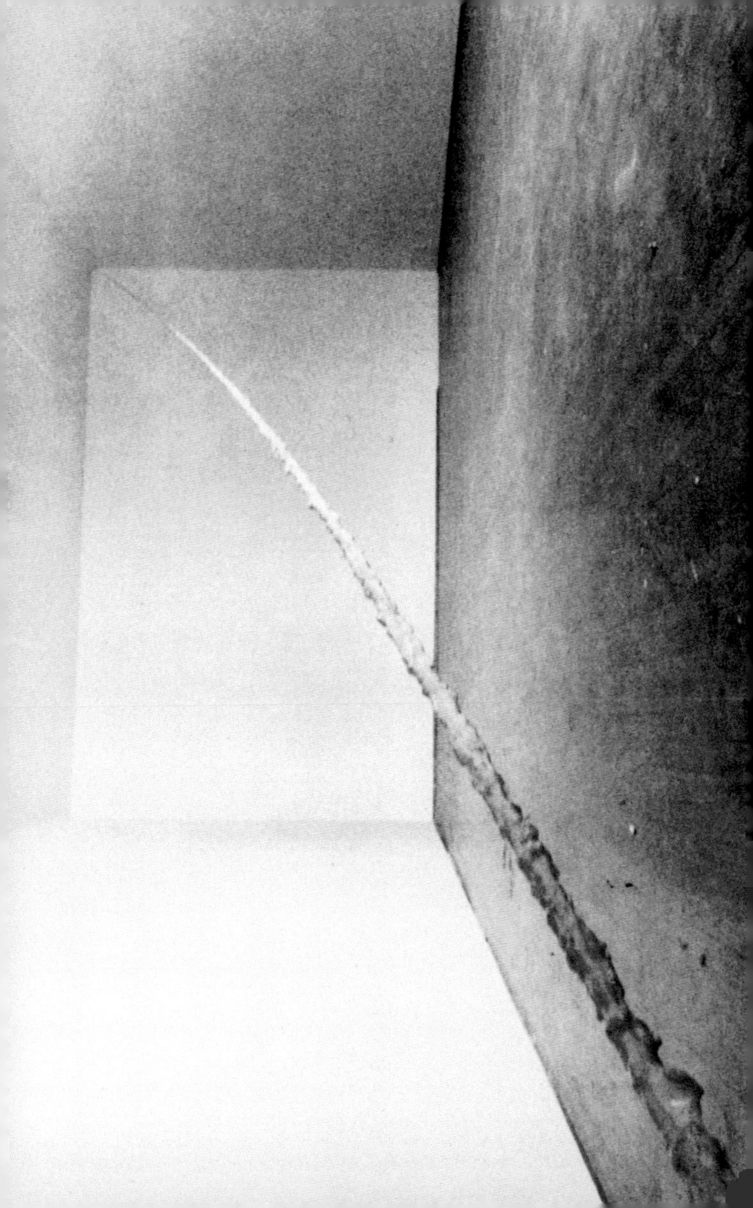

239 (not illustrated)
Valentine's Day piece
12 February 1972
Plastic, aluminum foil,
waxpaper, wax and
rose petals
2″x 2⅛″x 3″

238
Whatever You Like
2 January 1972
Plastic, wool cloth
and rabbit fur
11½″x 11″x 1⅜″

237
Leaded window No. 2
29 December 1971
Latex rubber
30 ¼″ x 20 ⅜″

236 (right)
Stairwell,
Paul's place
29 December 1971
Latex rubber
100″ x 142″ x 31″

235 (following spread)
Living room,
Paul's place
29 December 1971
Latex rubber
94⅝″ x 135½″ x 139″

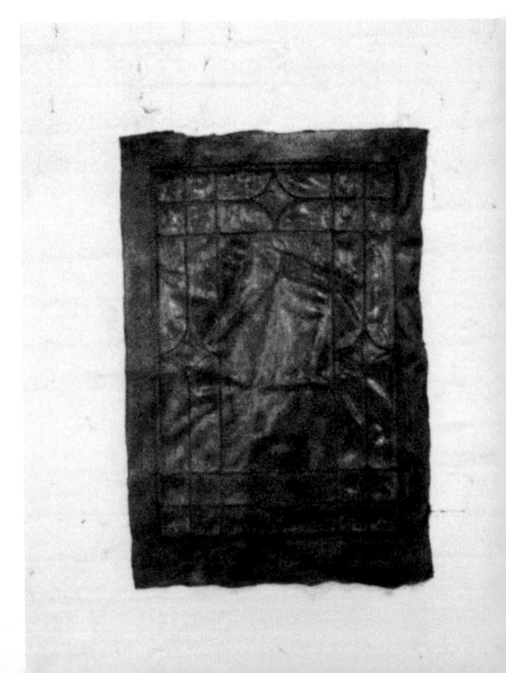

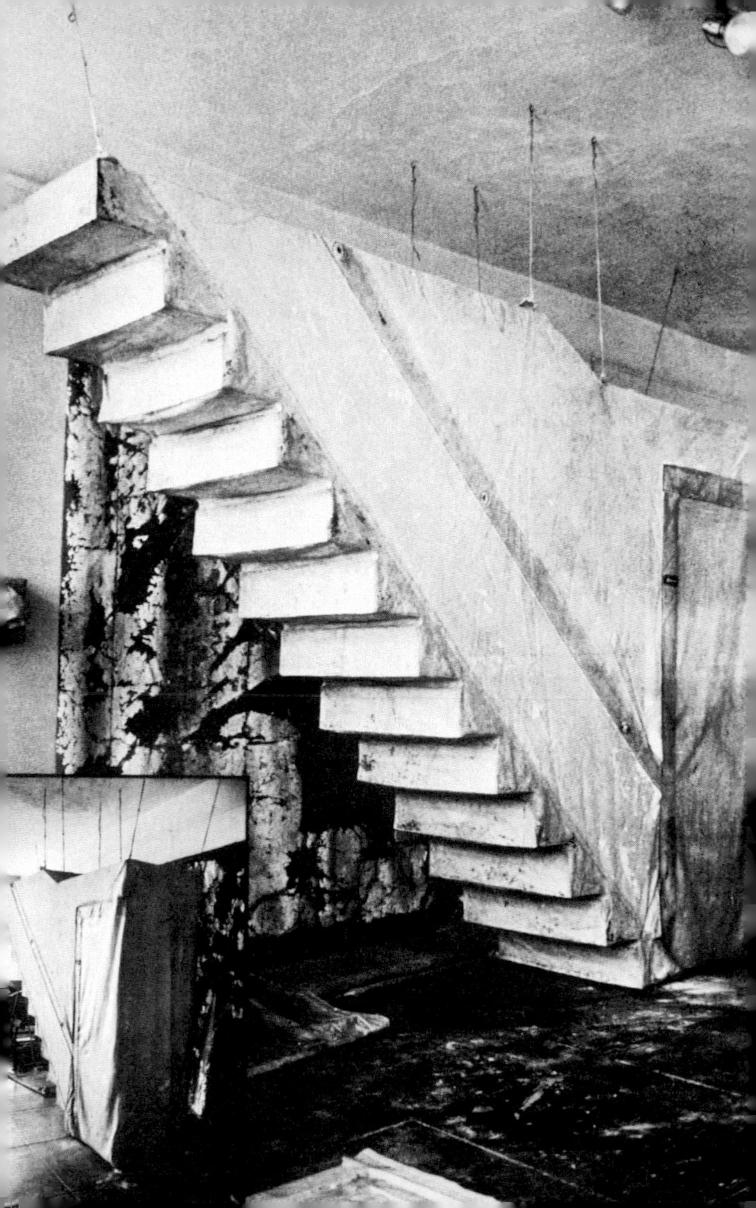

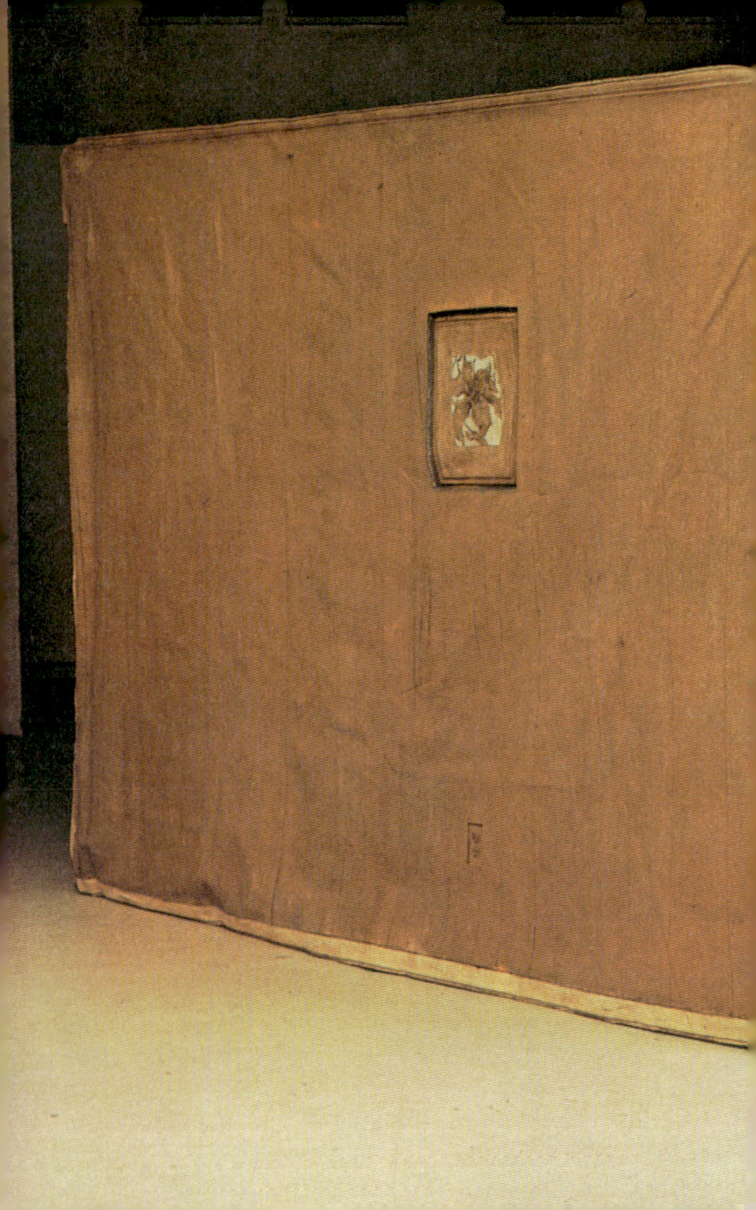

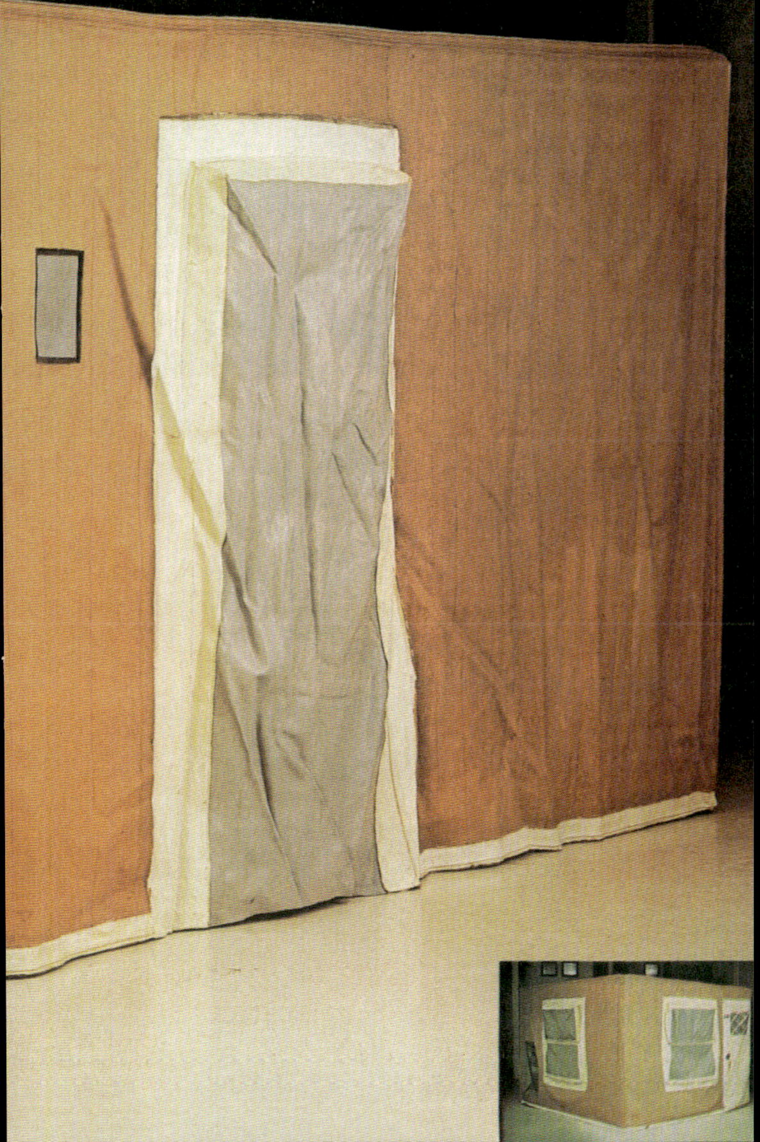

234
Marlene Xmas drawing
24 December 1971
Gauche and graphite on paper
11½″x 9½″

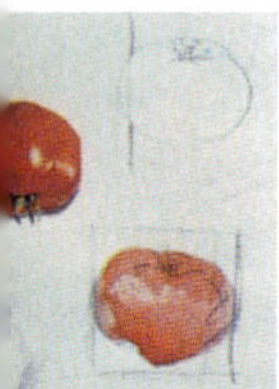

233
Kitchen cabinets No. 2,
Paul's place
22 December 1971
Latex rubber

Door, 79½″x 25″
2-door cabinet large, 37″x 38½″
Large drawer, 4¾″x 17½″
Small drawer, 4½″x 17⅛″
2-door cabinet small, 24″x 38¾″
1-door cabinet, 29¾″x 19″

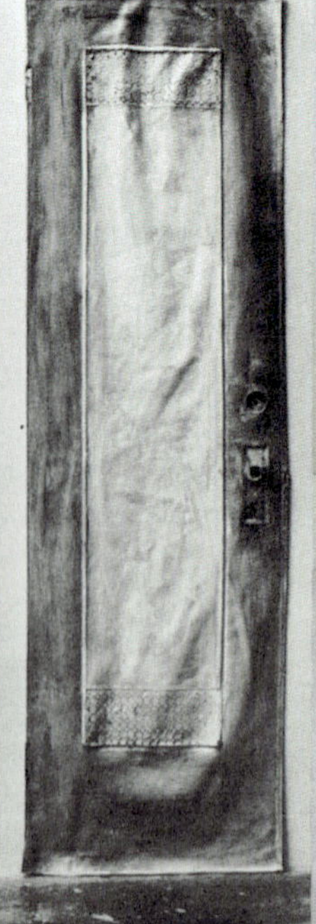

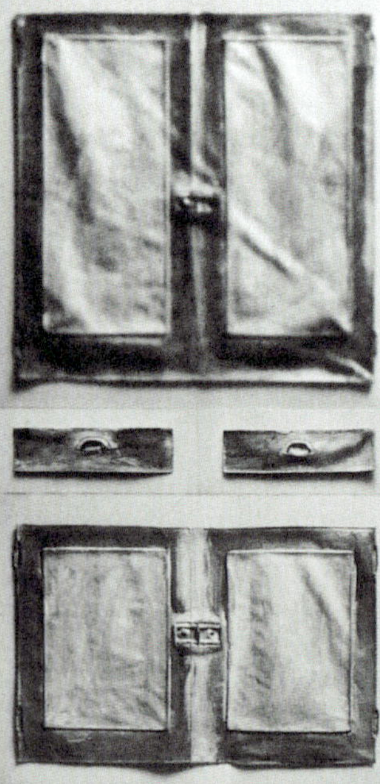

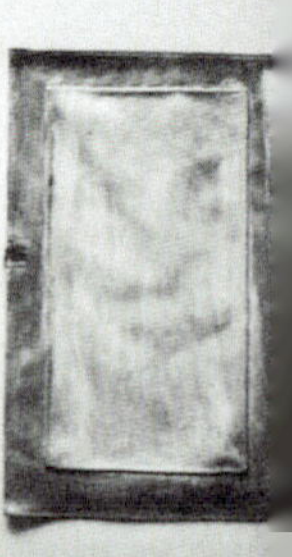

232
Leaded window
22 December 1971
Latex rubber
23″ x 16¼″

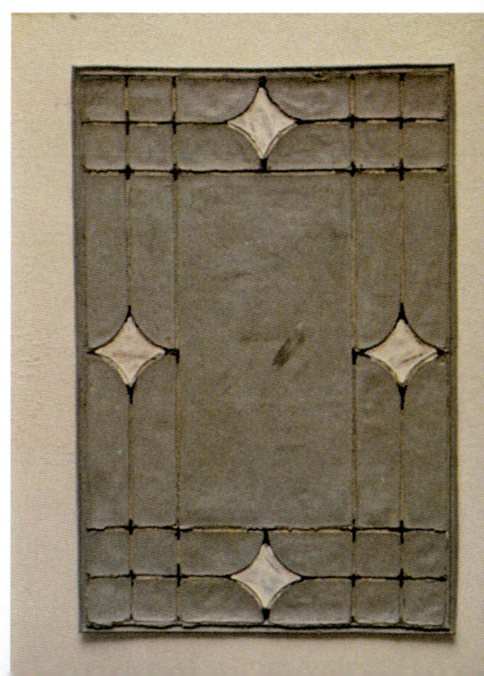

231
Light meters,
Paul's place
16 December 1971
Latex rubber
10″ x 18½″ x 10″

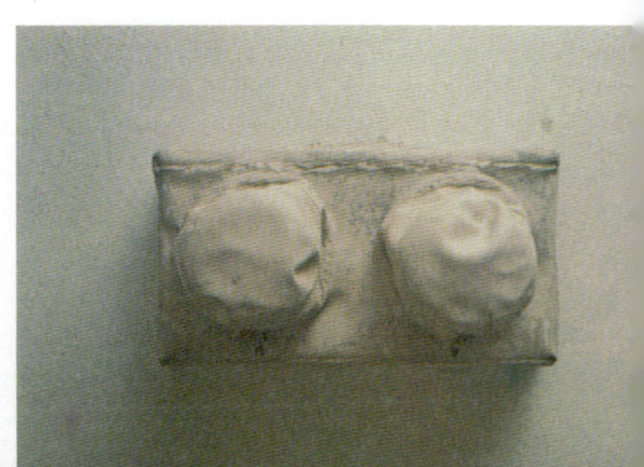

230
Upstairs hall window,
Paul's place
15 December 1971
Latex rubber
28¼″ x 24⅛″

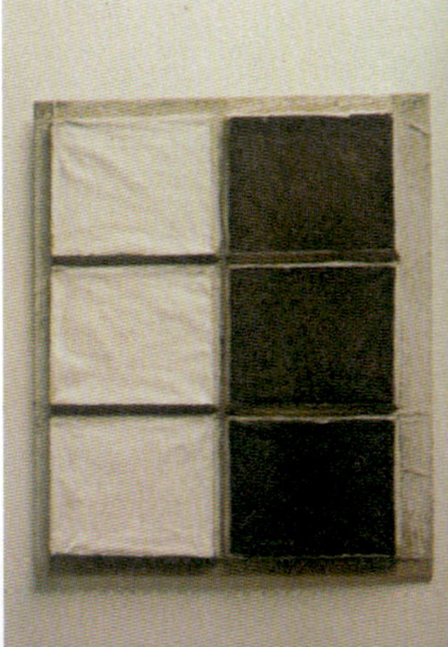

229
Gas can orange
15 December 1971
Latex rubber
15¼″ x 11⅝″

228 (not illustrated)
Pos gas can
15 December 1971
Latex rubber, 15¾″ x 11½″
Destroyed 8 June 1972

227 (not illustrated)
Small leaded window
14 December 1971
Latex rubber, 23"x 16"
Destroyed 8 June 1972

26
Marlene Feather Finger
. December 1971
Latex rubber fingers
with pen drawing on paper
0"x 26"

225 (not illustrated)
Gas can grey and Gas can white
14 December 1971
Latex rubber, each 14″x 11¾″
Both stolen 10 Jan. 1971

224
Kitchen sink,
Paul's place
12 December 1971
Latex rubber, 33″ x 58¾″

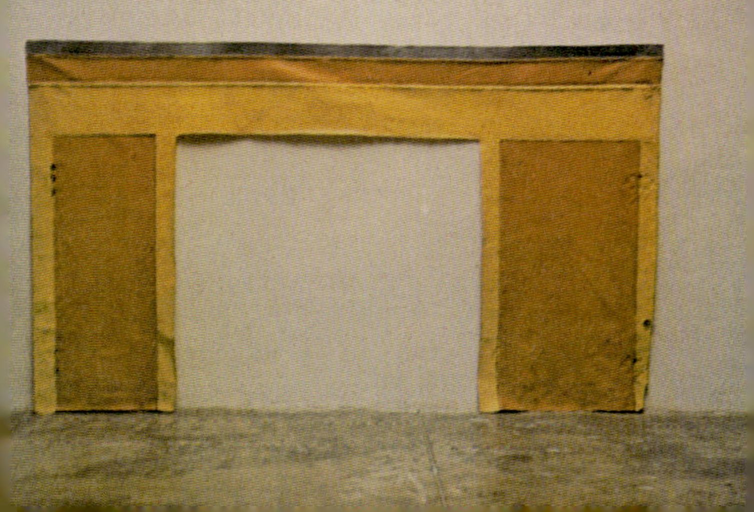

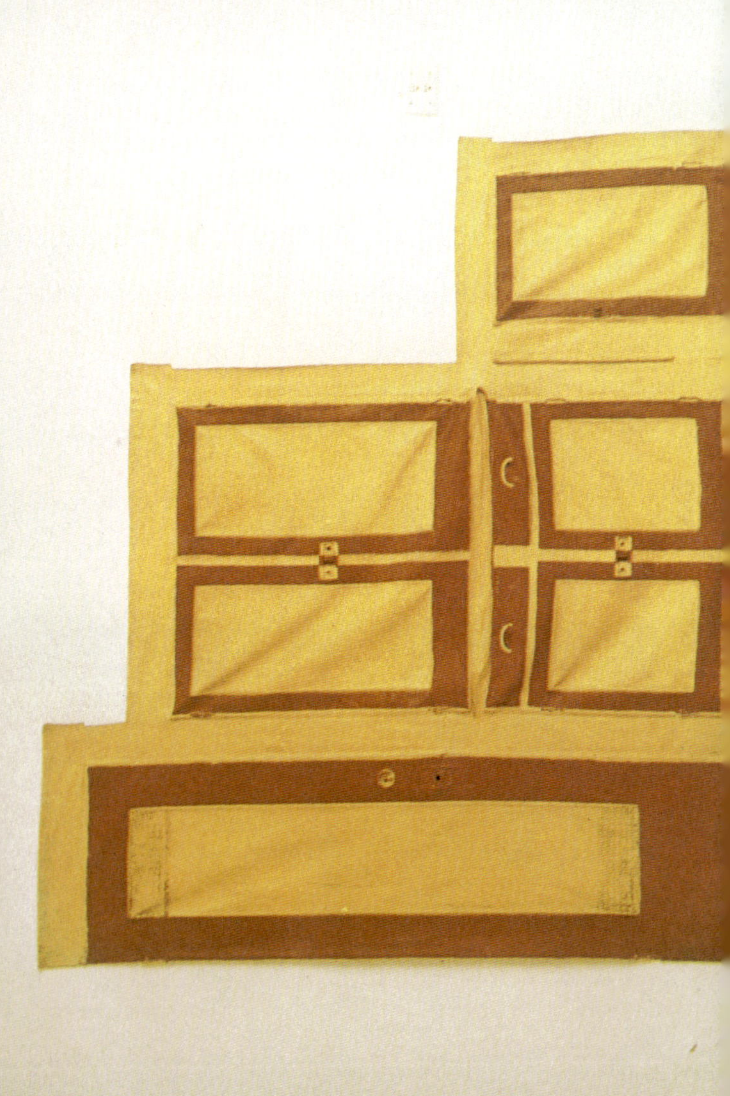

223
Kitchen cabinets,
Paul's place
12 December 1971
Latex rubber
84½″ x 98½″

222
Shadow of Its
Former Self
3 December 1971
Latex rubber and
cheesecloth, 96″ x 48″

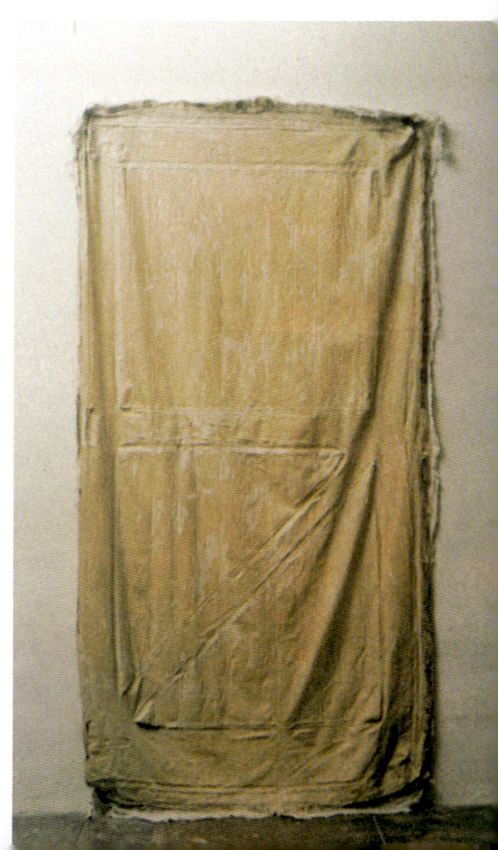

221 (not illustrated)
Fish net tests
15 November 1971
Latex rubber and netting
White, 29″x 12″
Brown, 25″x 13″
Destroyed Nov. 1972

220
Hanger
1 November 1971
Latex rubber, coat
hanger and nail
8½″x 16¼″x 1¼″

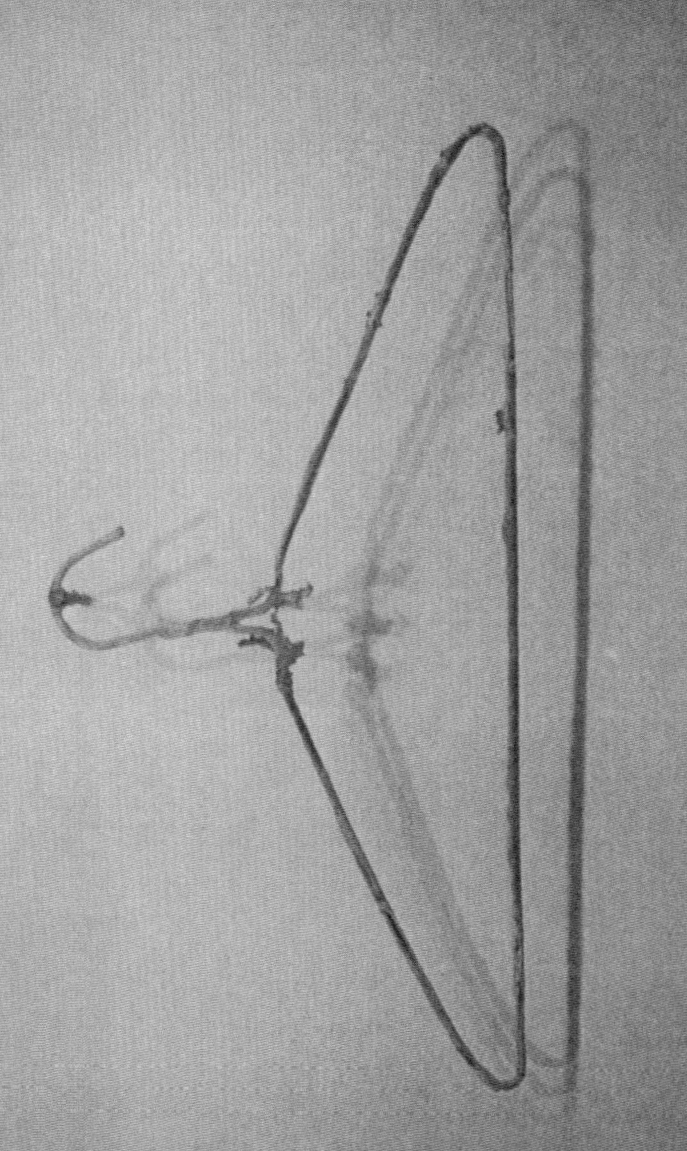

219
Red door edge
10 May 1971
Neon, 80″

218
Blue door edge
8 April 1971
Neon, 80″

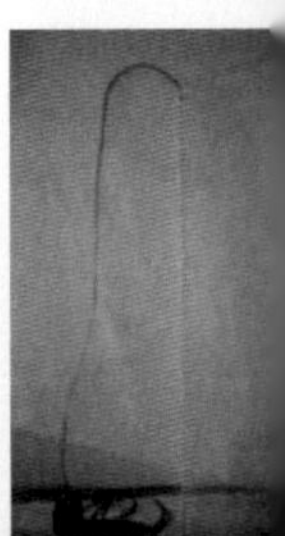

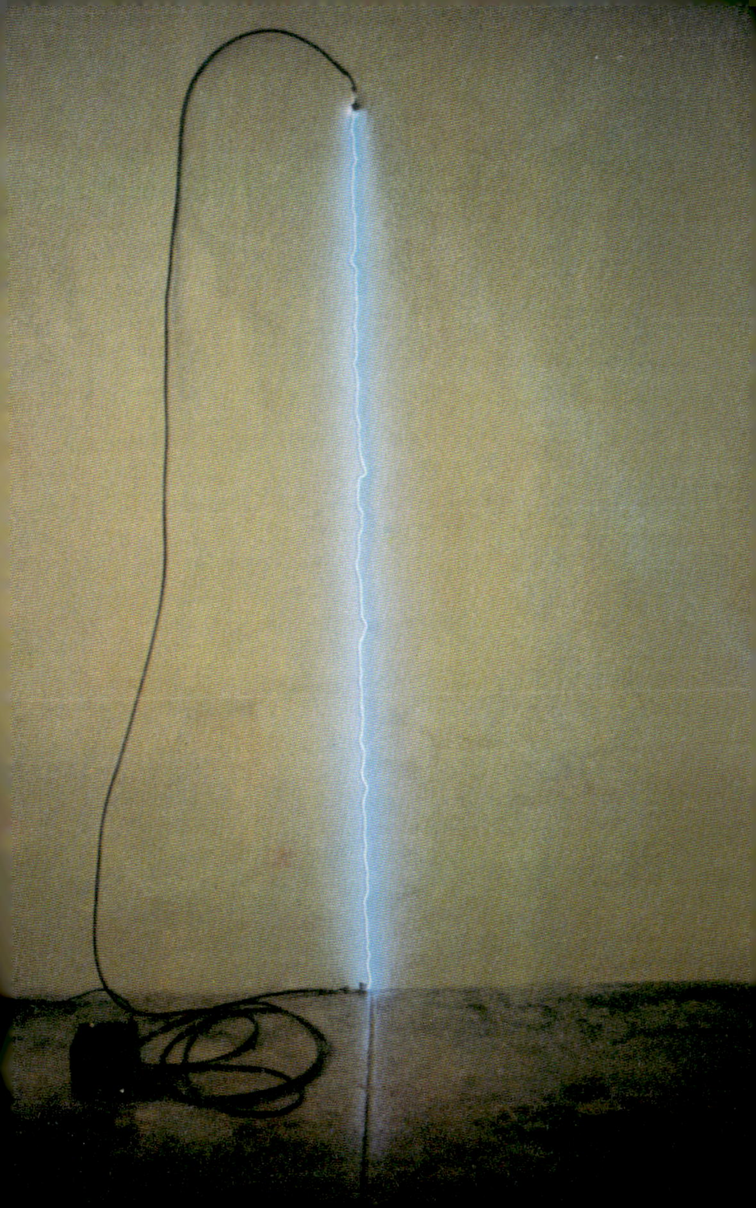

217
Transom window,
third floor
4 August 1971
Latex rubber
35½″ x 46½″

Note: 217 through 190
constitute the
Barclay House Series.

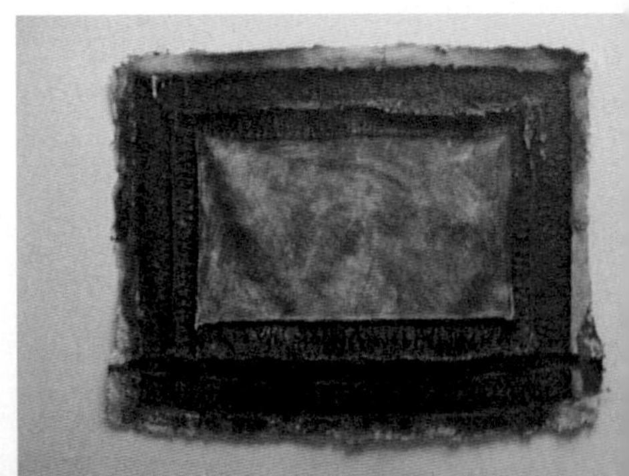

216
Window with
light blue,
third floor
4 August 1971
Latex rubber
31″x 37½″

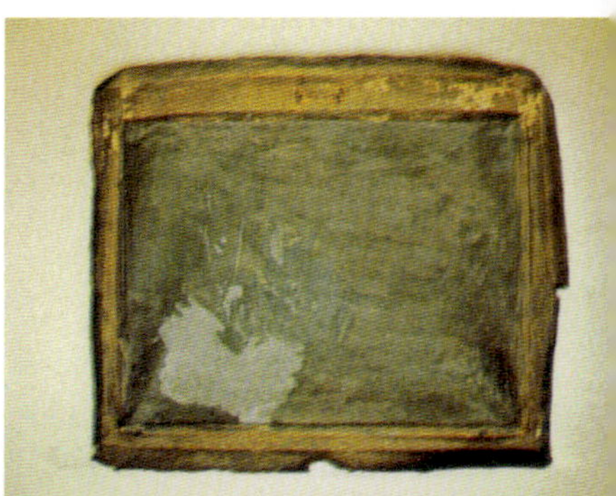

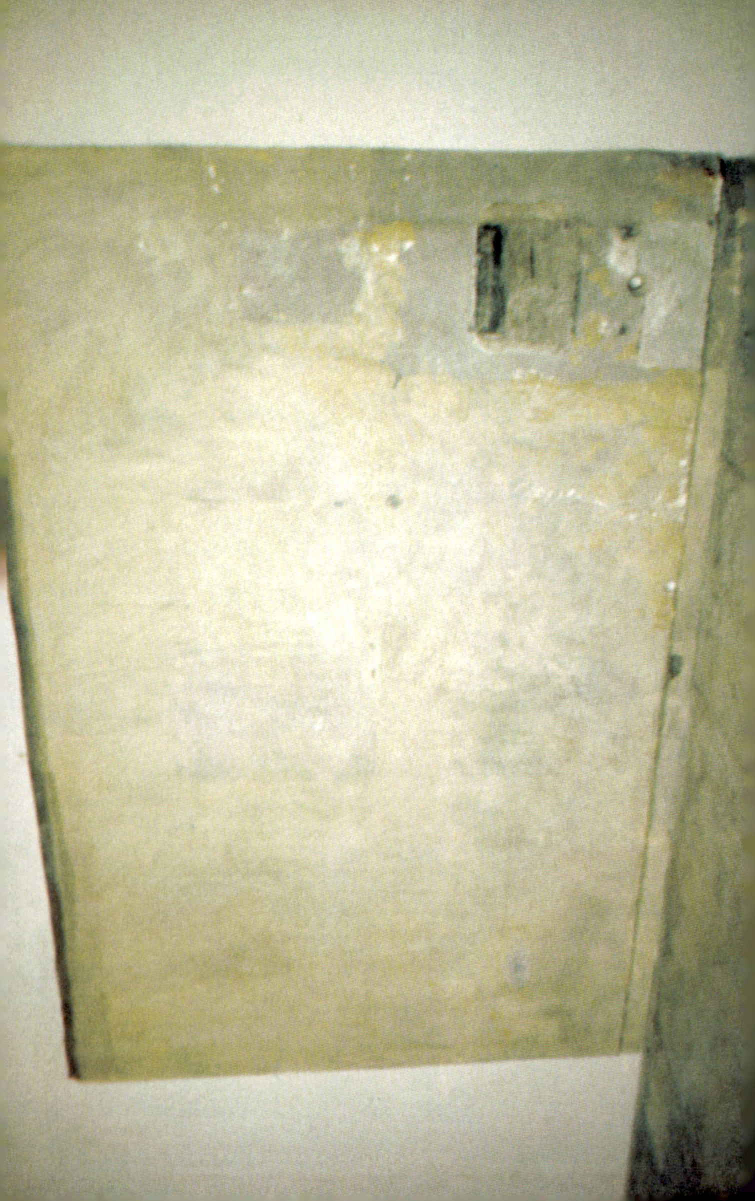

215 (below, 1973
photograph)

214 (with detail)
Long wall, third floor
4 August 1971
Latex rubber
106″ x 230″

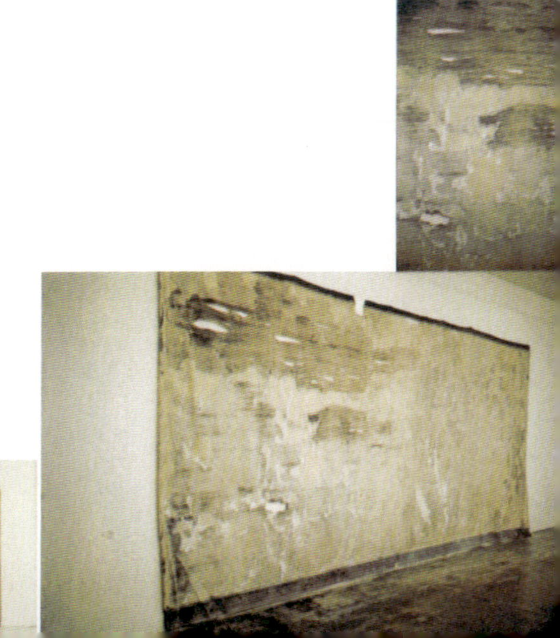

213
Scotch tape painting,
third floor
4 August 1971
Latex rubber, 50″x 65¼″

212
West hall painting,
third floor
4 August 1971
Latex rubber, 74¾″ x 84″

211
South room wall
painting, third floor
4 August 1971
Latex rubber
76½″ x 94½″

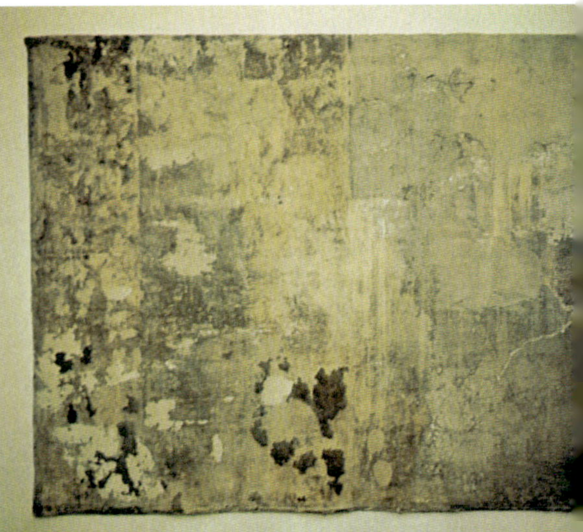

210
East room with
2 windows, third floor
4 August 1971
Latex rubber
107½″x 174″

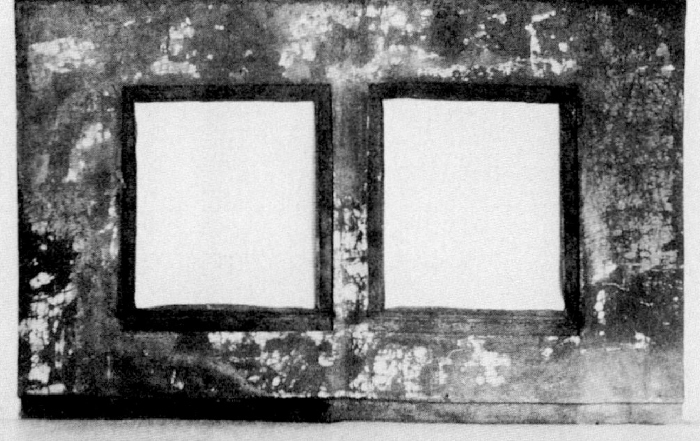

209
Closet doors,
third floor
4 August 1971
Latex rubber
104½″ x 63″

208
East hall wall,
third floor
(Grey wall)
4 August 1971
Latex rubber
104″ x 186½″

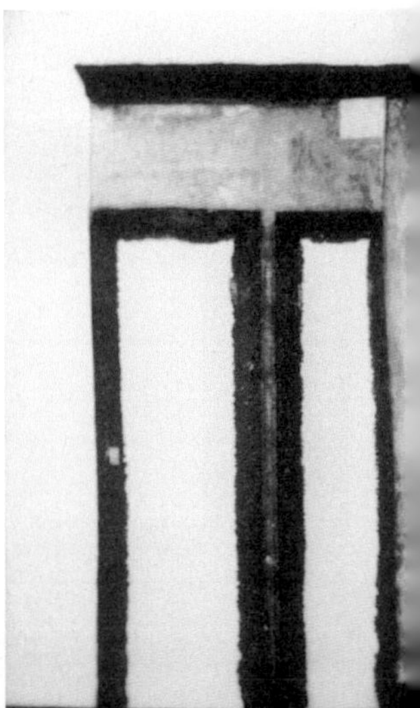

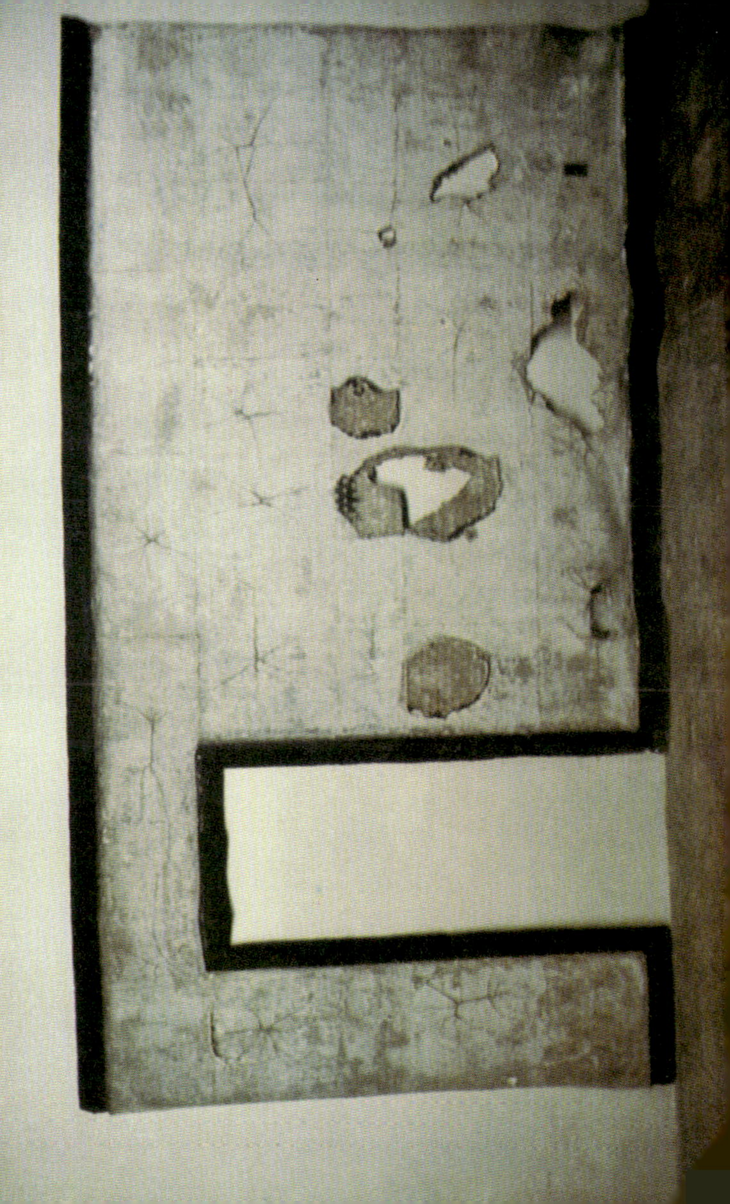

207
South door,
third floor
4 August 1971
Latex rubber
82½″ x 39½″

206
Paul's door,
third floor
4 August 1971
Latex rubber
82″ x 46½″

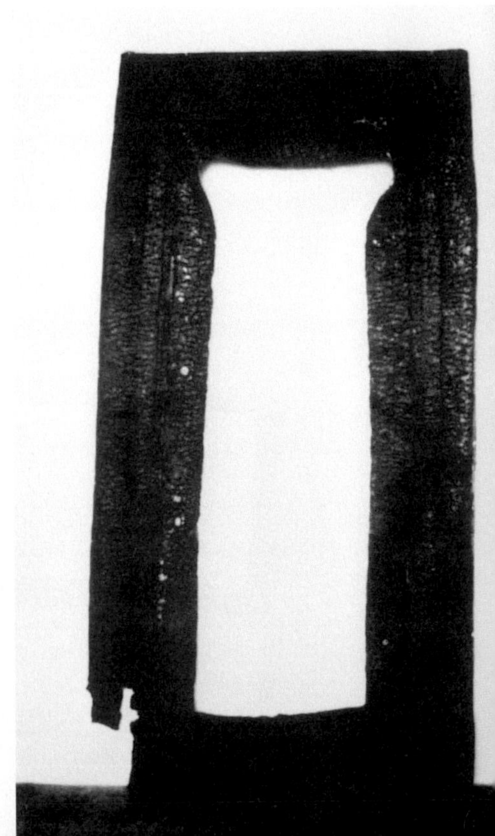

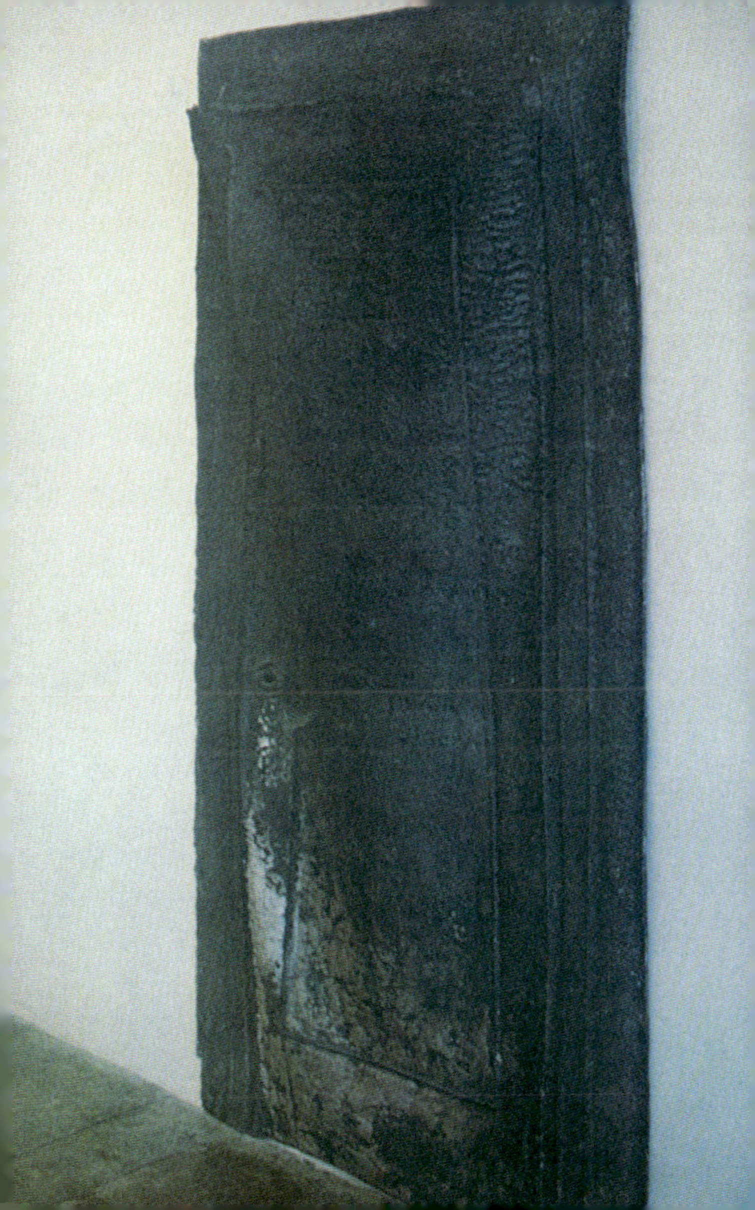

205
Two door jambs,
third floor
4 August 1971
Latex rubber
Both 84″x 48″approx.

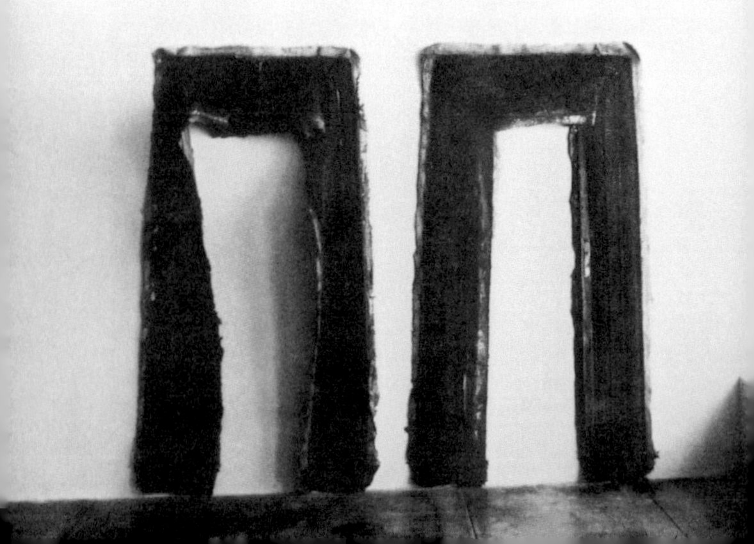

204
Door without center
panel, third floor
4 August 1971
Latex rubber, 79½″x 33″

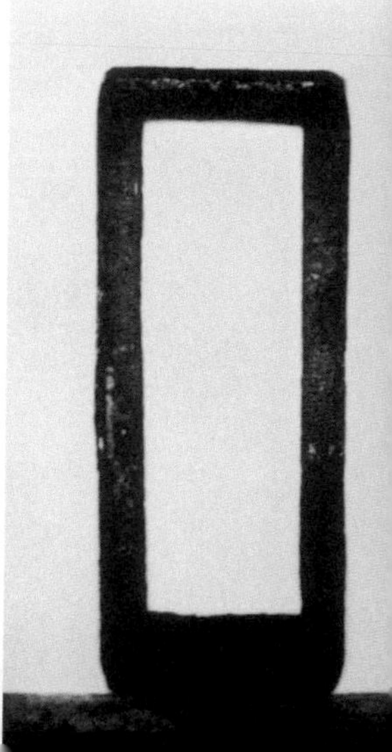

203
Telephone wall
painting, second floor
4 August 1971
Latex rubber, 110″x 56″

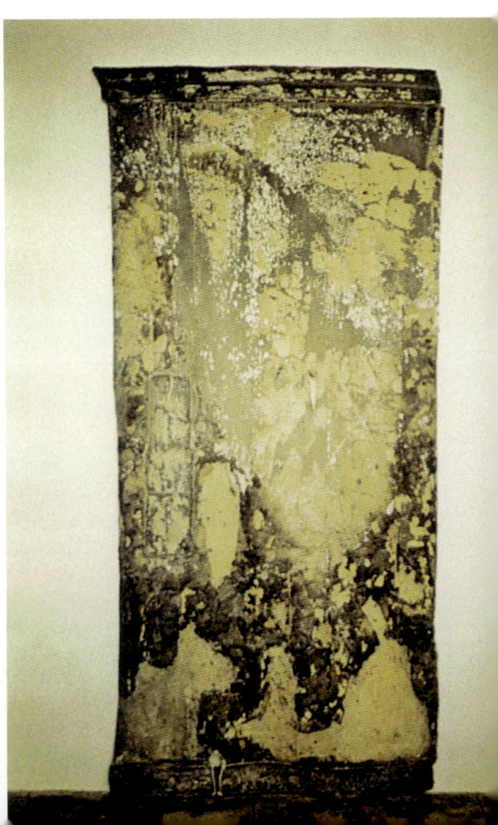

202
South hall wall,
second floor
4 August 1971
Latex rubber
110″x 304½″

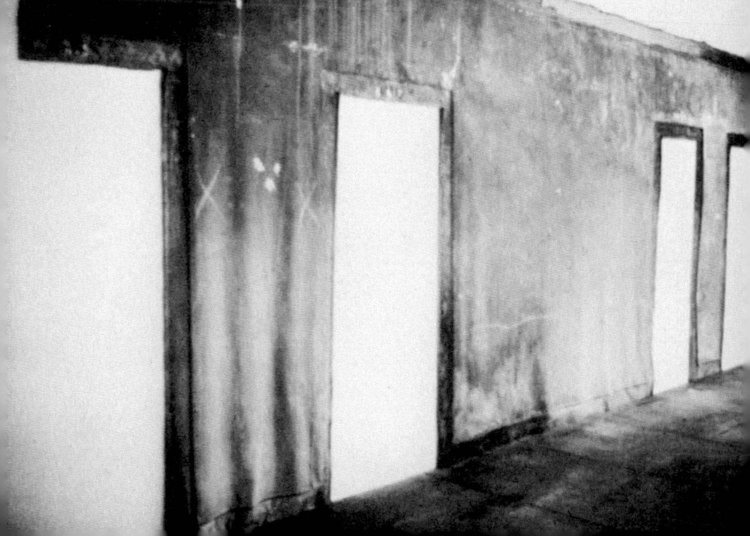

201 (with detail)
North hall wall,
second floor
4 August 1971
Latex rubber
110″x 376″

200
Door with hole,
second floor
4 August 1971
Latex rubber
80½″x 34″

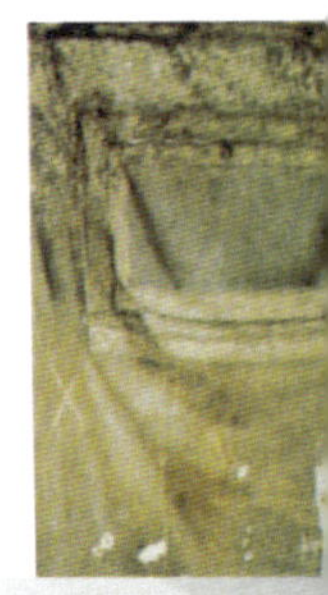

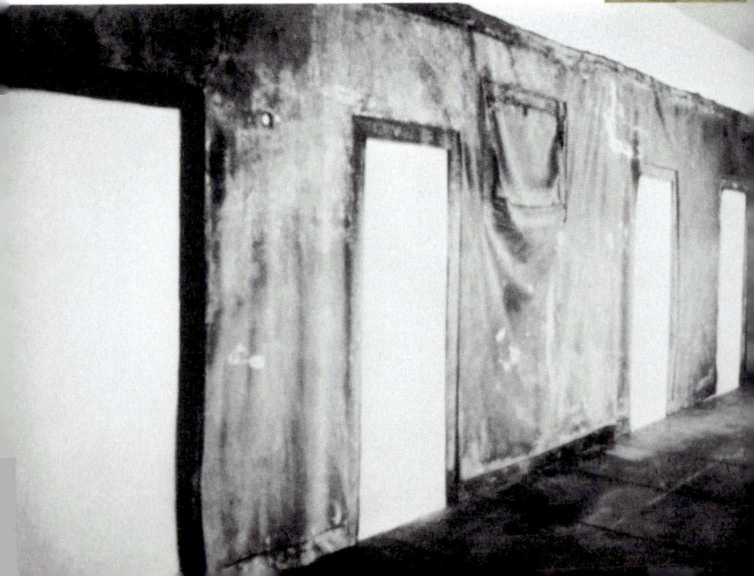

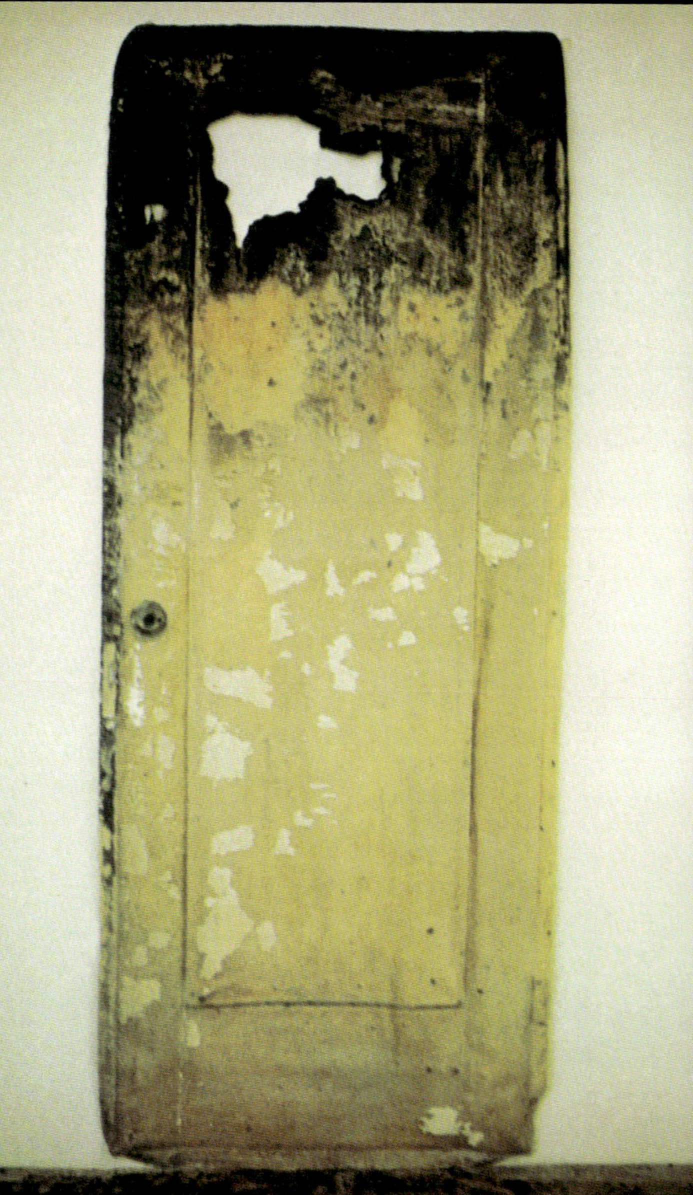

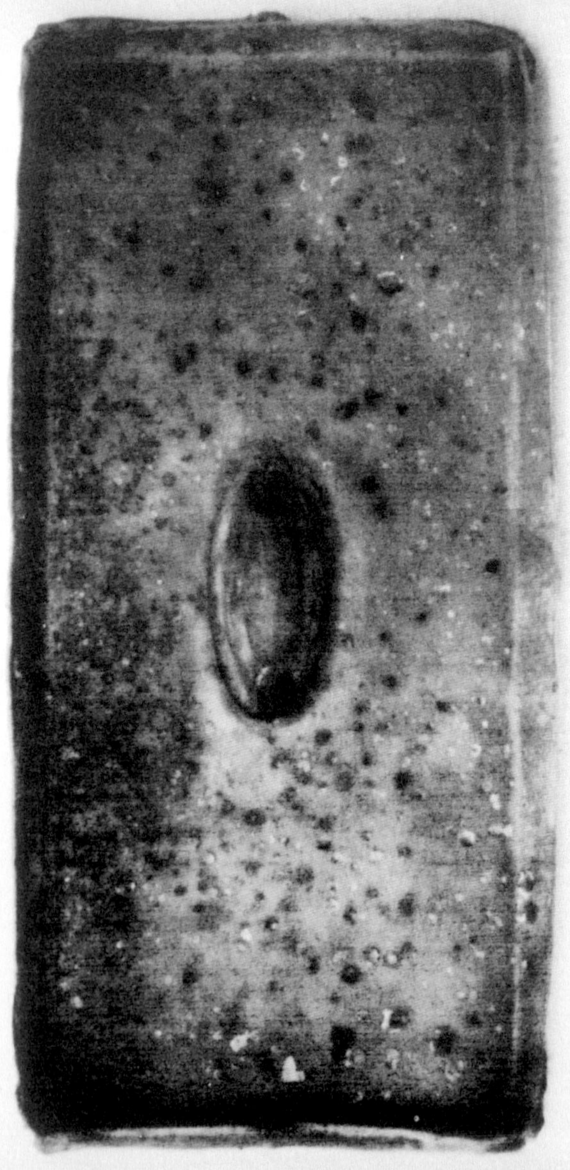

199
Drawer door,
second floor
4 August 1971
Latex rubber
7¼″ x 15¼″

198
Cabinet with door,
second floor
4 August 1971
Latex rubber
29½″ x 38½″

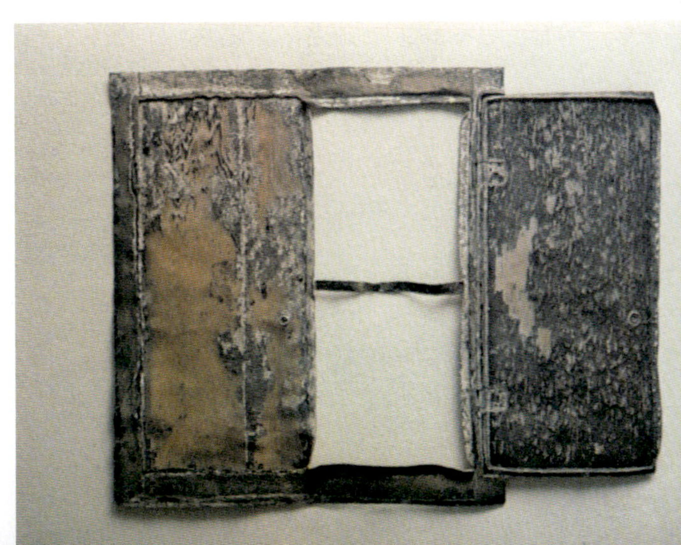

197 (with detail)
Sun room with window,
second floor
4 August 1971
Latex rubber, 110″x 176″

196
Tone-bar door,
first floor
4 August 1971
Latex rubber
79½″x 31½″

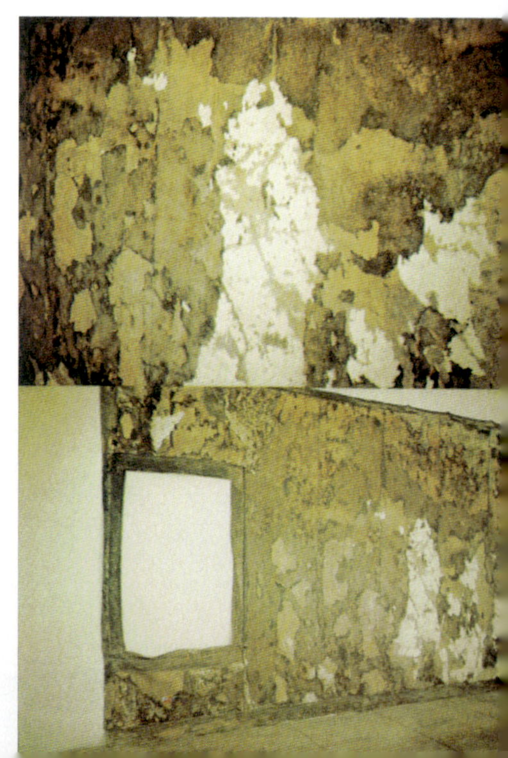

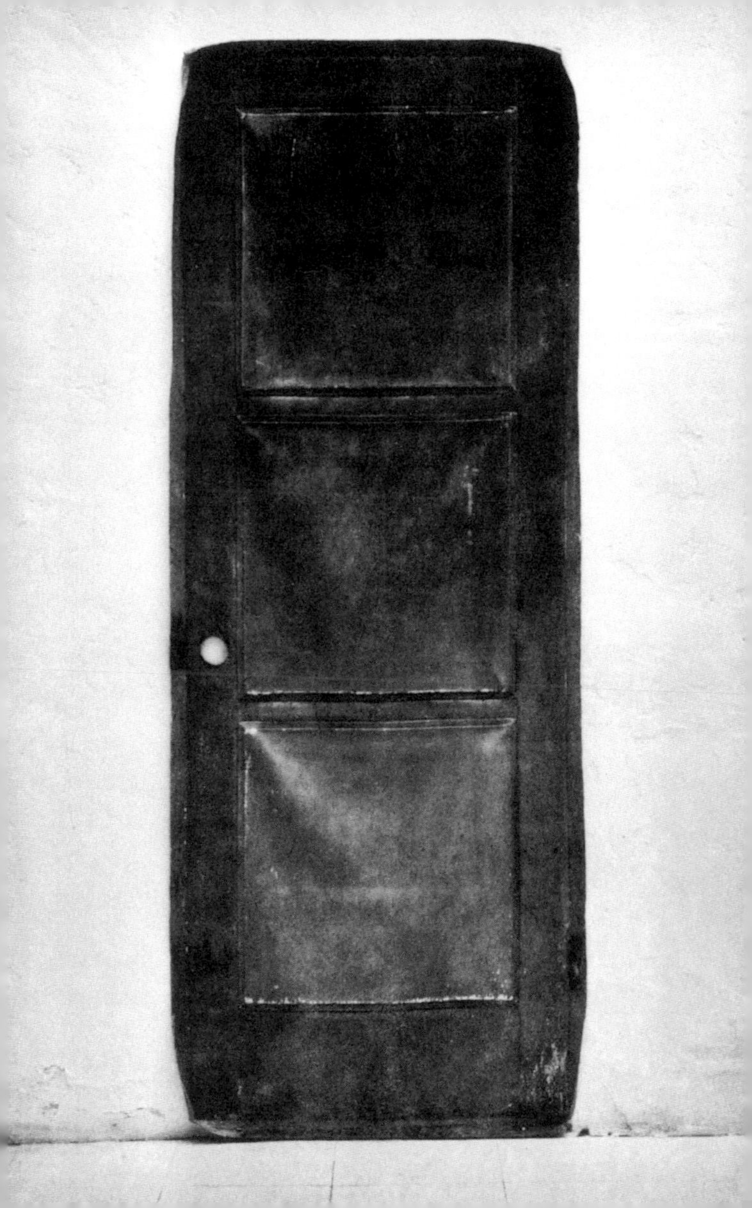

195
Hall painting,
first floor
4 August 1971
Latex rubber
107½″x 78″

194
Tone-bar room with
2 doors, first floor
4 August 1971
Latex rubber
109″x 125″

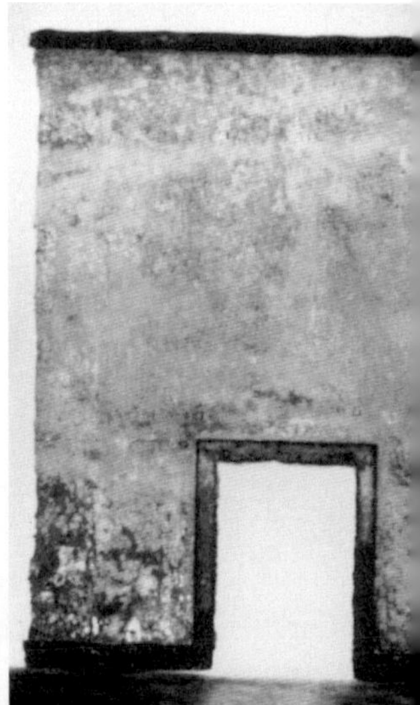

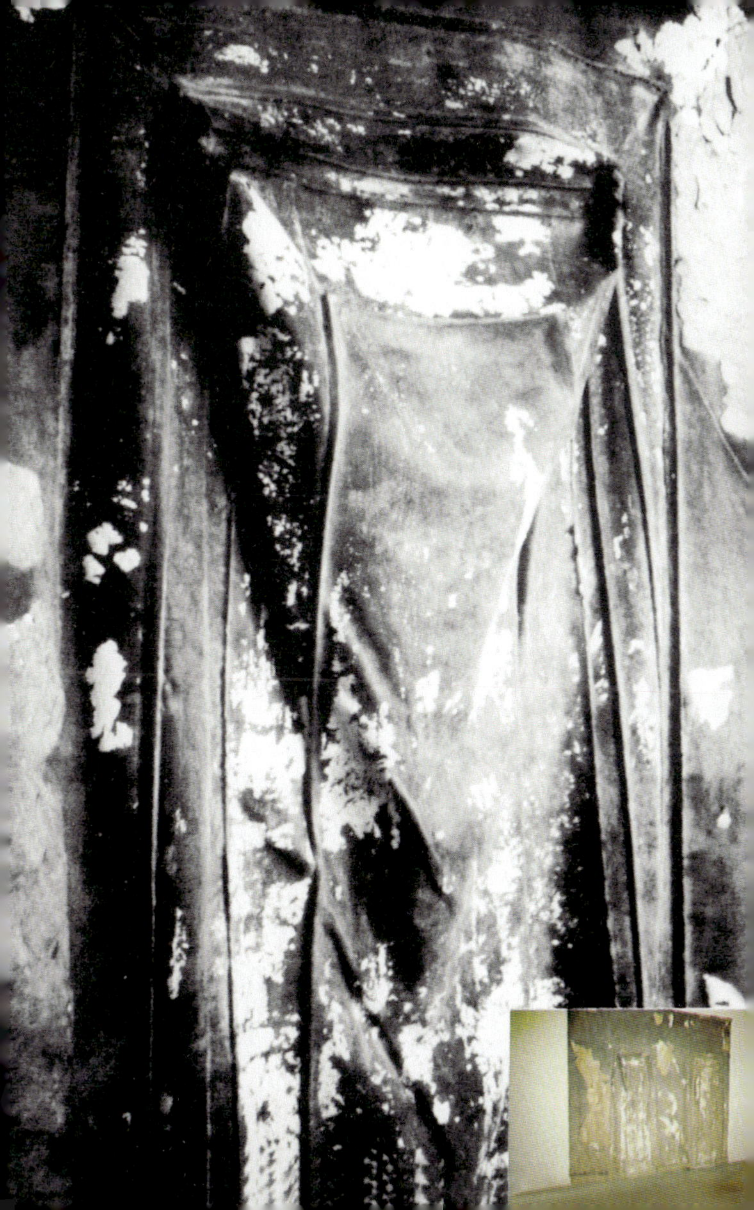

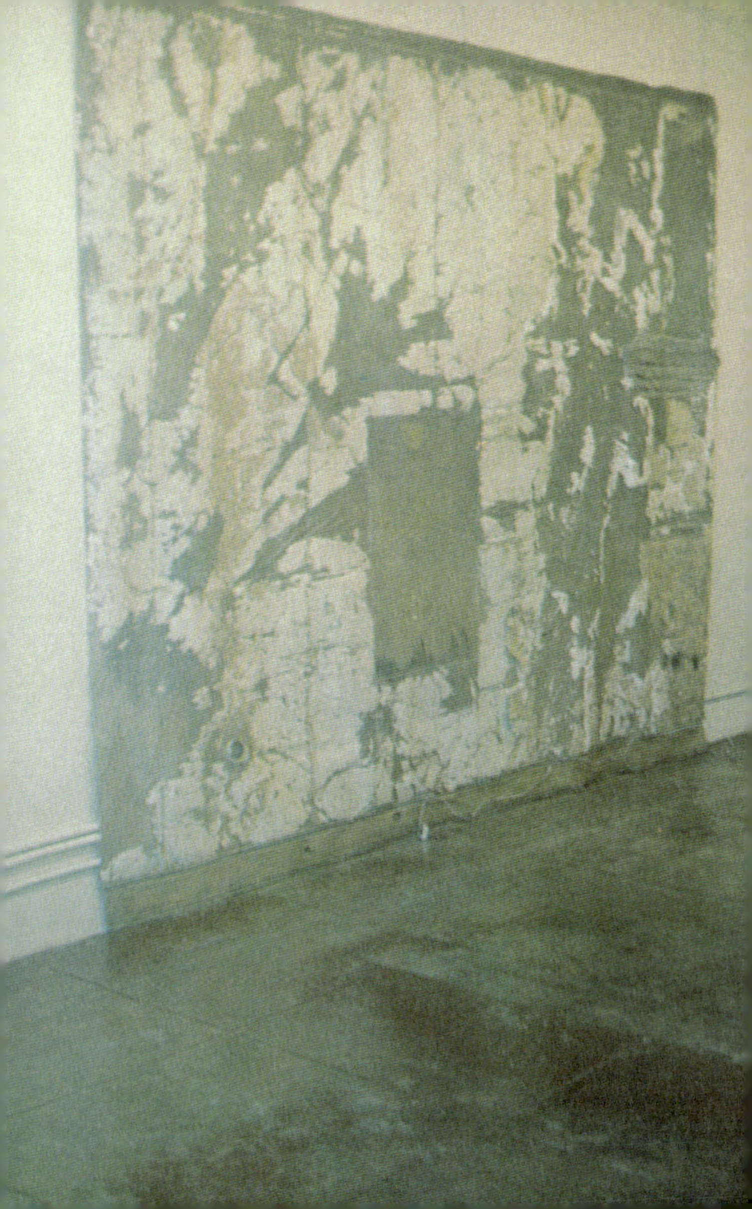

193
Powder room wall,
first floor
4 August 1971
Latex rubber
110″ x 140″

192
Small wall with slats,
first floor
4 August 1971
Latex rubber
110″ x 81½″

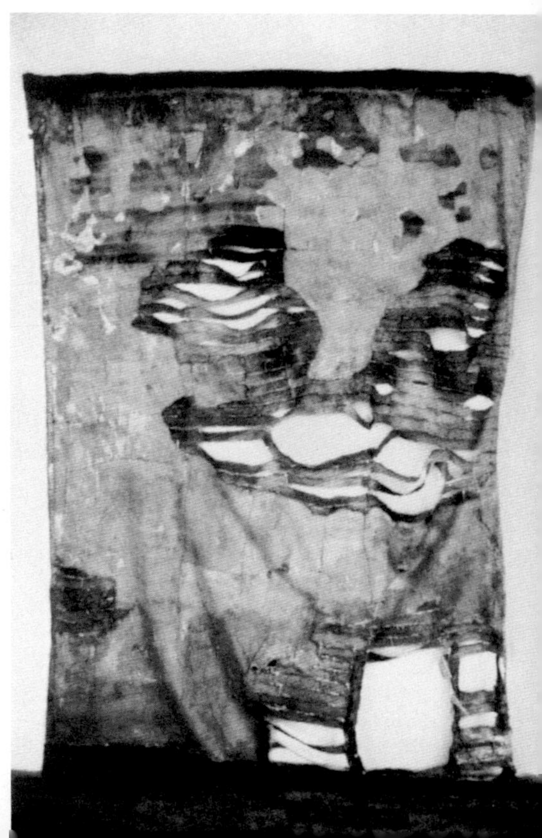

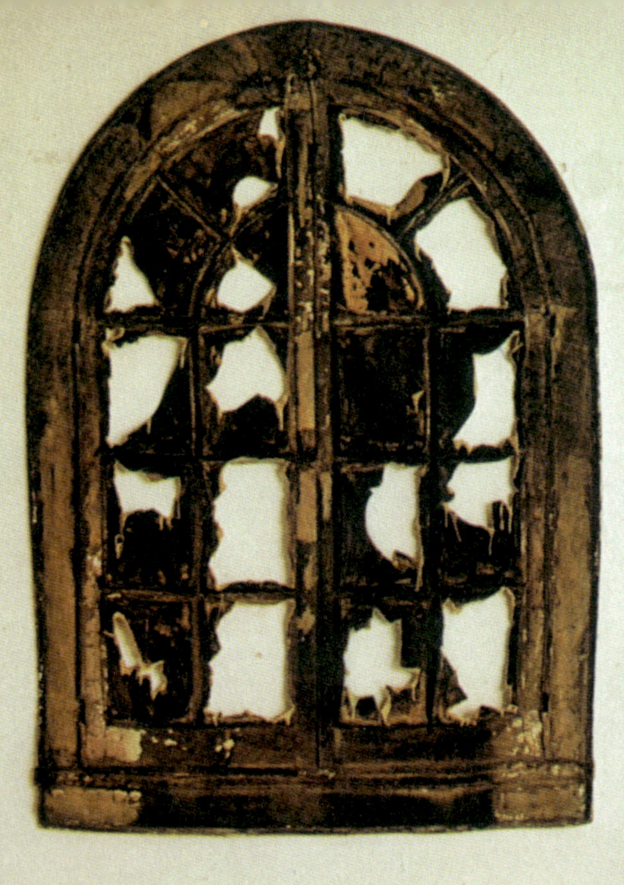

191
Broken window,
first floor
4 August 1971
Latex rubber
59″x 50″

190
103 (test),
Barclay House
4 August 1971
Latex rubber
3¾″x 39¼″

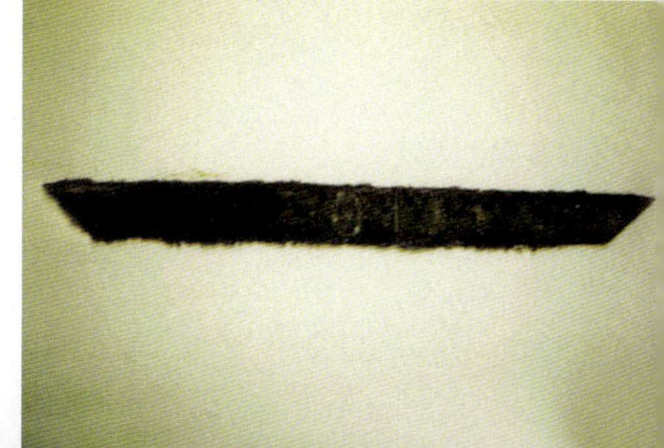

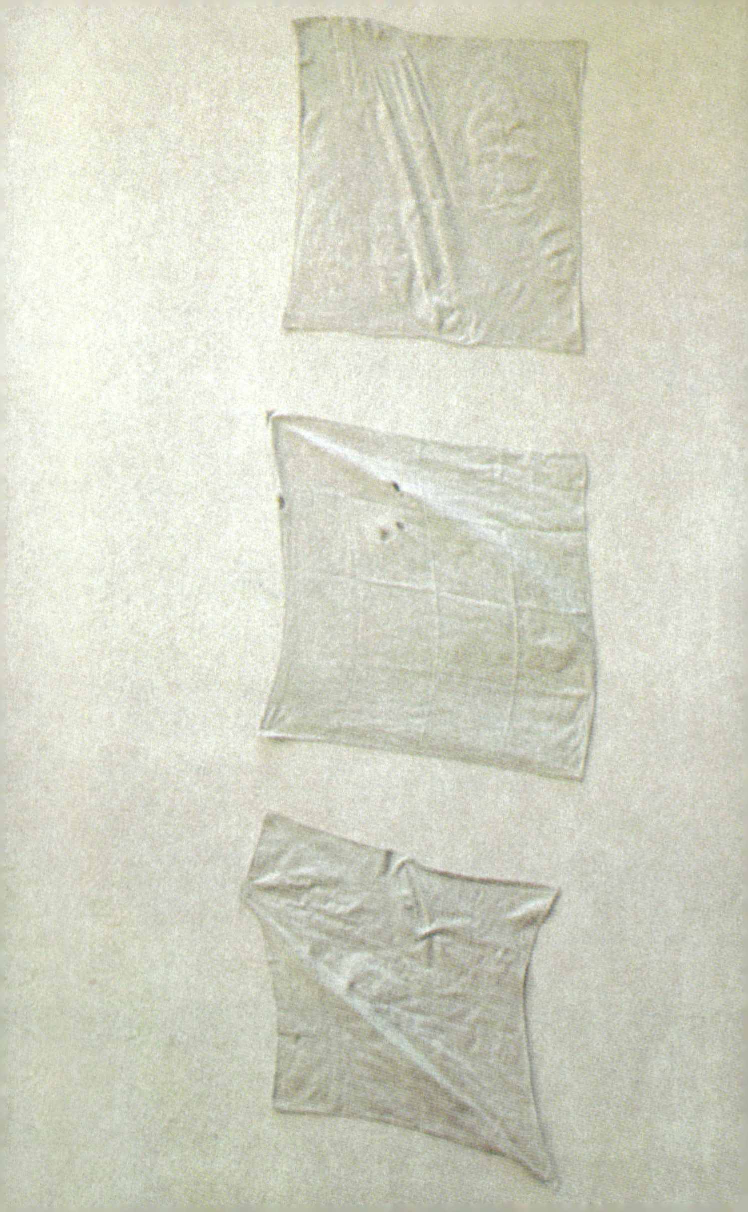

189
Three handkerchiefs
unlimited multiple
4 August 1971
Latex rubber
17″ x 18½″ (left)
17½″ x 18½″ (center)
15½″ x 17″ (right)

188
Green Bolus
July 1971 to 5 February 1972
Polyester resin and
acrylic lacquer, 48″ x 15 ⅛″ x 4″

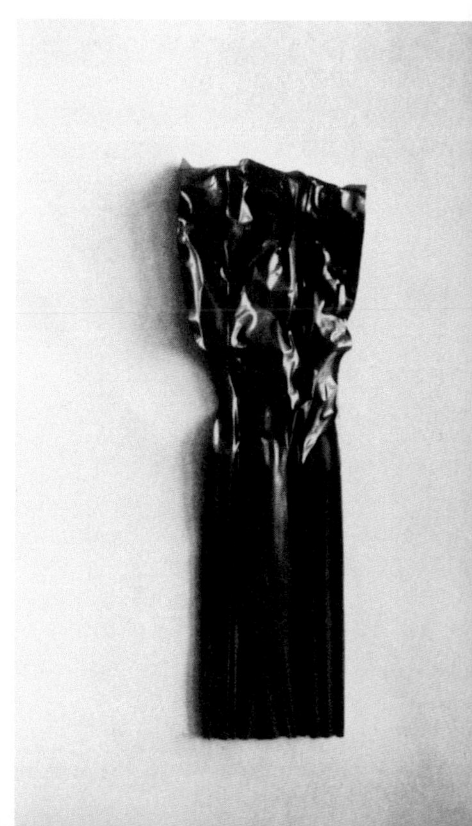

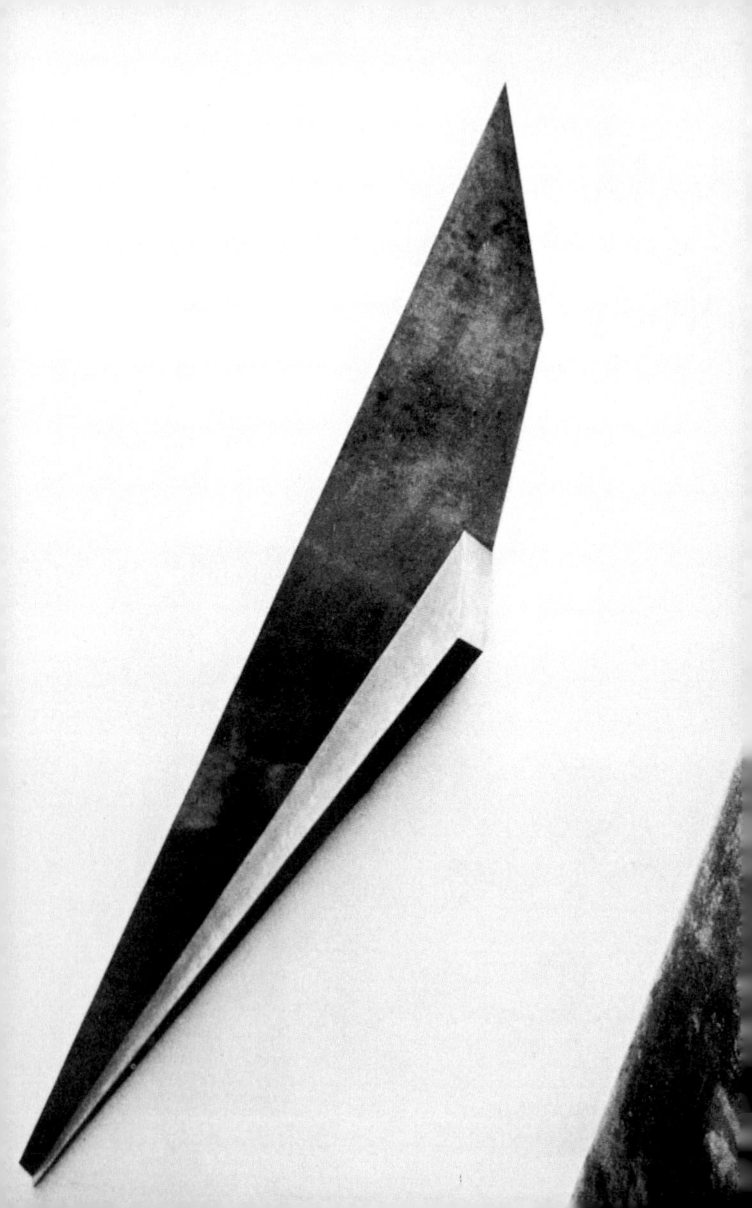

187.
Aluminum piece
July 1971 to
1 February 1972
Sheet aluminum
18½"x 128½"x 6"

186 (not illustrated)
Cold Roll
Unfinished July 1971
Acrylic on canvas, 51¾"x 72"

185
Space No. 1 Neon
3 July 1971
Neon, 97½″

184 (not illustrated)
Vert neon piece (green)
28 June 1971
Neon, 21″
Destroyed 24 Sept. 1971

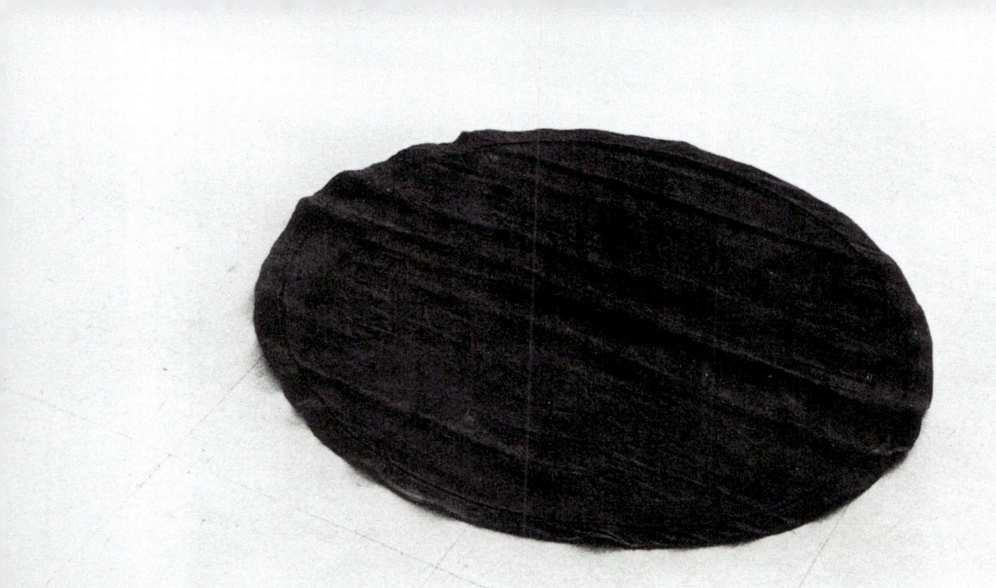

183
Blue neon piece
28 June 1971
Neon, 30″

182
Manhole cover
28 June 1971
Latex rubber
24″ x 32″

Manhole Neg.
28 June 1971
Latex rubber
14″ x 19″ x 3¼″

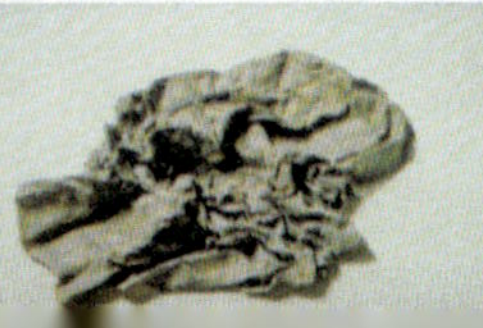

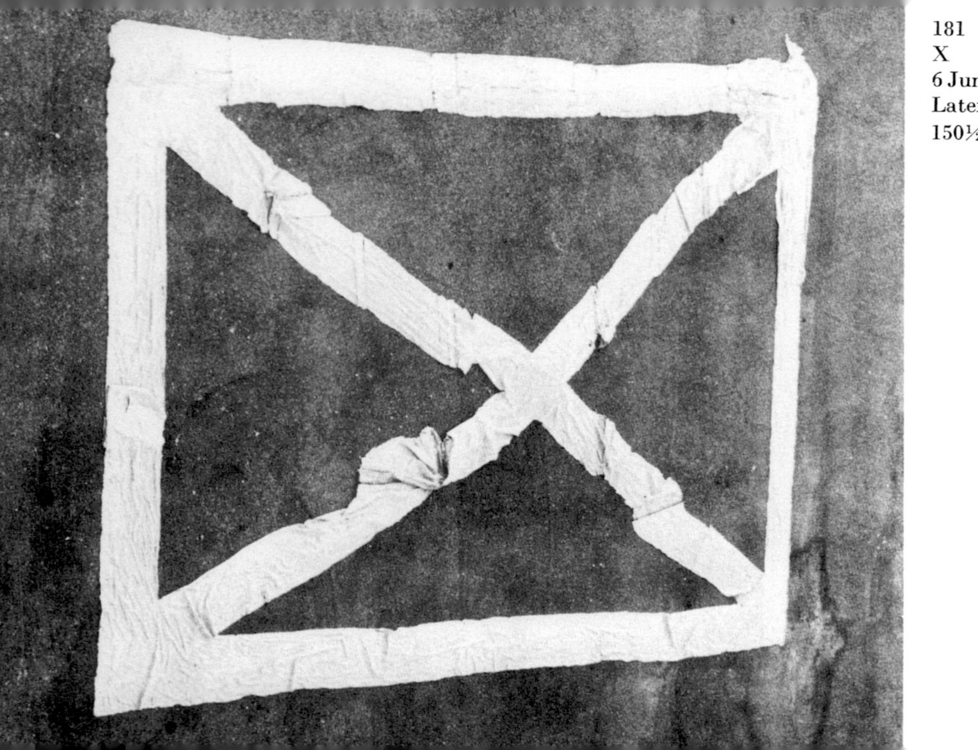

181
X
6 June 1971
Latex rubber
150½" x 214"

180
Loft window
5 June 1971
Latex rubber
113″ x 60″

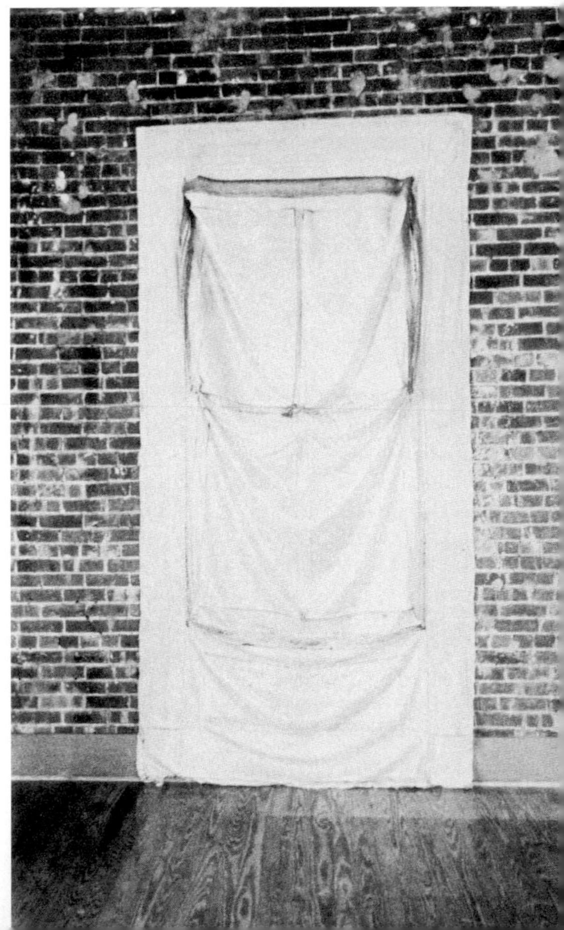

179
Ralph's Door
4 June 1971
Latex rubber
92¾″ x 43″

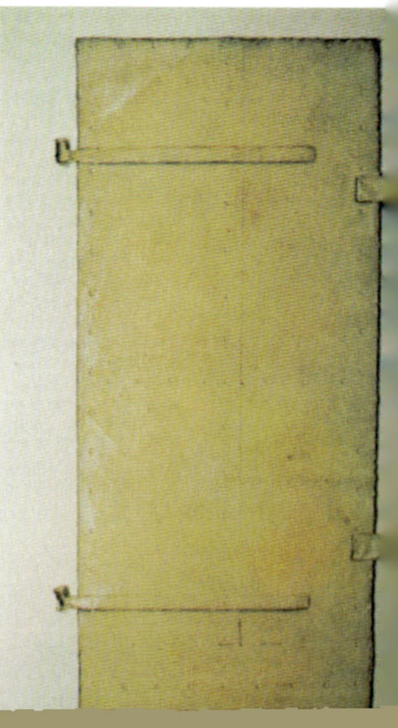

178
Brick painting
(from Wall Rubbing No. 1)
3 June 1971
Latex rubber
and mixed media
34¼″ x 48″

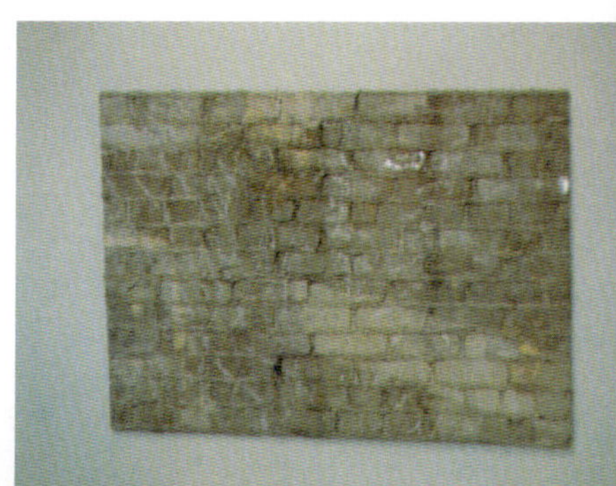

177 (not illustrated)
Site wall piece
3 June 1971
Latex rubber
17"x 74"

176
Hanging bricks
3 June 1971
Latex rubber
53"x 19"x 4"

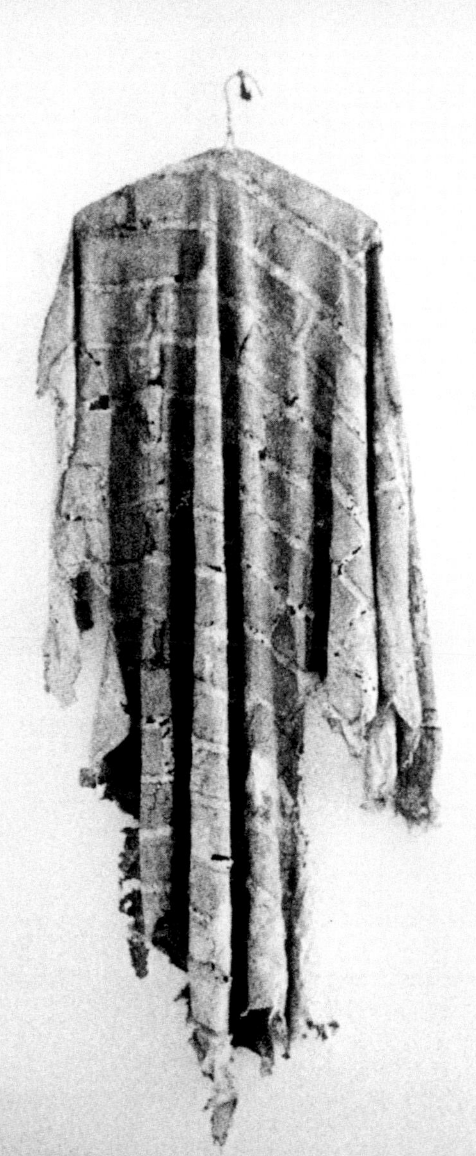

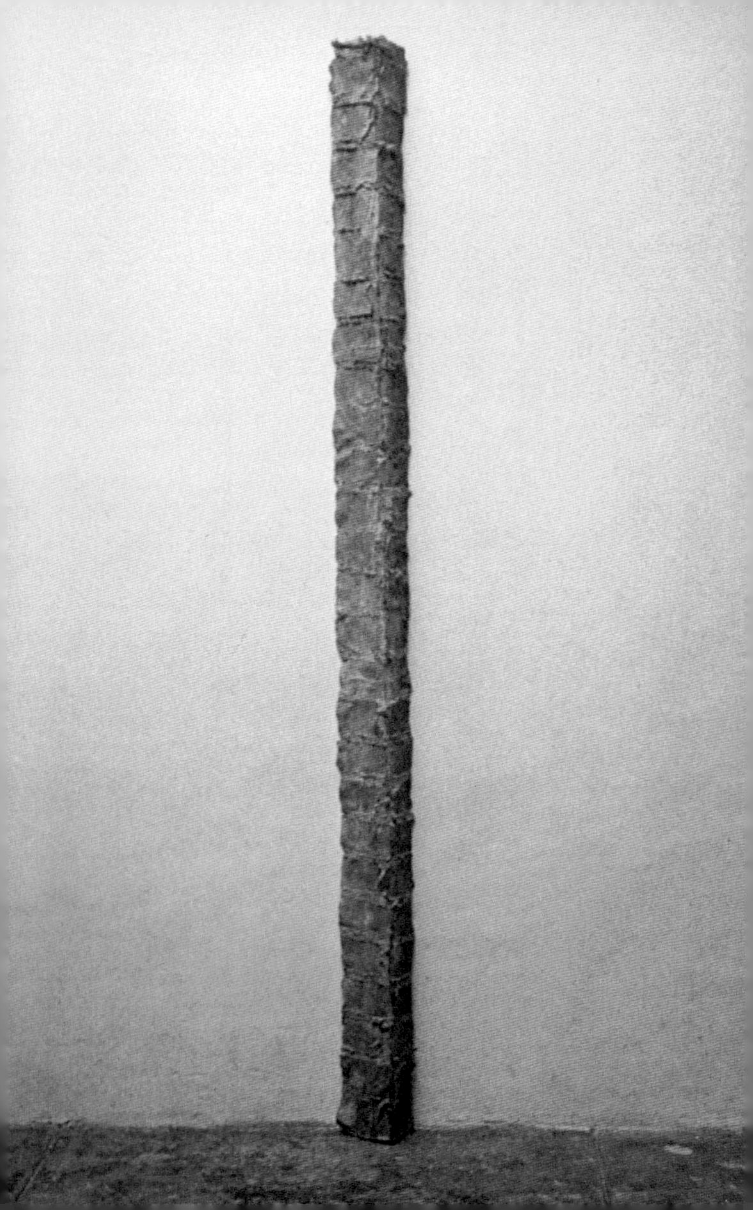

75
Bricks, small corner
June 1971
Latex rubber
0¼″x 5″x 2¾″

174
Bricks, large corner
2 June 1971
Latex rubber
155″x 4″x 7″

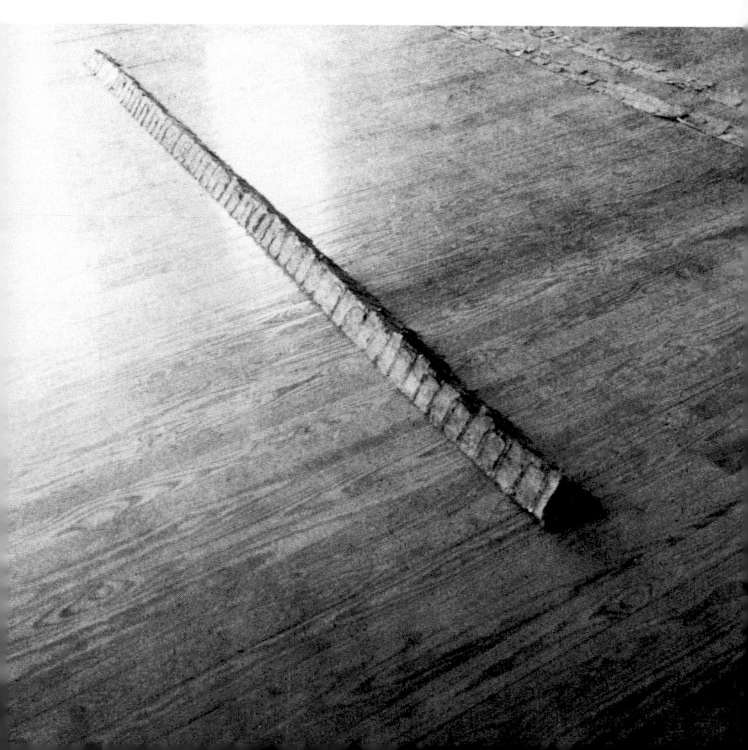

173
15°
2 June 1971
Latex rubber
360″x 6½″
and 324½″x 6½″

172
Around the House
16 May 1971
Latex rubber
36″x 2436″ approx.

171
Across the Street
14 May 1971
Latex rubber

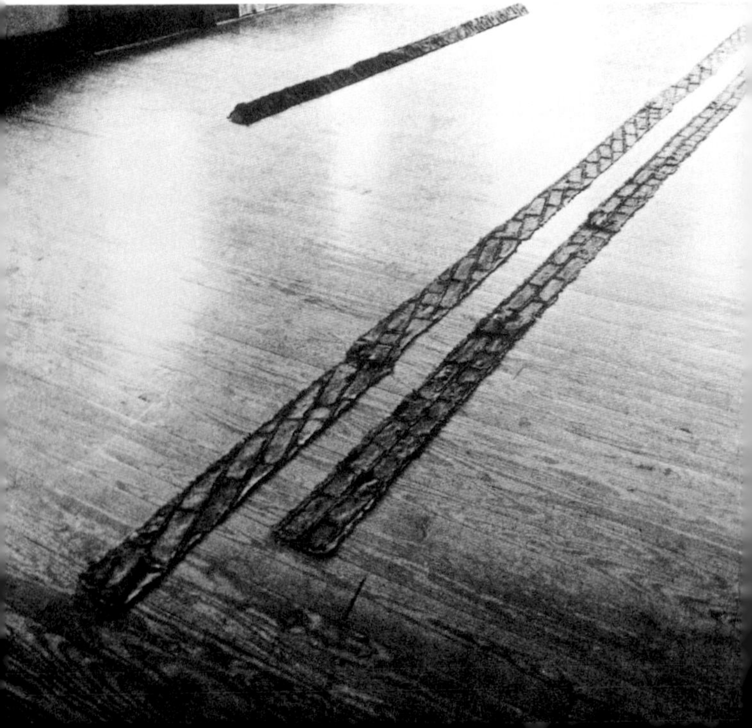

172
Around the House
16 May 1971
Latex rubber
36″x 2436″ approx.

171
Across the Street (positive)
14 May 1971
Latex rubber, 120″x 360″

Curb to Curb (negative)
2 May 1971
Latex rubber, 138″x 316″,
minus curbs

170
Garage Door
13 May 1971
Latex rubber
84″x 48″

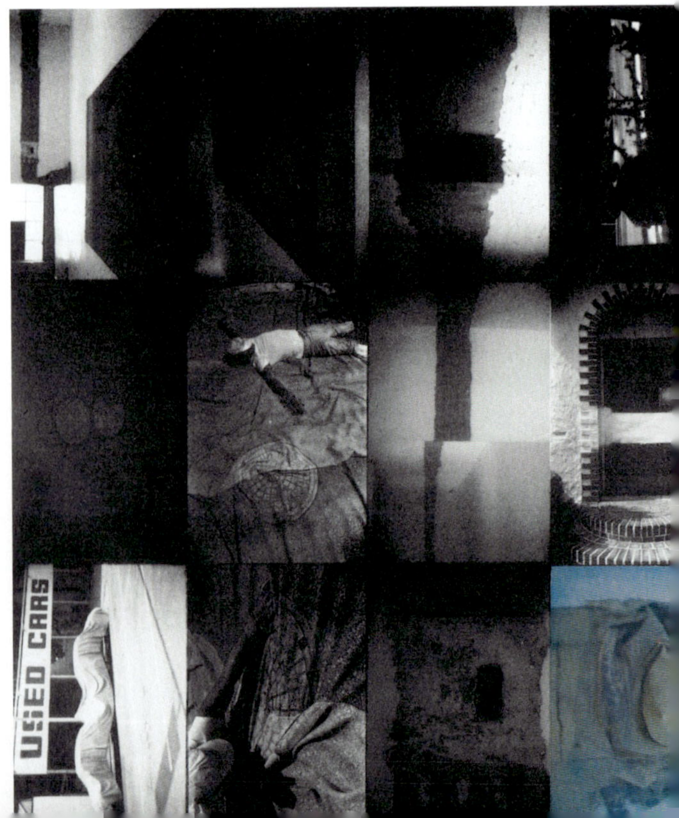

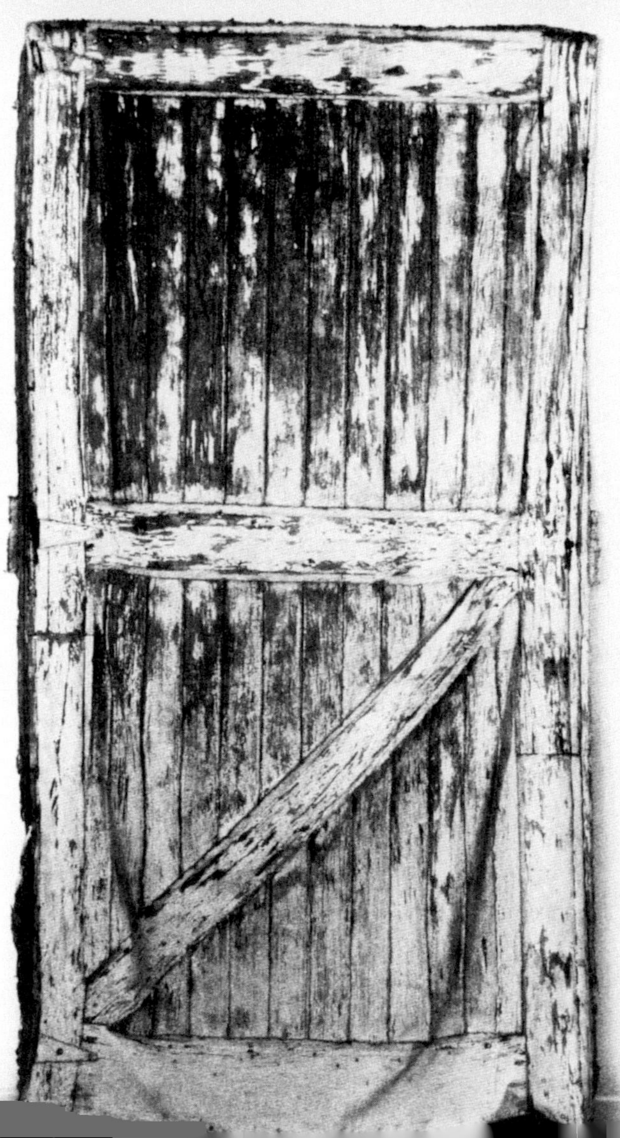

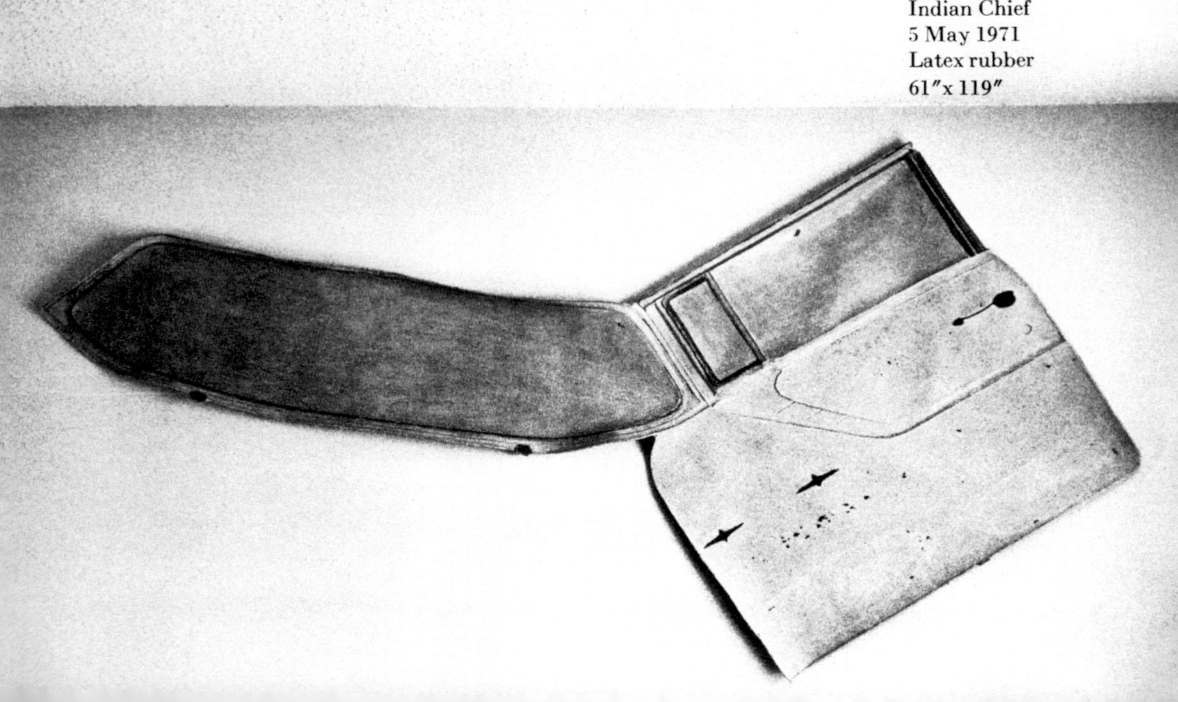

169
Indian Chief
5 May 1971
Latex rubber
61″ x 119″

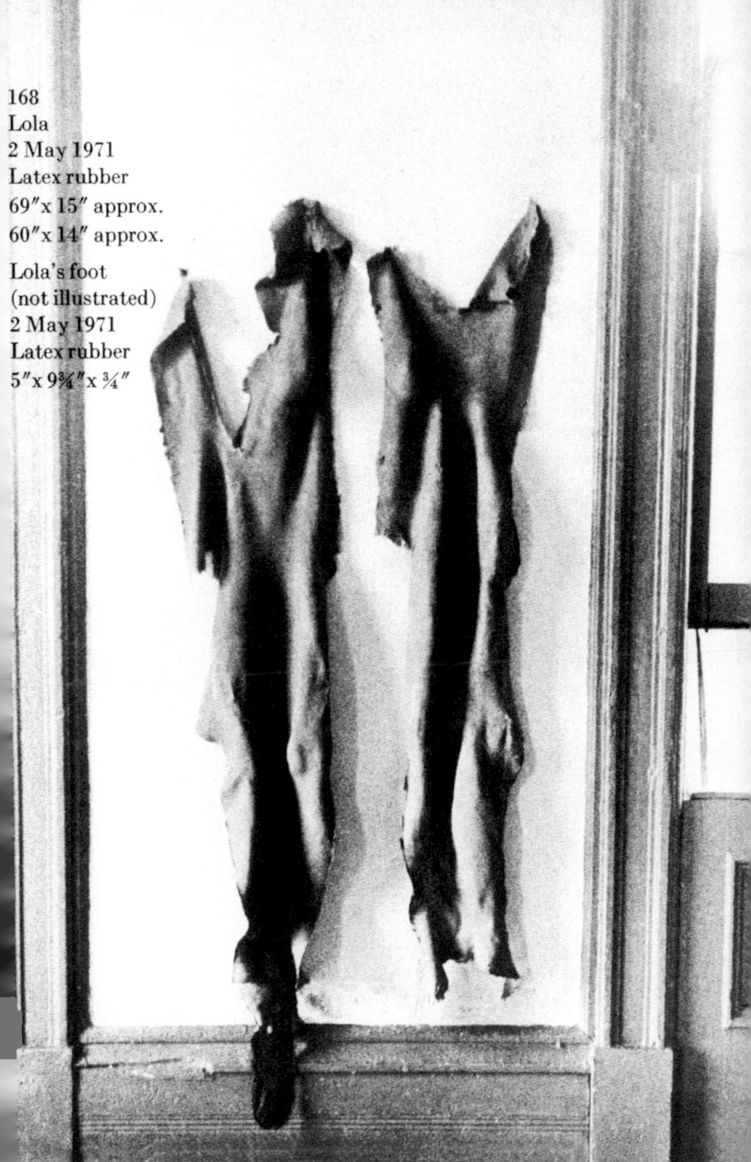

168
Lola
2 May 1971
Latex rubber
69″x 15″ approx.
60″x 14″ approx.

Lola's foot
(not illustrated)
2 May 1971
Latex rubber
5″x 9¾″x ¾″

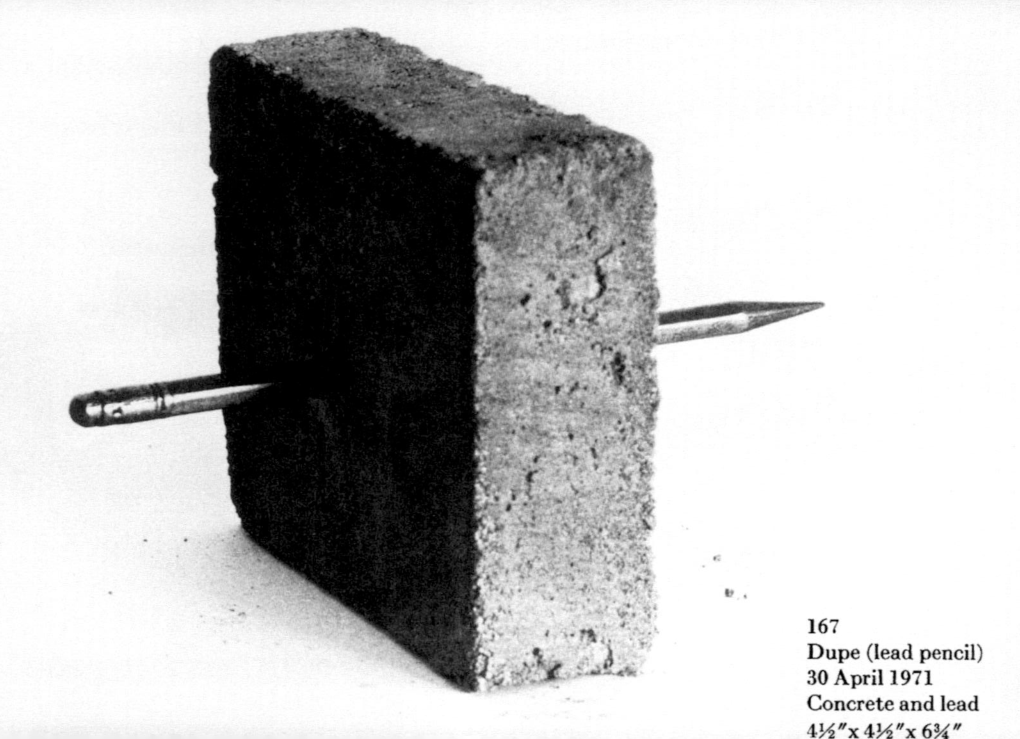

167
Dupe (lead pencil)
30 April 1971
Concrete and lead
4½" x 4½" x 6¾"

166
Blunt Arrival (light bulb)
30 April 1971
Concrete and lead
3¼"x 3¼"x 4¼"

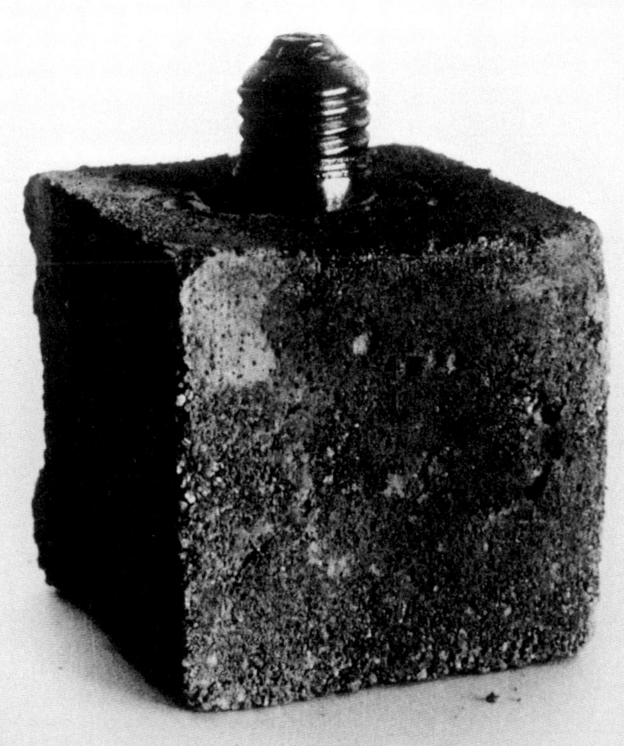

165
Long Sock
30 April 1971
Flexible polyester resin
and bronze powder
15¾″x 3¼″

Handle Sock
30 April 1971
Polyester resin
and sand
15½″x 3¼″x 2″

164
Saulle's Place
23 April 1971
Latex rubber and burlap
144″x 600″x 10″ approx.

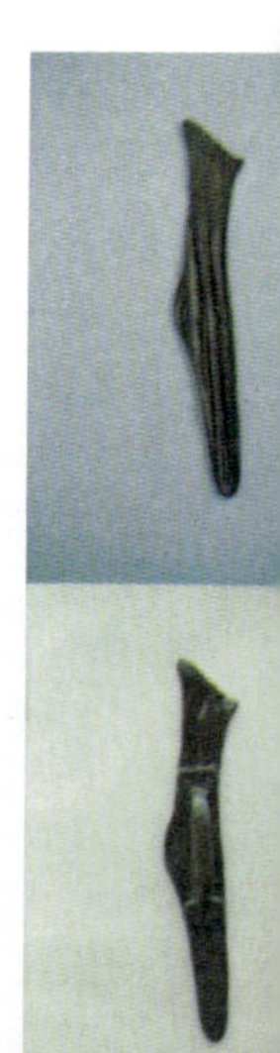

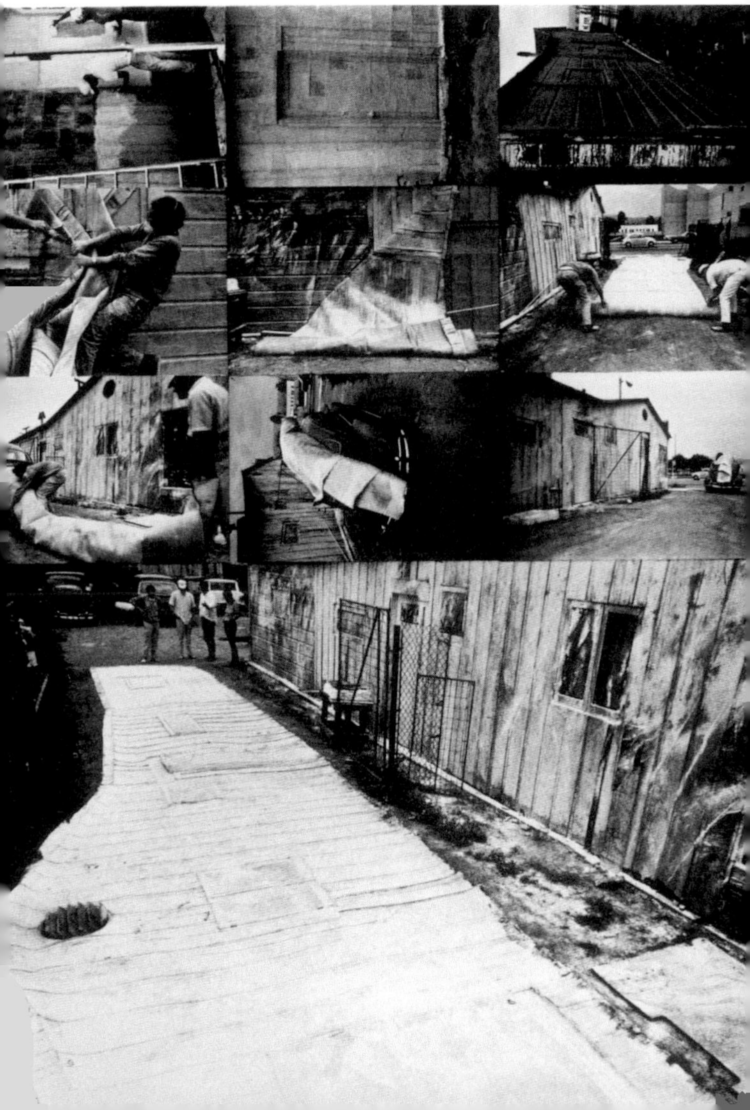

163
Blue screen door
11 March 1971
Polyester resin
and fiberglass
76½"x 31¾"x 1½"

162
Clear screen door
11 March 1971
Polyester resin
77"x 40½"x 2½"
Destroyed 4 May 1971

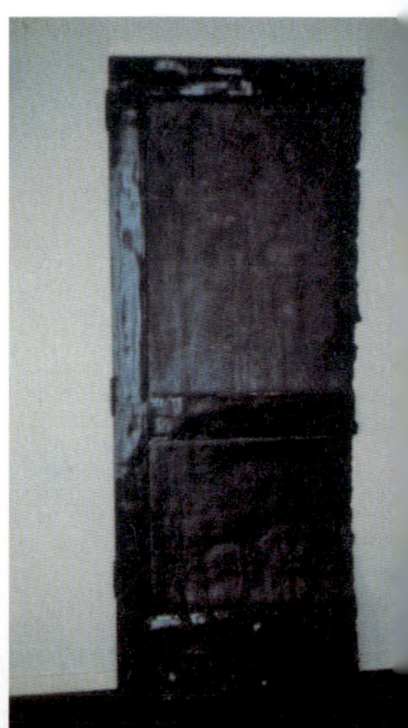

161
Sucker Sock
4 March 1971
Polyester resin
7¾″x 10″

160
Owl's Navel Revealed
4 March 1971
Polyester resin
2⅛″x 2⅛″x 1¼″

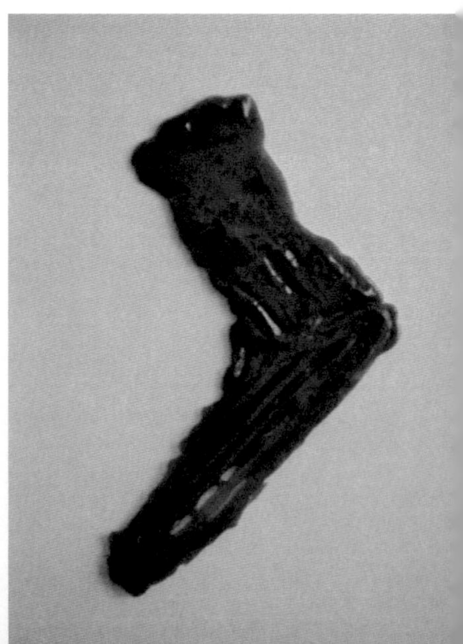

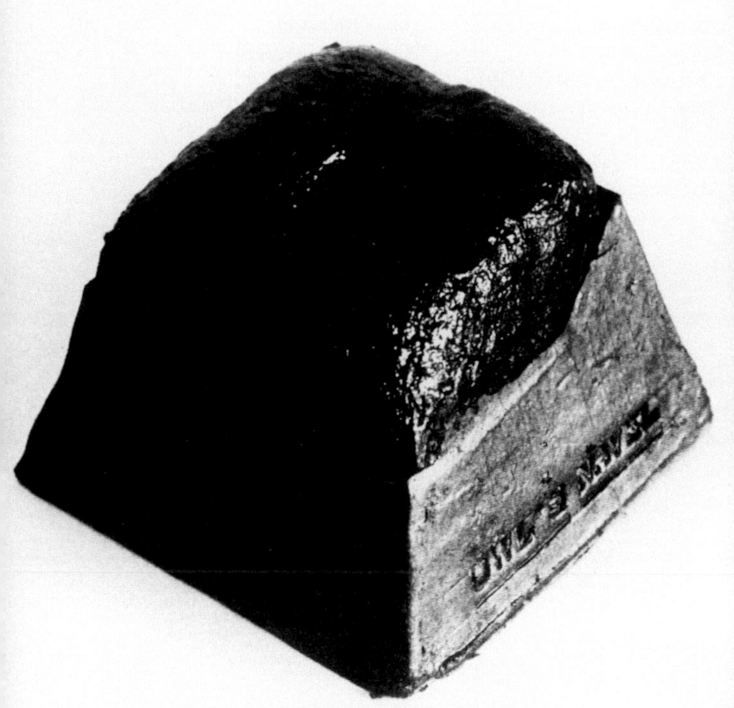

159 (not illustrated)
91 life drawings
2 February to 3 March 1971
Charcoal, graphite and
conté on paper
All 18″x 12⅜″
53 destroyed 20 Nov. 1973

158 (with detail)
Natural resin screen door
2 March 1971
Polyester resin and fiberglass
79″x 42″x 3″

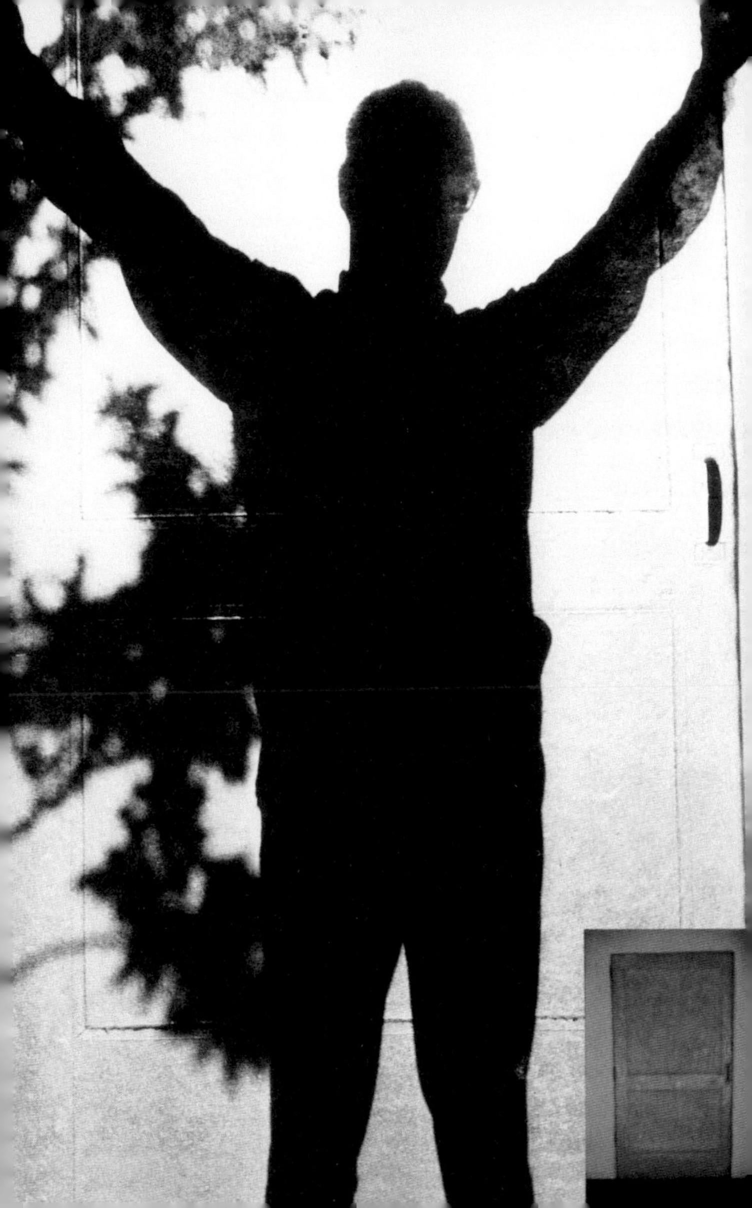

157
Allusion
(Walking Wheel)
2 March 1971
Mixed media
59"x 11¼"x 5½"

156
Foam screen door
26 February 1971
Polyester resin, fiberglass,
and polyurethane foam
78"x 41½"x 4"

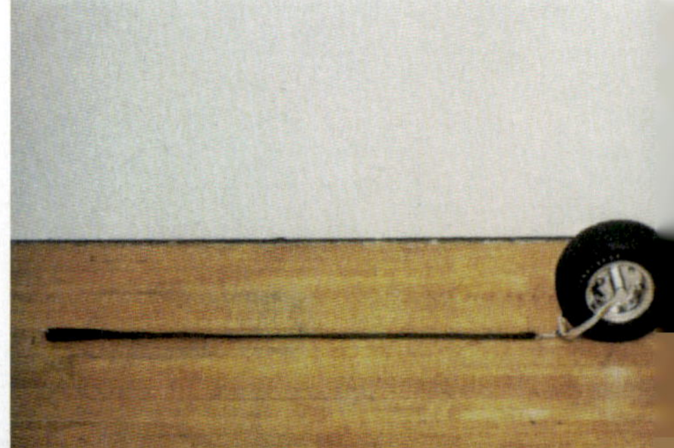

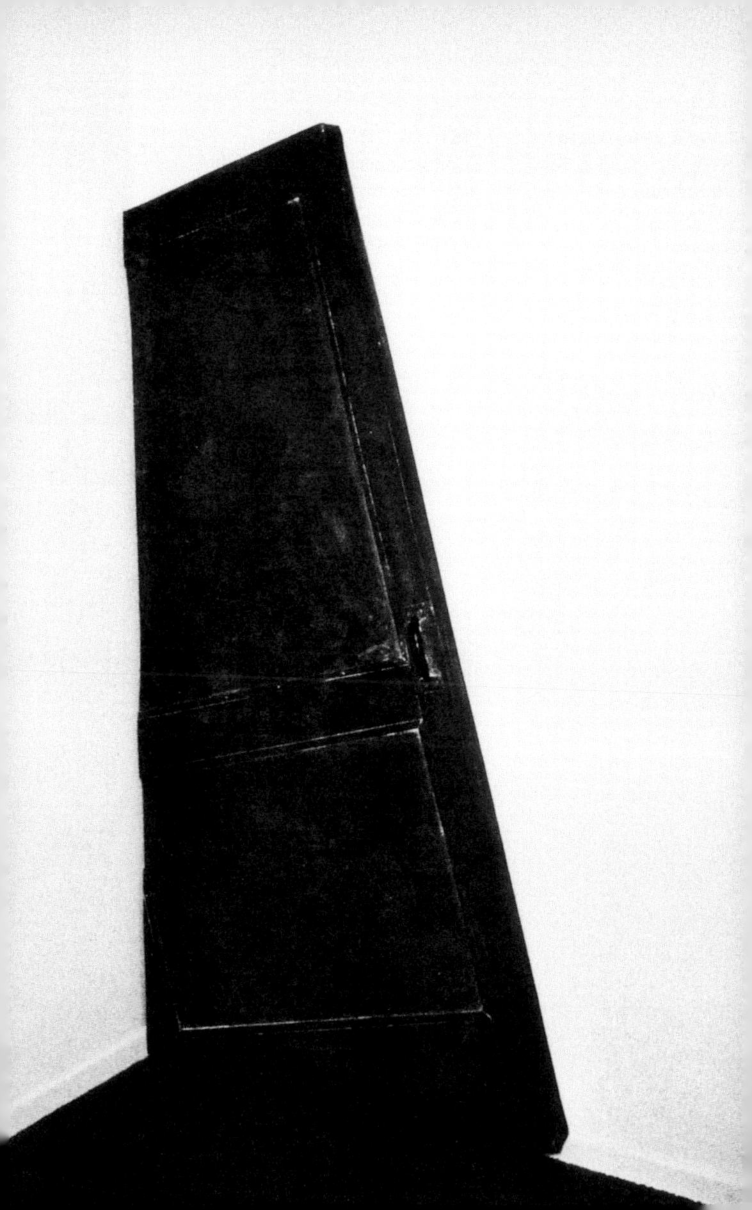

155 (not illustrated)
Free-pour screen door
23 February 1971
Polyester resin
78"x 43"x 2¾"
Destroyed 16 June 1971

154
Concrete screen door handle
20 February 1971
Concrete and steel
11¼"x 6¼"x 3"

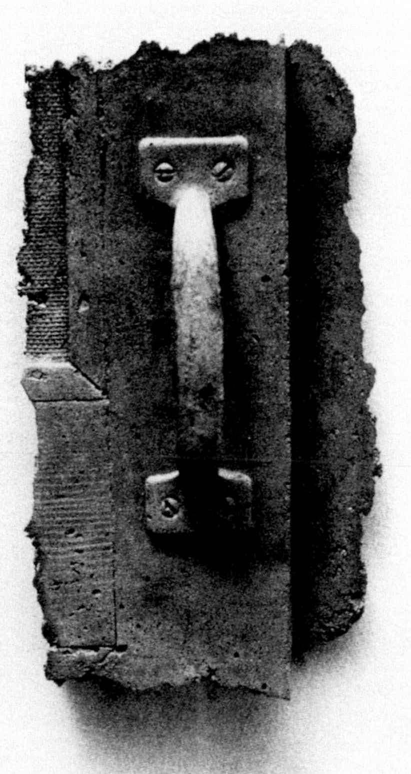

153
Concrete screen door with hole
20 February 1971
Concrete and steel, 80"x 45"x 5"

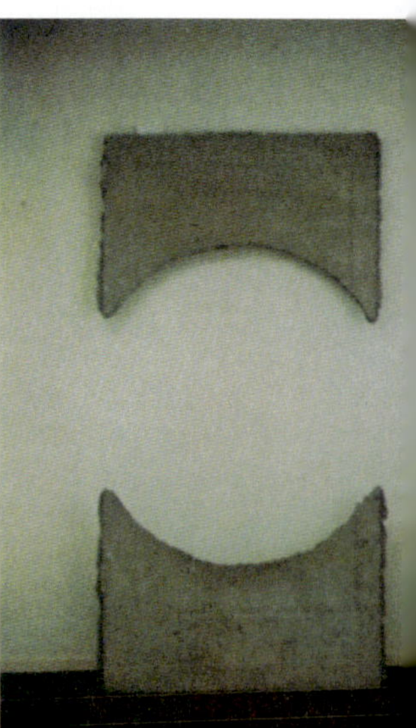

152
Opaque door edge
24 February 1971
Polyester resin, fiberglass
and acrylic lacquer
30"x 2"x 1¾"

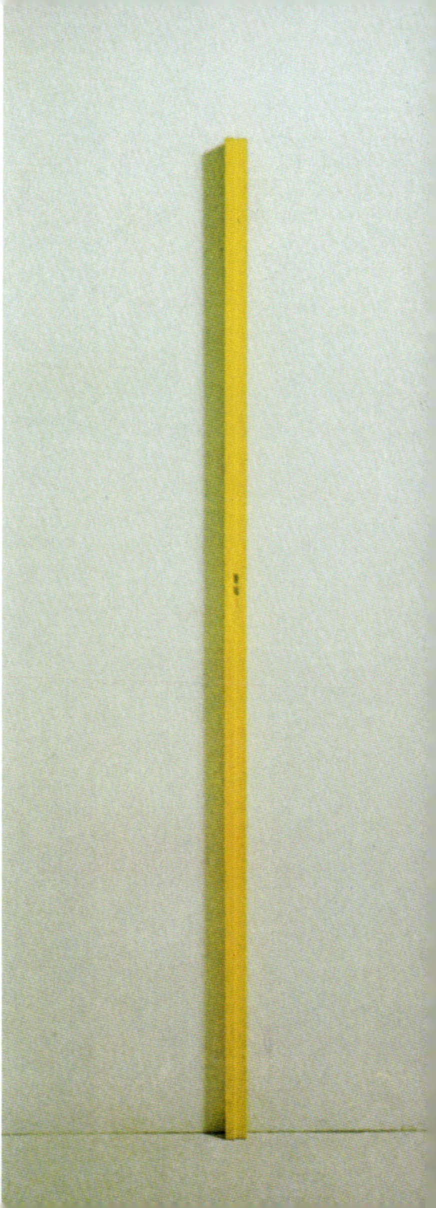

151
Door edge
19 February 1971
Polyester resin and fiberglass
80″x 2″x 1¾″

.50 (not illustrated)
Kiss
.9 February 1971
Lead and acrylic lacquer
⅛"x 1"x ⅜"

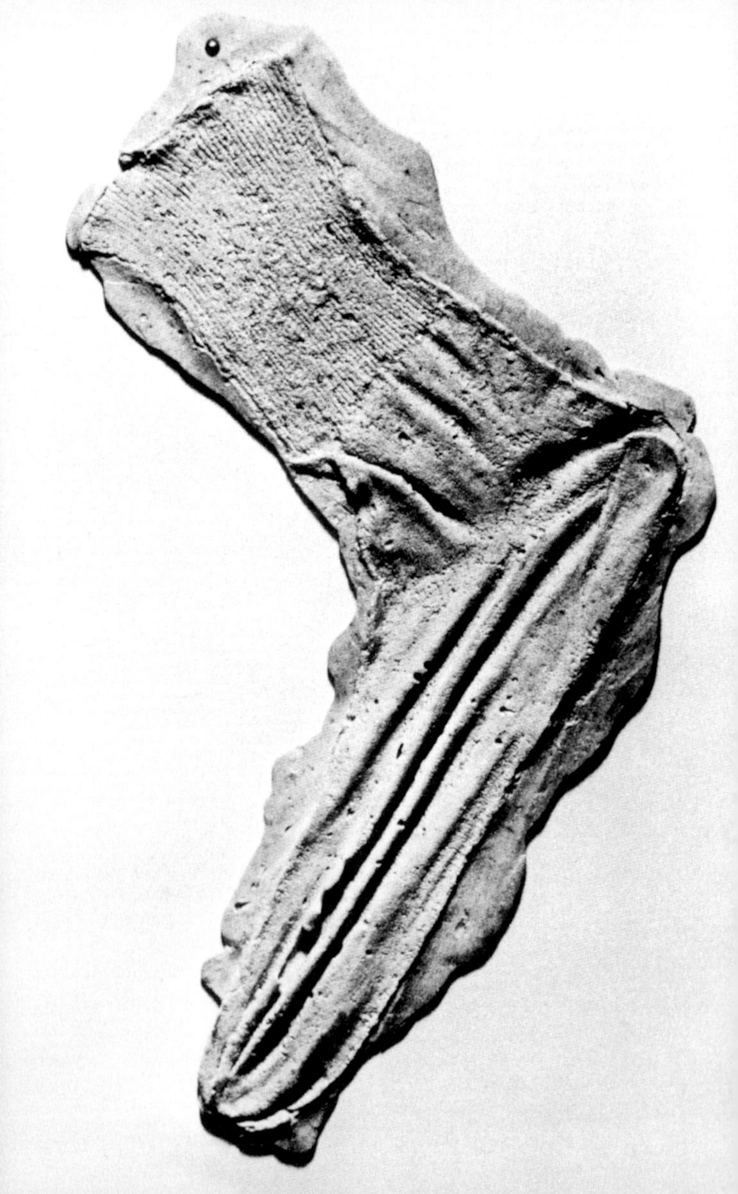

149
Rubber sock
18 February 1971
Cast rubber, 12″x 8″

148
Cast socks
14-18 February 1971
Wax

Falling Sock, 11¾″x 14⅞″
Rauschenberg Sock, 10¾″x 11¾″
Fish Sock, 15¾″x 8½″
Reptile Sock, 10⅞″x 12½″
Dual Sock, 17⅜″x 13″
Drip Sock, 15⅝″x 4¼″

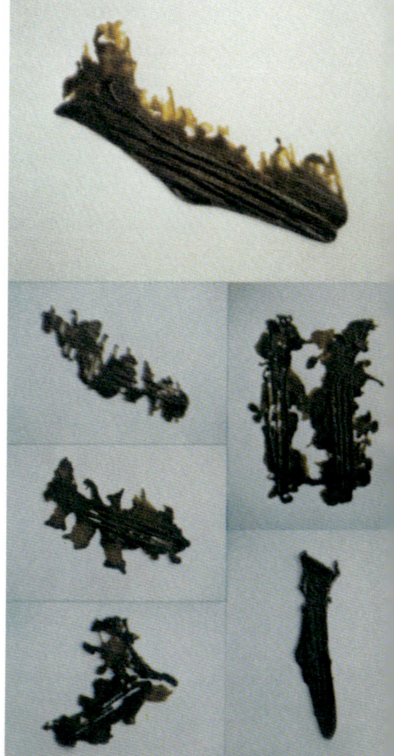

147
Marlenescape
14 February 1971
Watercolor
3¾″ x 5¼″

146
R. M. Rill
7 February 1971
Lead 2″ x 8″

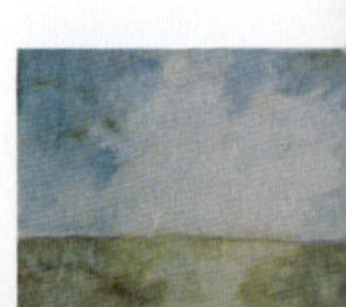

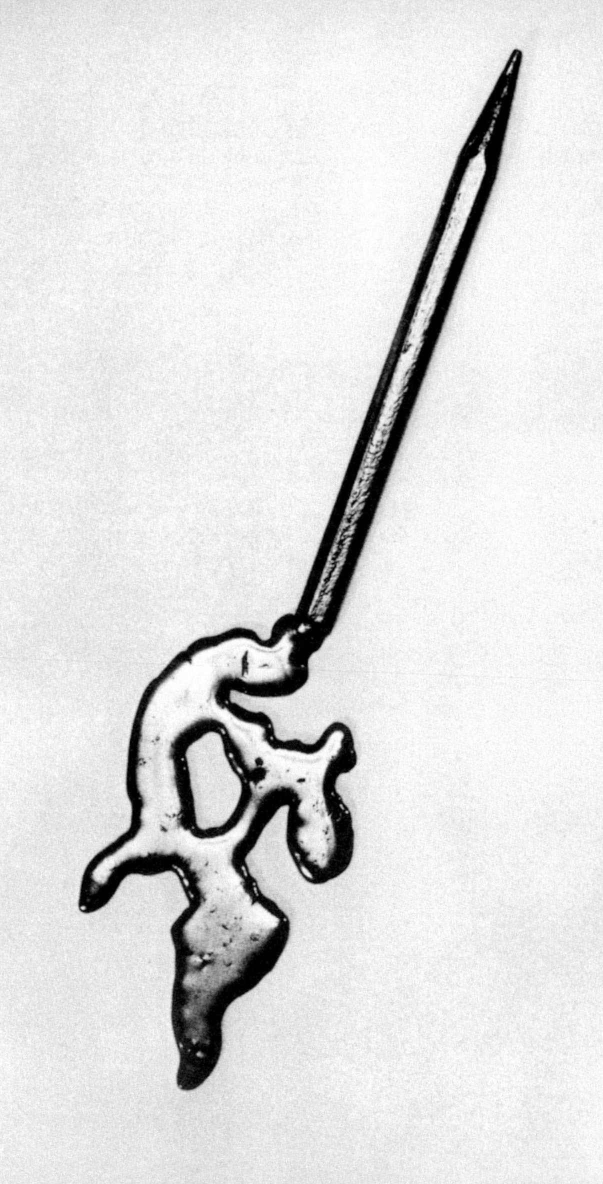

145
Trinket $1.00
4 February 1971
Lead, ½″x ½″x ¹¹⁄₁₆″

144 (not illustrated)
Moving object (untitled)
2 January 1971
Oil on canvas, 36″x 36″
Destroyed 20 Dec. 1972

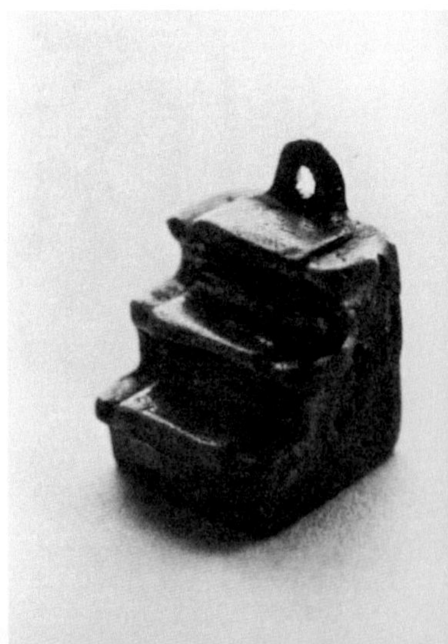

143

50 painting sketches
Gouache and pencil on paper
8 April 1970 to 16 November 1972
(also see next page)

1. 8 April 1970, 4⅝″x 6½″
2. 8 April 1970, 4⅜″x 5⅞″
3. 8 April 1970, 5⅞″x 4⅛″
4. 8 April 1970, 4⅛″x 5⅝″
5. 8 April 1970, 4⅜″x 5¾″
6. 23 Nov. 1970, 4½″x 3½″
7. 24 Nov. 1970, 4½″x 3¾″
8. 23 Nov. 1970, 4½″x 3⅜″
9. 23 Nov. 1970, 4⅛″x 3½″
10. 23 Nov. 1970, 4½″x 3⅜″

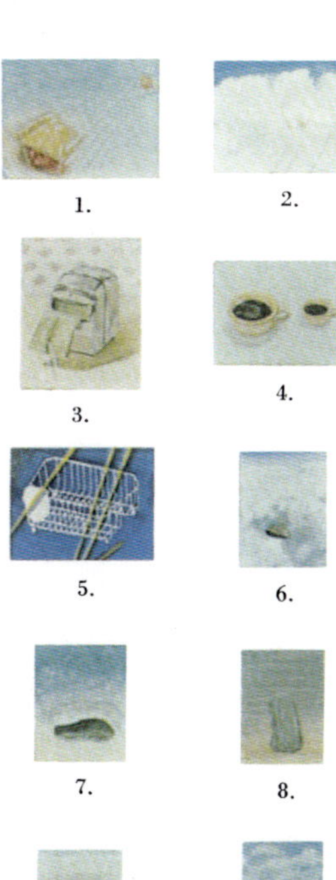

1.

2.

3.

4.

5.

6.

7.

8.

9.

10.

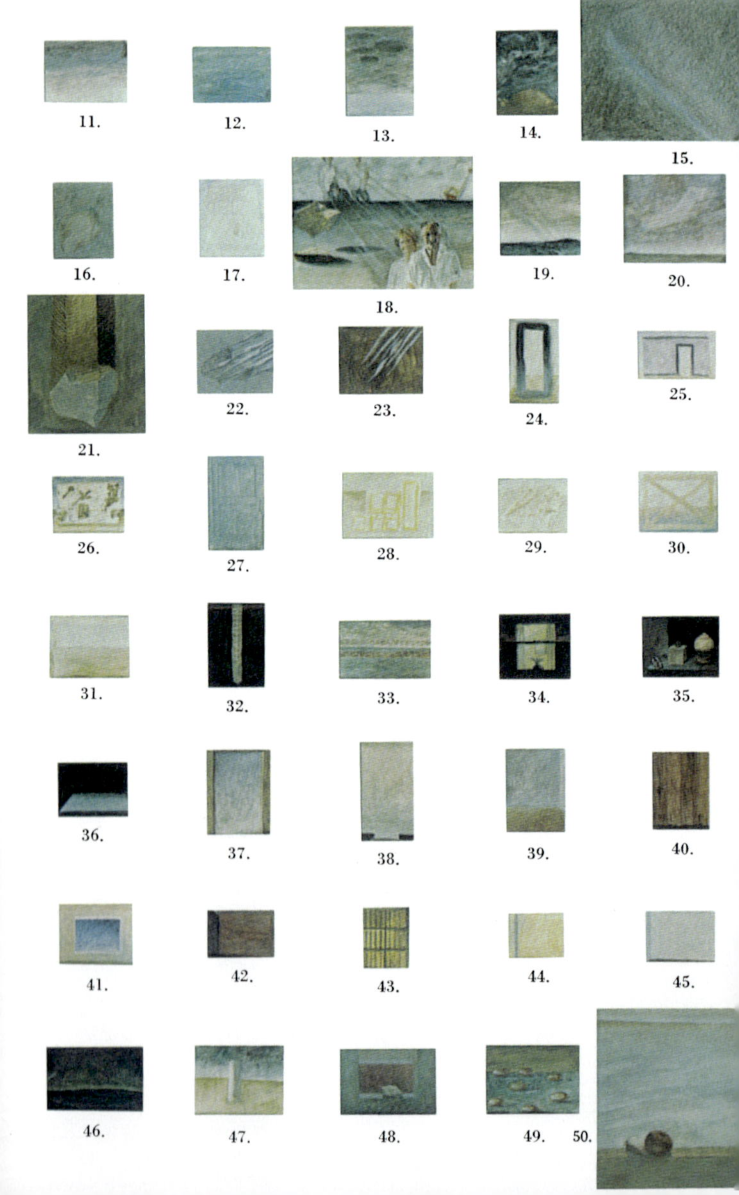

11.

12.

13.

14.

15.

16.

17.

18.

19.

20.

21.

22.

23.

24.

25.

26.

27.

28.

29.

30.

31.

32.

33.

34.

35.

36.

37.

38.

39.

40.

41.

42.

43.

44.

45.

46.

47.

48.

49.   50.

11. 23 Nov. 1970, 3¼"x 4½"
12. 23 Nov. 1970, 3⅛"x 4⅜"
13. 23 Nov. 1970, 4¾"x 3¾"
14. 23 Nov. 1970, 4½"x 3½"
15. 12 Jan. 1971, 3¼"x 4½"
16. 12 Jan. 1971, 4⅛"x 3⅜"
17. 16 Jan. 1971, 4¼"x 3⅝"
18. 16 Jan. 1971, 7⅛"x 9⅛"
19. 16 Jan. 1971, 4" x 4½"
20. 16 Jan. 1971, 4¾"x 5⅝"
21. 18 Jan. 1971, 7½"x 6½"
22. 19 Jan. 1971, 3½"x 4¼"
23. 19 Jan. 1971, 3¾"x 4⅝"
24. 27 Dec. 1971, 4½"x 2¾"
25. 27 Dec. 1971, 2⅝"x 4¼"
26. 27 Dec. 1971, 3"x 4"
27. 27 Dec. 1971, 5"x 3⅛"
28. 28 Dec. 1971, 3⅝"x 4¾"
29. 28 Dec. 1971, 3"x 3⅛"
30. 6 Jan. 1972, 3⅜"x 4¼"
31. 6 Jan. 1972, 3½"x 4⅜"
32. 6 Jan. 1972, 4½"x 3⅛"
33. 6 Jan. 1972, 3¼"x 5"
34. 6 Jan. 1972, 3½"x 4"
35. 9 Jan. 1972, 3¼"x 4¼"
36. 9 Jan. 1972, 2⅞"x 3⅞"
37. 12 Jan. 1972, 4½"x 3½"
38. 12 Jan. 1972, 5¼"x 2⅞"
39. 14 Jan. 1972, 4½"x 3¼"
40. 15 Jan. 1972, 4⅛"x 3⅛"
41. 15 Jan. 1972, 3¼"x 4⅛"
42. 15 Jan. 1972, 2⅝"x 3¾"
43. 15 Jan. 1972, 3¼"x 2⅝"
44. 16 Jan. 1972, 2½"x 3"
45. 16 Jan. 1972, 2¾"x 3⅞"
46. 16 Nov. 1972, 3½"x 5¼"
47. 16 Nov. 1972, 3¾"x 4⅞"
48. 16 Nov. 1972, 3⅝"x 5¼"
49. 16 Nov. 1972, 3¾"x 5⅛"
50. 16 Nov. 1972, 3½"x 4¾"

142
Seven models for large moving pieces
23 August to 16 October 1970
Clay

1. 4⅛"x 1¾"x 1⅜",
   lost 1971
2. 4"x 5⅝"x 1"
3. 3"x 6⅞"x 1⅛"
4. 3"x 3½"x 1"
5. 1"x 3¾"x 3½"
6. 3"x 3¼"x 3¼"
7. ⅞"x 2⅛"x 1⅝"

Mechanical drawings for moving pieces
(not illustrated)

No. 1, 2 and 3
27 August 1970
Pencil on paper
21½"x 20"

No. 7
16 September 1970
Pen on paper
7⅜"x 10½"

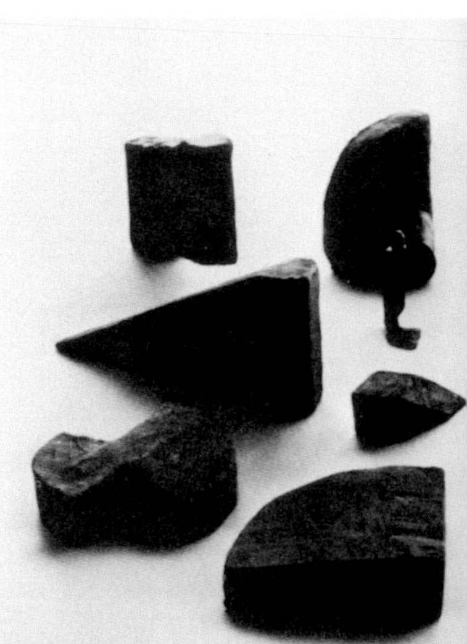

141
Projected space between my legs
16 October 1970
Concrete and steel

Thin one, 45½″x 7″x 2″ (left)
Base point left, 44″x 9½″x 2″ (center)
Base point right, 43¾″x 8½″x 1¾″ (right)
Fat short one, 42½″x 8½″x 1¾″,
destroyed Oct. 1970
Edition of 3, molds destroyed Nov. 1970

140
Aluminum foil pieces
5 April to 19 October 1970
Aluminum foil

Colonel Chicken, 1⅝″x 5¼″x 1⅜″,
destroyed Dec. 1970
Art Polish, 4¼″x 3″x 1¾″
Owl's Navel, 2¼″x 2⅜″x 1⅝″
Top O'Tradition, 3⅜″x 3⅜″x 2¼″
Trilobite, 5¼″x 4″x 1⅝″

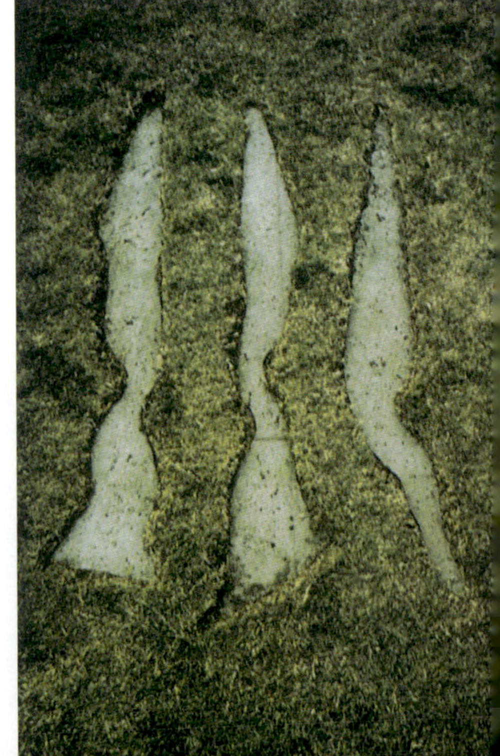

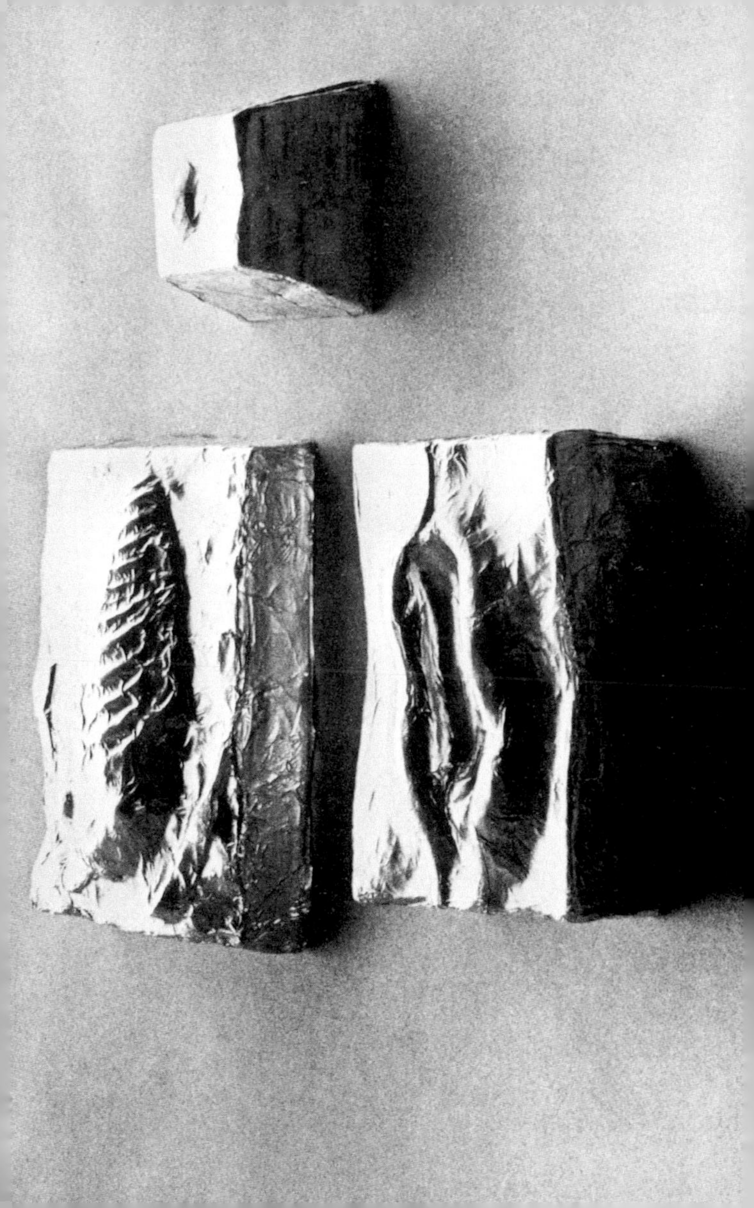

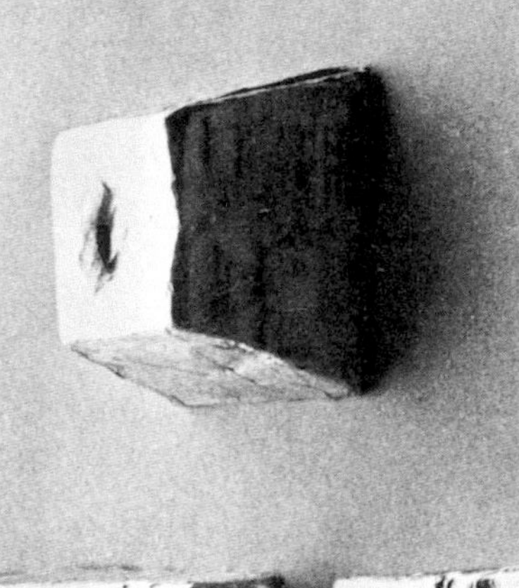

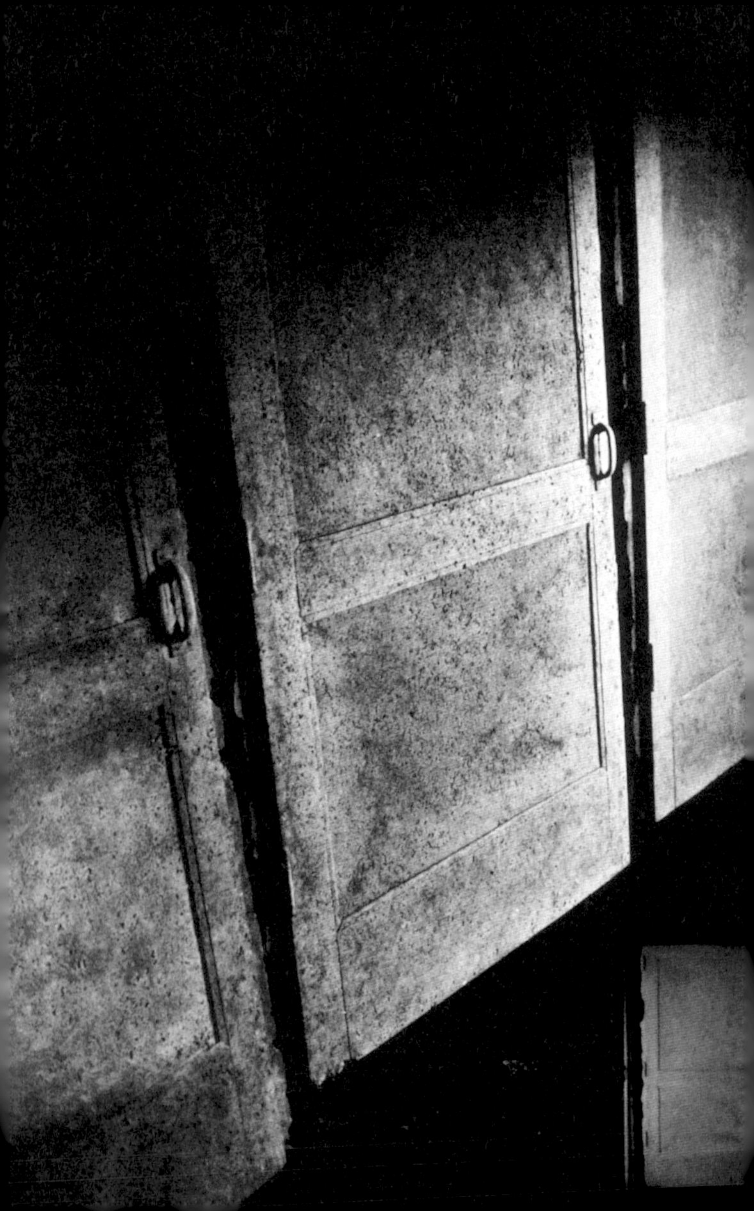

139
Concrete screen doors
9 October 1970 to
22 January 1971
Concrete and steel
30"x 45"x 5" approx.
Edition of 5

138
Madonna Door
5 October 1970
Polyvinyl chloride
84"x 28"x 11"

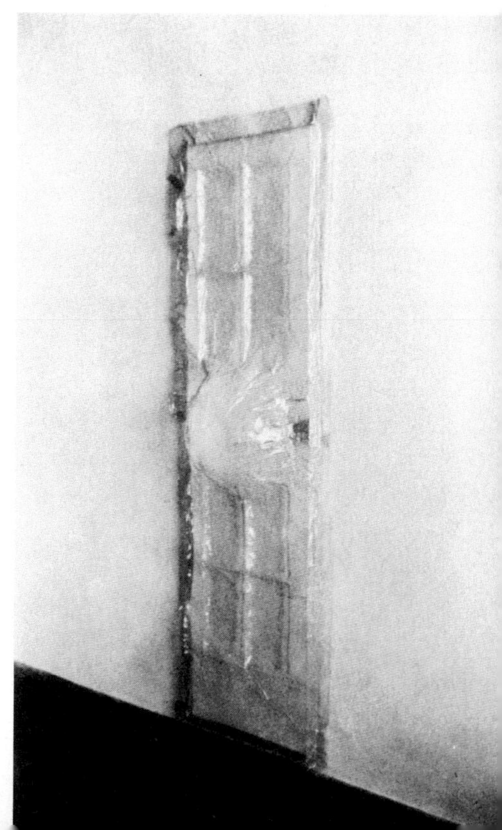

137
Madonna Door study
1 October 1970
Polyvinyl chloride, resin
wood and glass
79½″x 21″x 10″
Disassembled 5 Oct.1970

Refurbished (below)
5 August 1971, pvc replaced
by latex rubber

136
Lizard Soup No. 2
20 September 1970
Cadmium-plated resin
and acrylic
3¾″x 3¾″x 4″

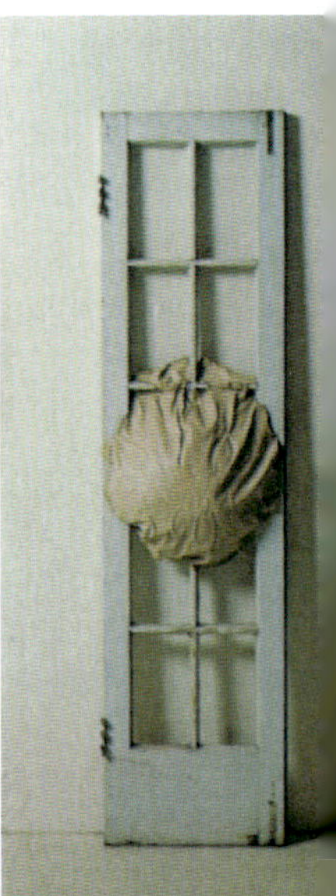

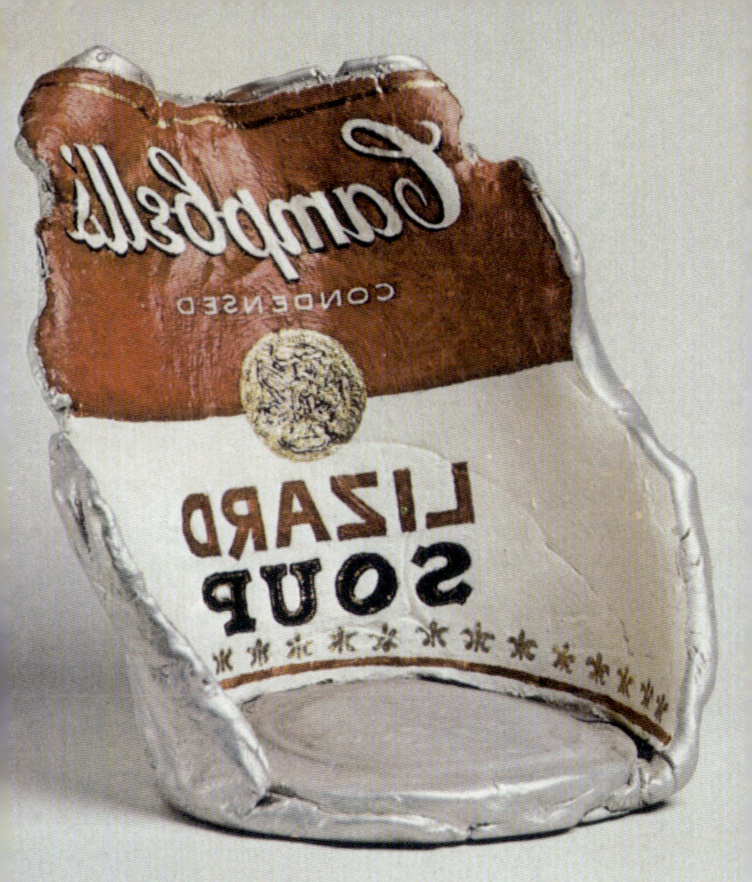

Campbell's
CONDENSED
LIZARD
SOUP

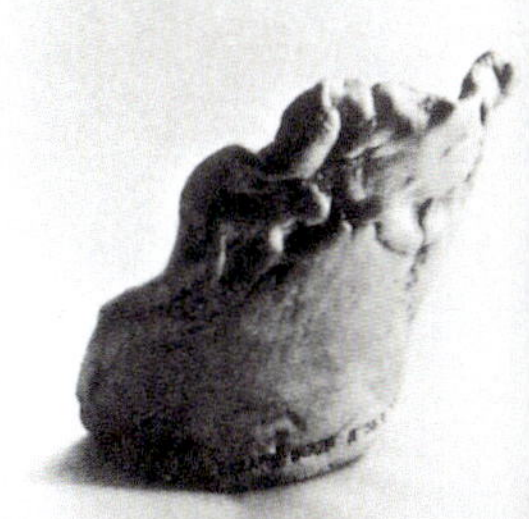

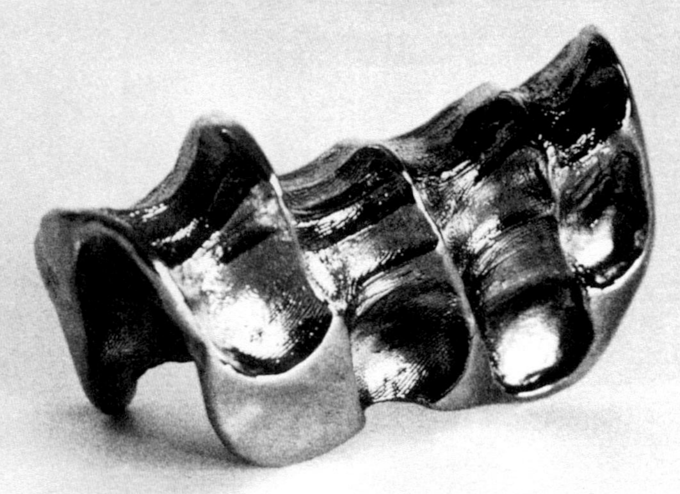

135
Monkey Grip
20 September 1970
Nickel-plated resin
1⅜" x 3⅝" x 2⅜"

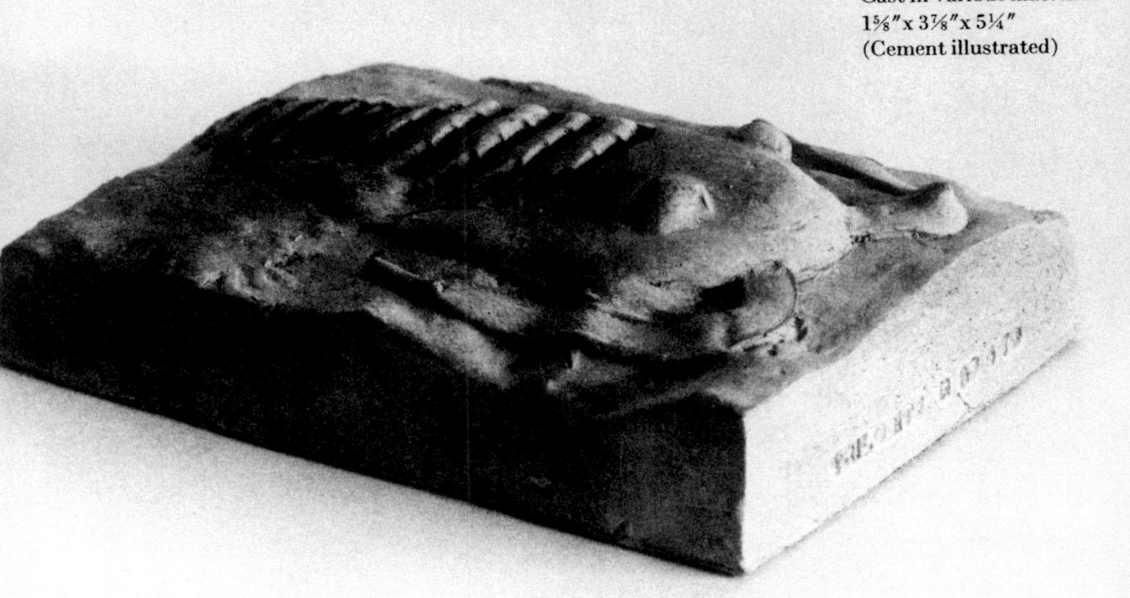

134
Trilobite
20 September 1970
Cast in various materials
1⅝" x 3⅞" x 5¼"
(Cement illustrated)

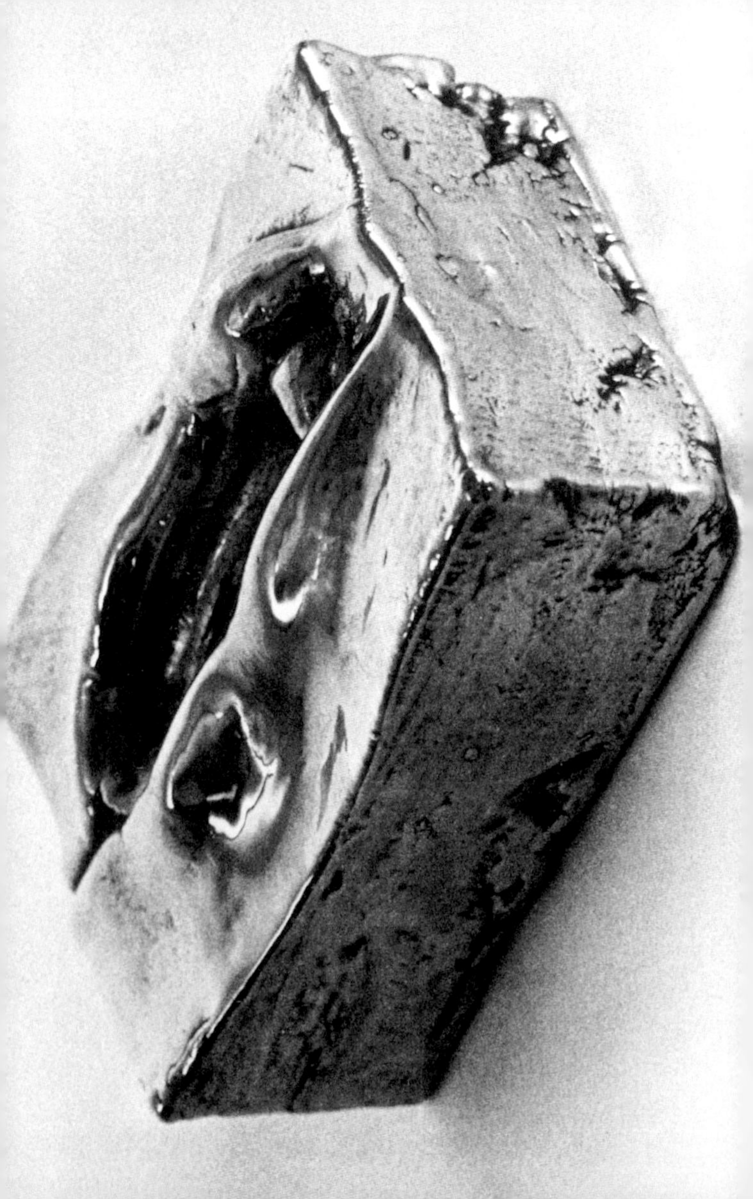

133
Art Polish
17 September 1970
Copper-plated resin
1⅞″x 2⅞″x 4¼″

132
Art Polish Study
17 September 1970
Nickel-plated resin
2″x 3⅛″x 4¼″

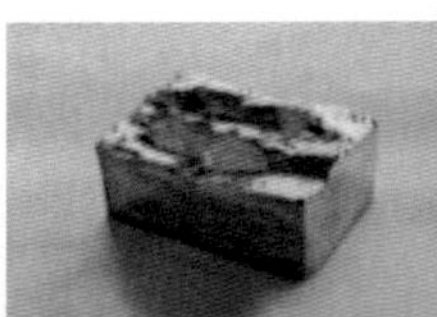

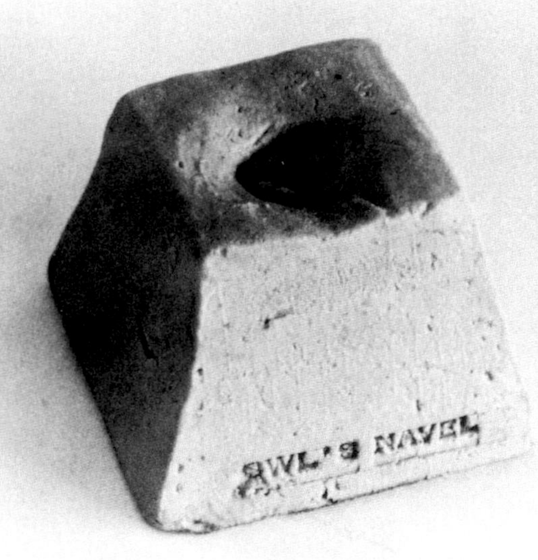

OWL'S NAVEL

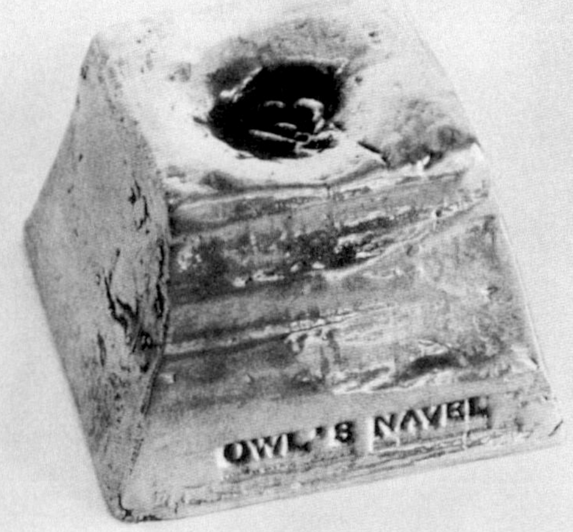

OWL'S NAVEL

31
Owl's Navel
7 September 1970
Cast in various materials:
⅝″x 2¼″x 2¼″
illustrated; solid rubber,
copper-plated and black
chromium-plated resin)

130 (not illustrated)
4 O'Clock Breeze
7 September 1970
Aluminum window screen,
newspaper and wool
41″x 45½″x 4″
Destroyed Dec. 1971

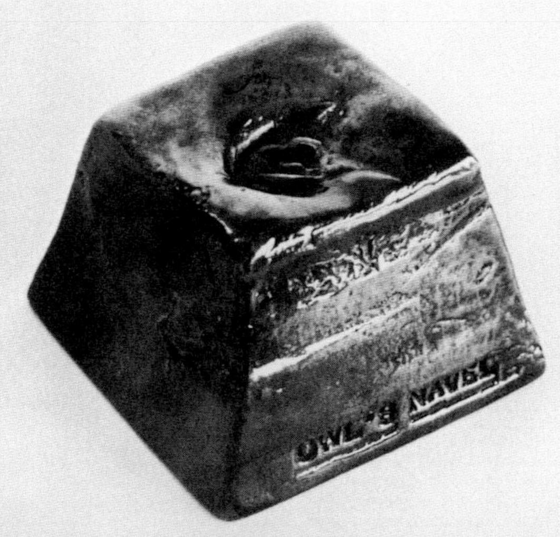

129-126
Carbon transfer drawings
7 September 1970
Carbon on paper

(129)
Fingerscape
7¾"x 10¾"

(128)
Untitiled
15½"x 22½"

(127, not illustrated)
On three hole paper
11"x 8½"

(126, not illustrated)
With Stella mat
6"x 5"
Destroyed 1 Jan. 1972

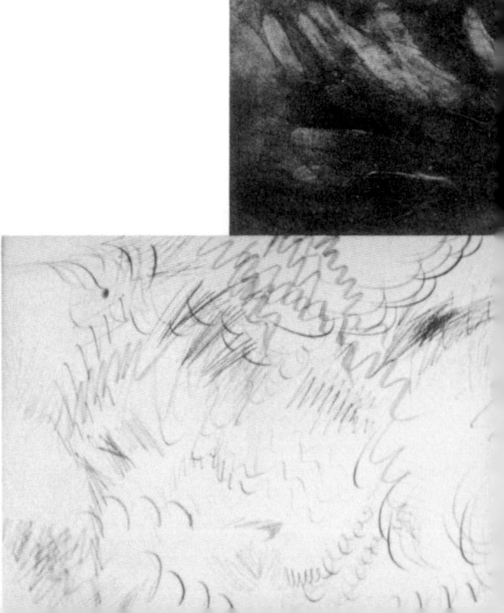

125
T. S. Eliot
7 September 1970
Collage
16″ x 22¾″

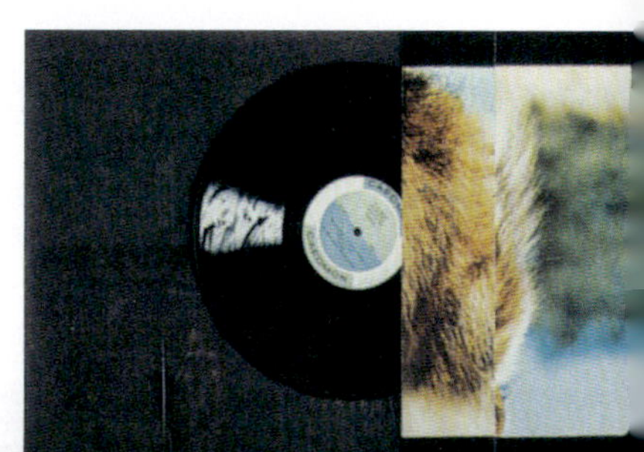

124
Drew's 'Nam jungle jumpers fit me, too
6 September 1970
Mixed media
46½″ x 24½″

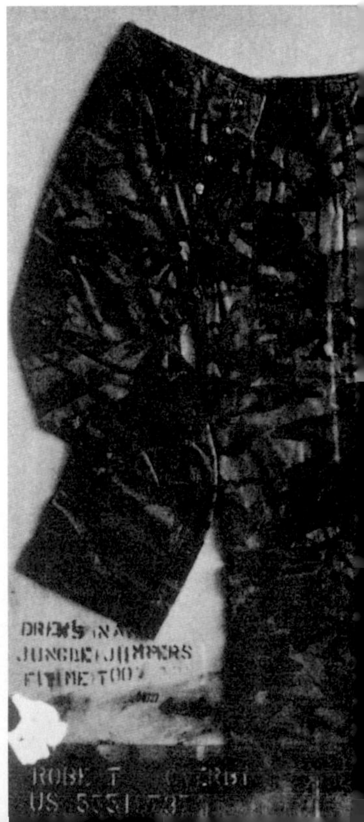

123
Imperial Analogy, By George!
2 September 1970
Graphite and ink on paper
20″ x 24″

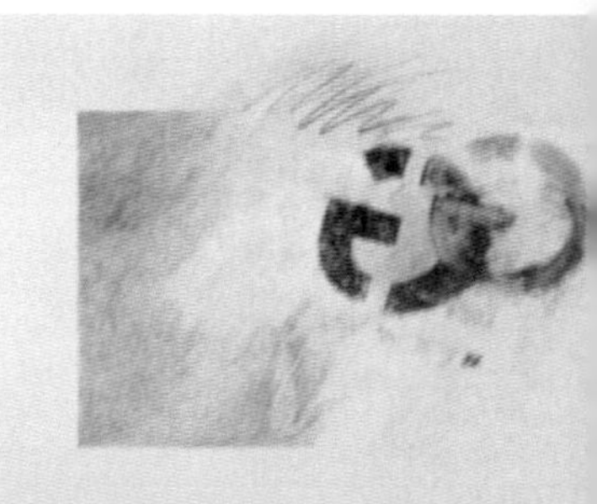

122-121
Two monoprints

(122)
G for General Audiences
on newspaper
20 August 1970
29″x 22¾″

(121)
Alphabet Blur
19 August 1970
25¾″x 19¾″

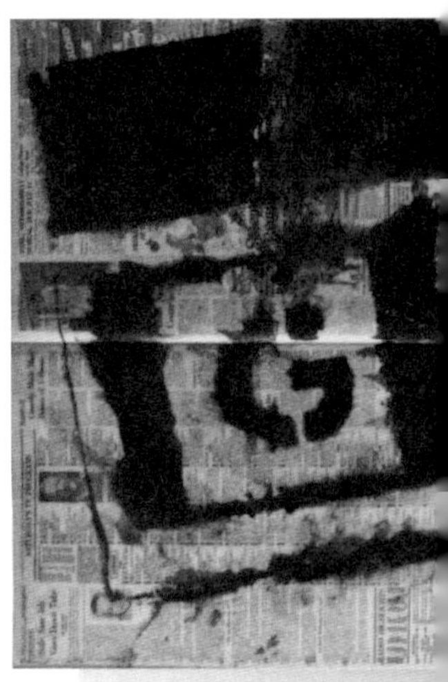

120 (not illustrated)
Space between my legs drawings
(4 drawings—2 each per sheet)
18 August 1970
Graphite on paper, 42"x 31"
Destroyed 30 Oct. 1970

119 (not illustrated)
Post About When
18 August 1970
Graphite on paper
8½"x 11"
Lost Oct. 1970

118
Horizon Line Detail
15 August 1970
Acrylic and resin on canvas
14″x 22″

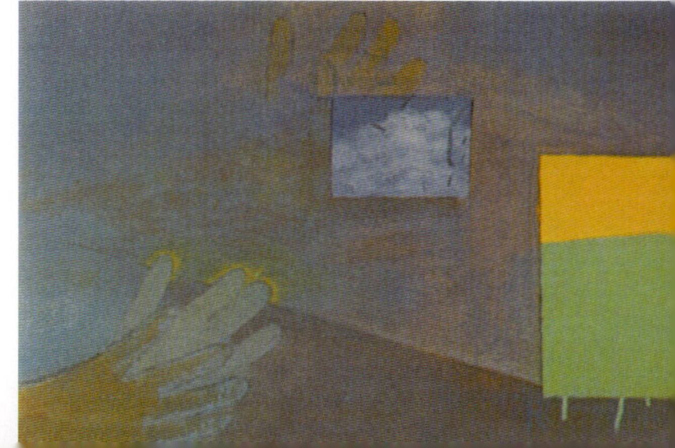

117
Landscape Painting
12 August 1970
Acrylic and resin on canvas
52½″x 59″

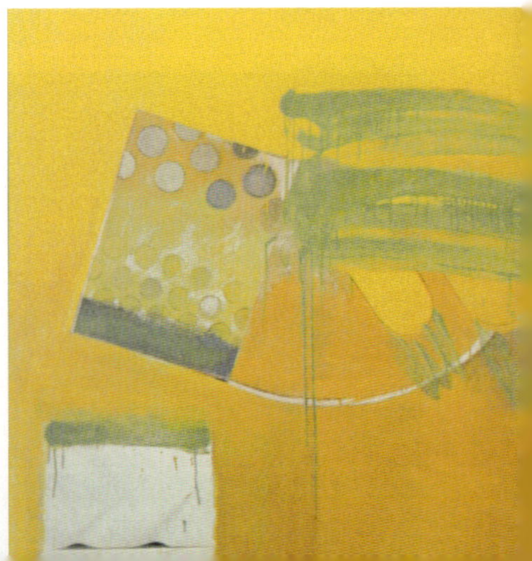

16
Landscape series
9-10 August 1970
Collage
All 11″x 8½″

1. Yellow Finger Tips
2. Horizon Confusion
3. Push-Pull (not illustrated)

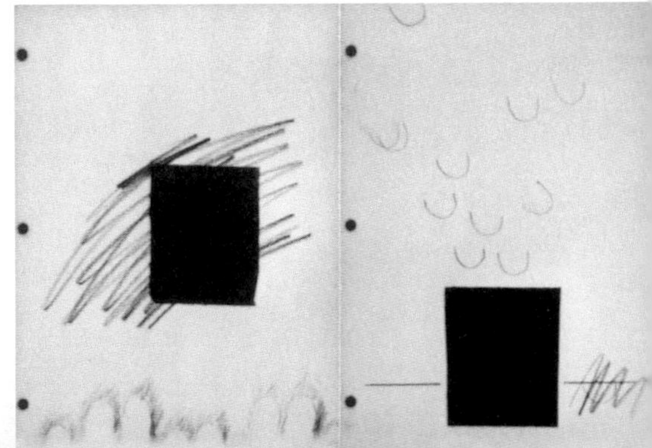

115
Plaid No. 4/i
14 August 1970
Polyvinyl chloride
and resin
47"x 57½"

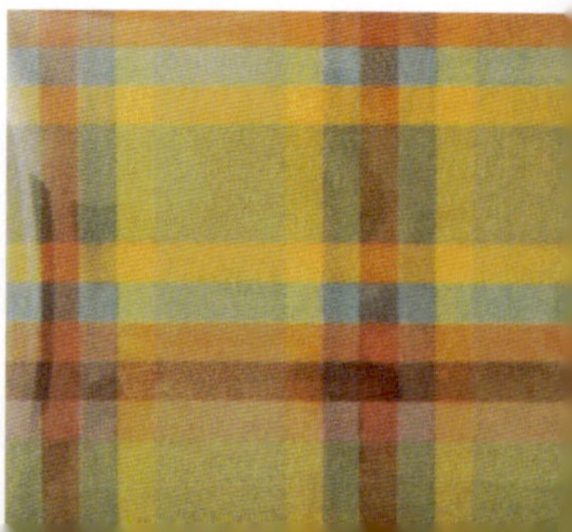

114
Plaid No. 4/a
14 August 1970
Polyvinyl chloride
and resin
47″x 57½″

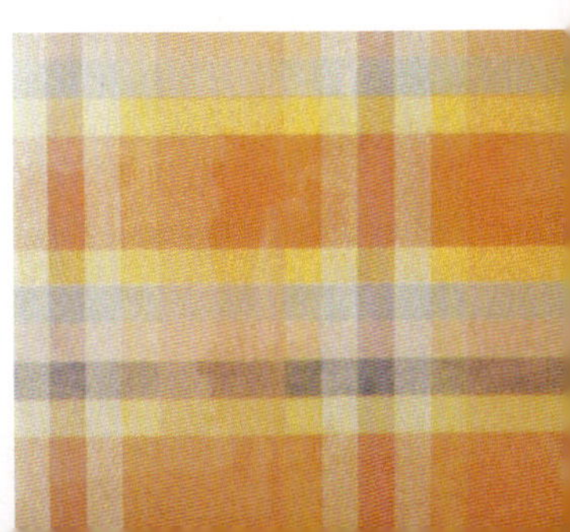

111
Plaid No. 4
13 August 1970
Polyvinyl chloride
and resin
47″x 57½″

112
Diabolical Blue Finger
4 August 1970
Graphite, chalk, marker
and watercolor on paper
12″x 16½″

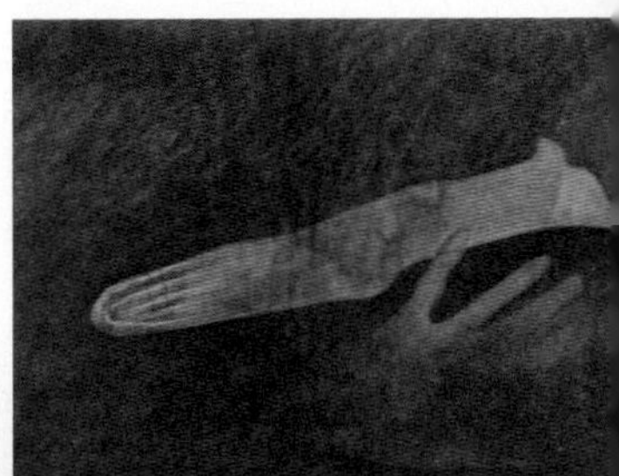

111
Bright Tomorrows Frame
3 August 1970
Graphite and marker on paper
20″x 16½″

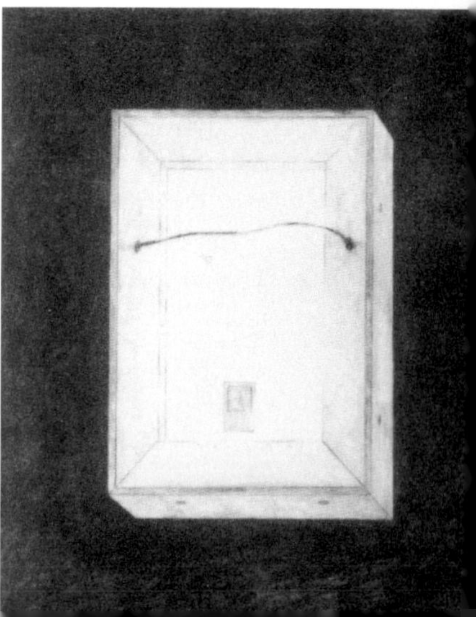

110
Stephanie's Sox are Blue
4 August 1970
Graphite, marker and
watercolor on paper
17¼" x 17¼"

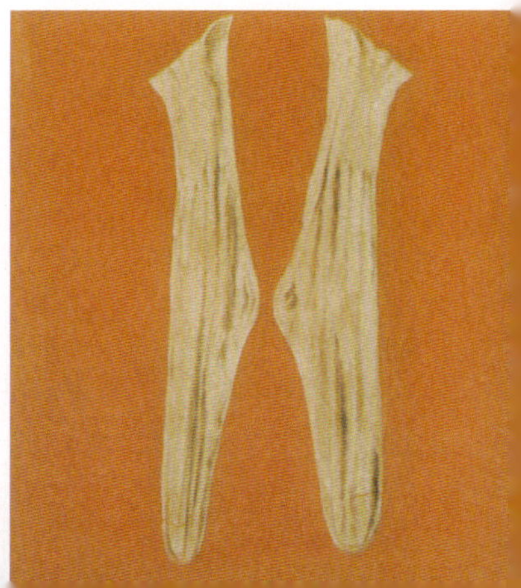

109
Stephanie's Sox
1 August 1970
Graphite, marker and
watercolor on paper
20″ x 24″

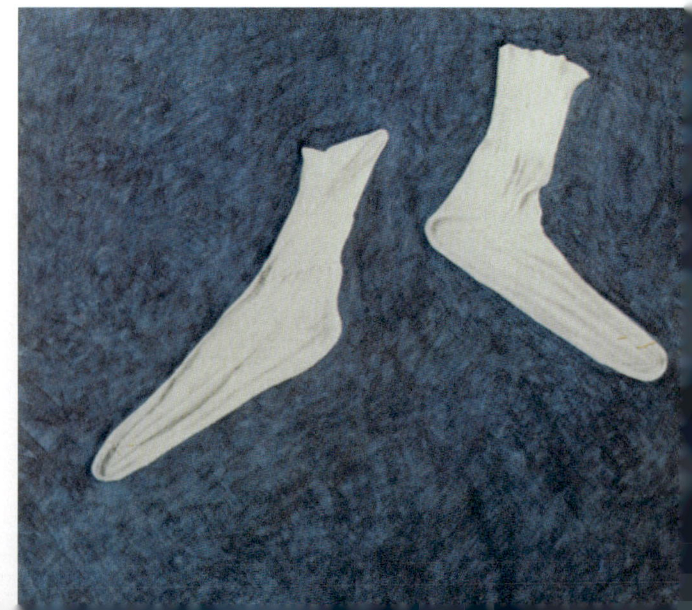

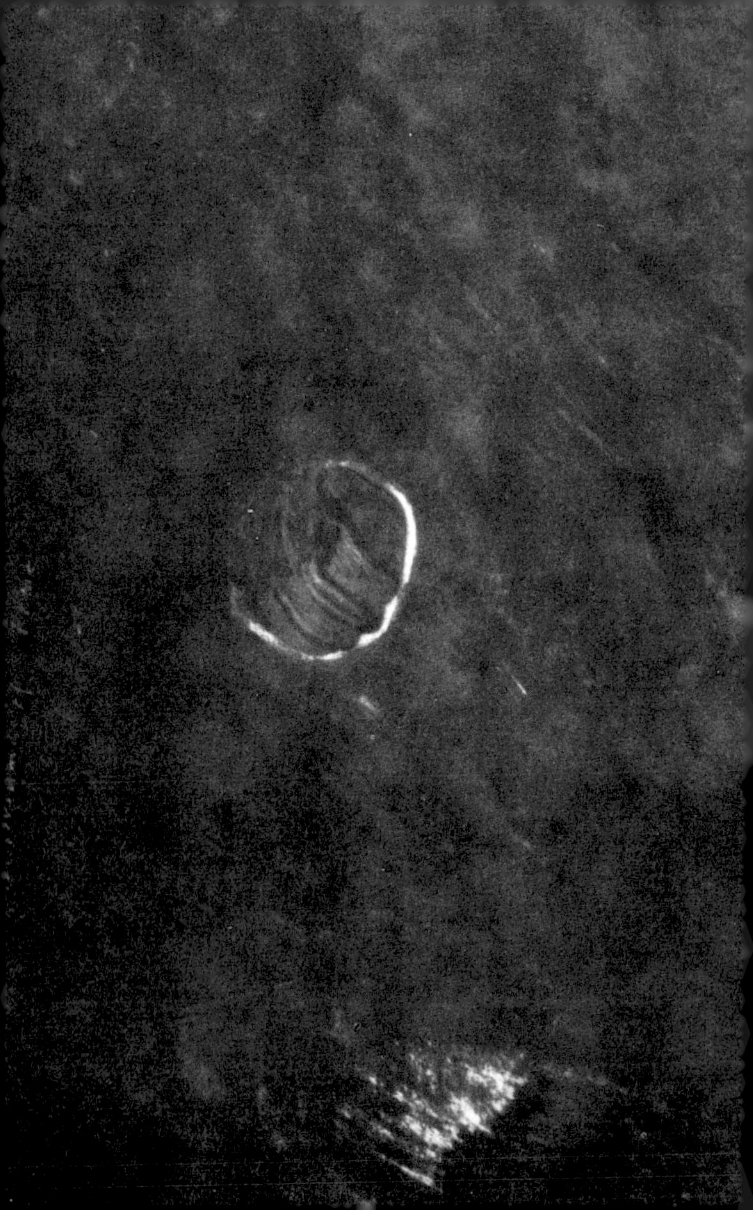

106
Delirium of Time
1 August 1970
Graphite and marker on paper
6″x 8½″

106
Delirium of Edge
1 August 1970
Graphite and marker on paper
26″x 20″

105
Five handkerchief sketches
26 July 1970
Graphite, marker and
gouache on paper
20″x 26″ and 20″x 24¼″
Three destroyed Nov. 1972
Kerchief with blocks
20″x 24¼″
Study for Stone (illustrated)
20″x 26″

104
Your nose gets scribbled on—
26 July 1970
Graphite on paper
20″x 26″

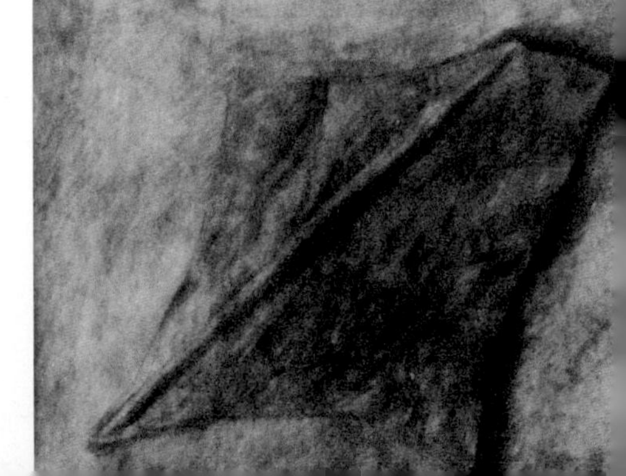

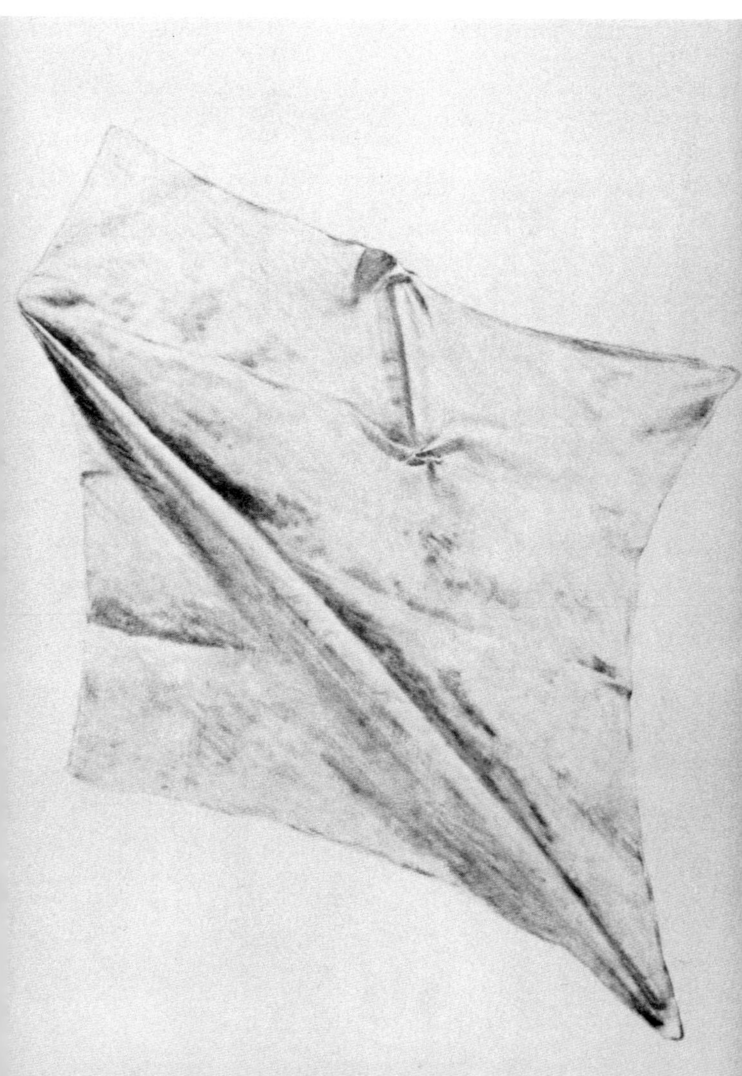

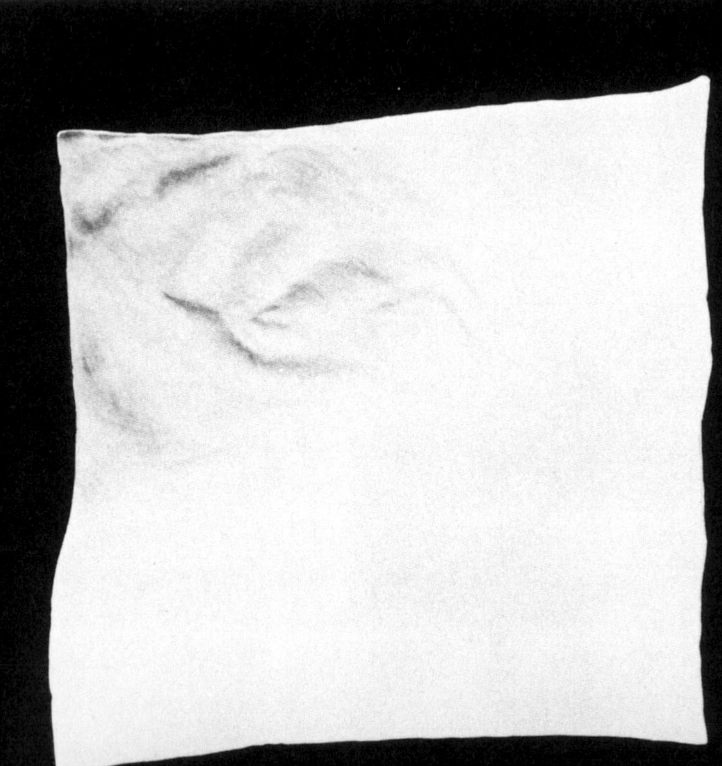

103
The Brown Noses Have It
26 July 1970
Graphite and marker
on paper
36"x 20"

102
Passage
10 July 1970
Polyvinyl chloride and
metal soap pad
36"x 3½"x 1¾"

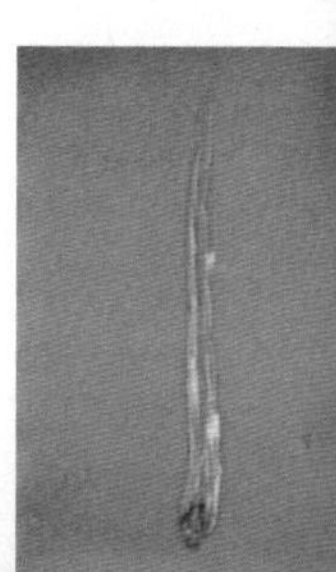

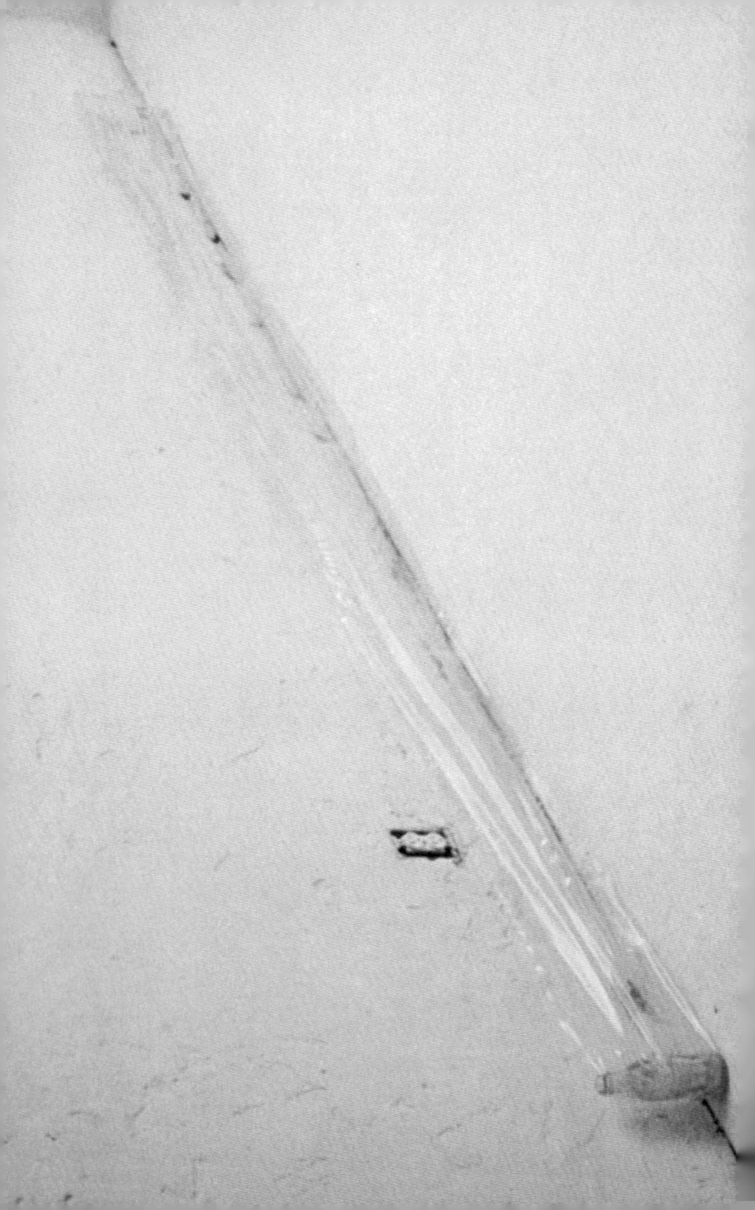

100
Large Yellow and Silver Stretch
16 July 1970
Polyvinyl chloride and resin
59″x 81″x 3″

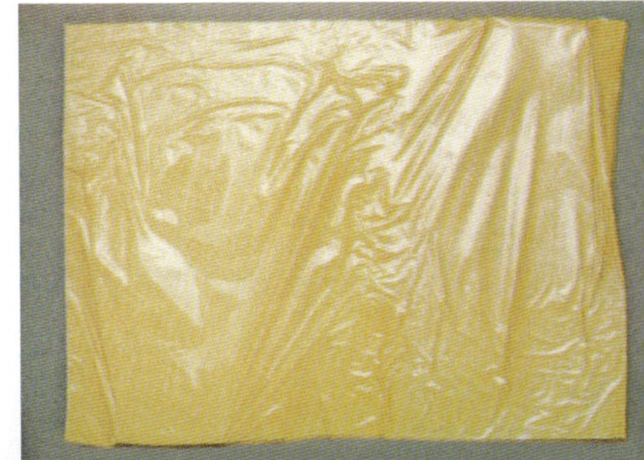

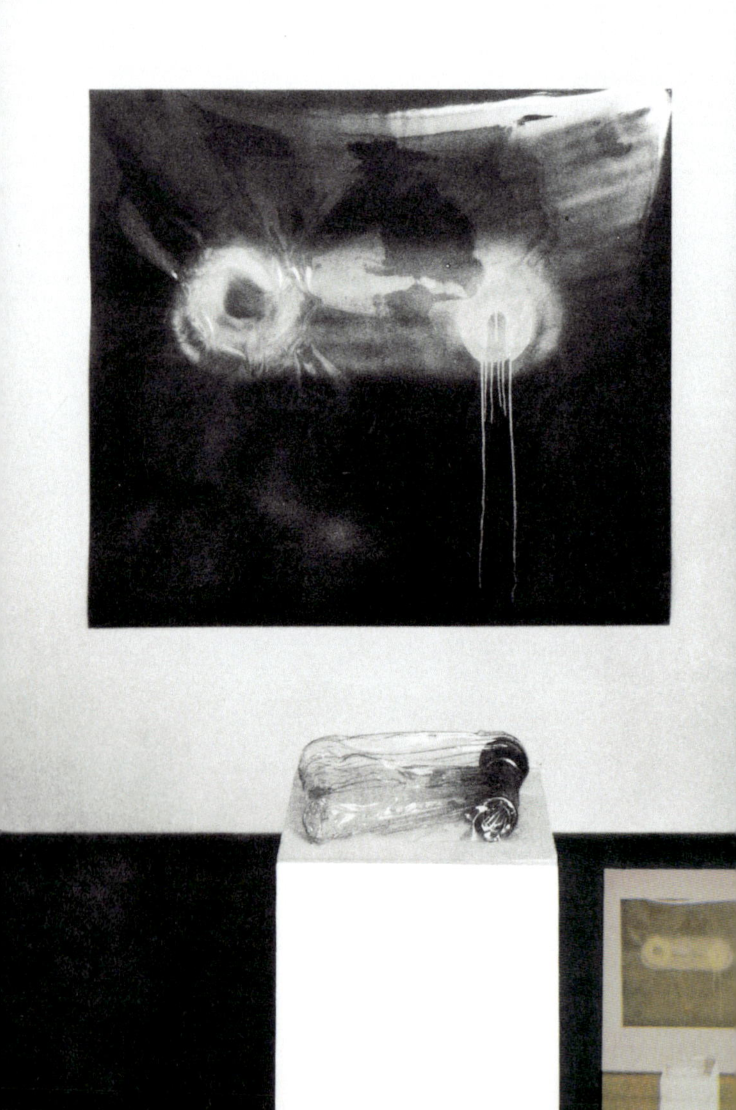

99
Sunny-Side-Up
15 July 1970
Polyvinyl chloride,
resin and flashlight
51″x 57½″x 72″ approx.

98
Blue Stretch No. 2
15 July 1970
Polyvinyl chloride
and resin
56¼″x 60″x 6½″

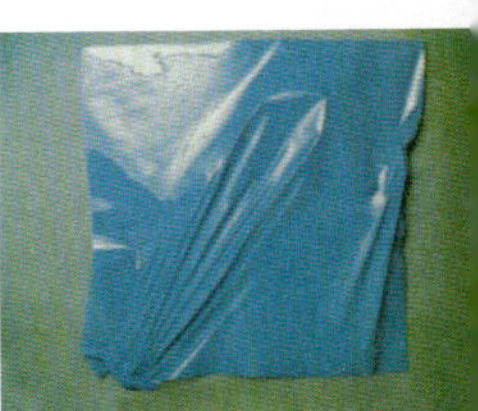

97
Test for Blue Stretch No. 2
15 July 1970
Polyvinyl chloride
46″x 59½″x 3½″
Destroyed Nov. 1972

96
Sky-Hi
14 July 1970
Polyvinyl chloride
and resin
54″x 48″

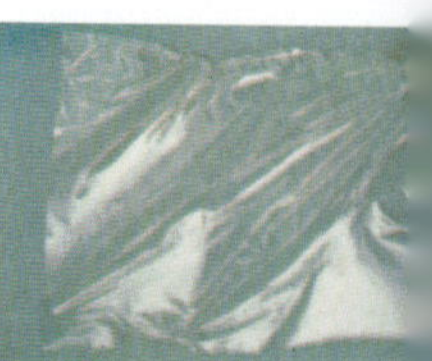

95
S-S-S-S
14 July 1970
Polyvinyl chloride,
aerosol can and acrylic
13"x 28"x 3"

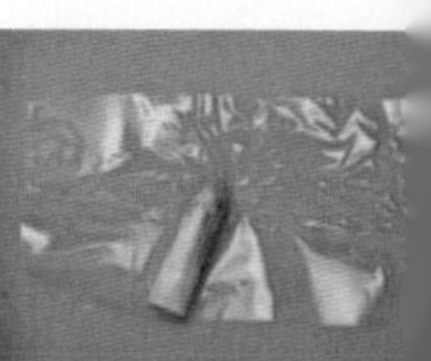

94
Red Stretch No. 2
14 July 1970
Polyvinyl chloride
and resin
62″x 54″x 3½″

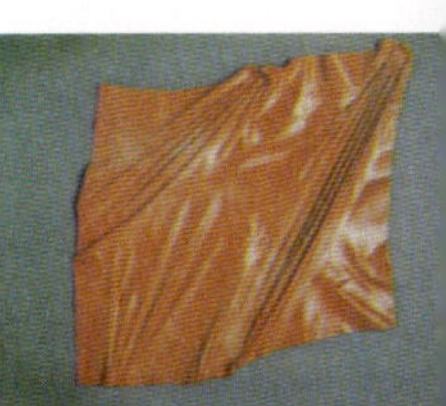

93
Plaid No. 15
13 July 1970
Polyvinyl chloride
and resin
38½″ x 50″ x 4″

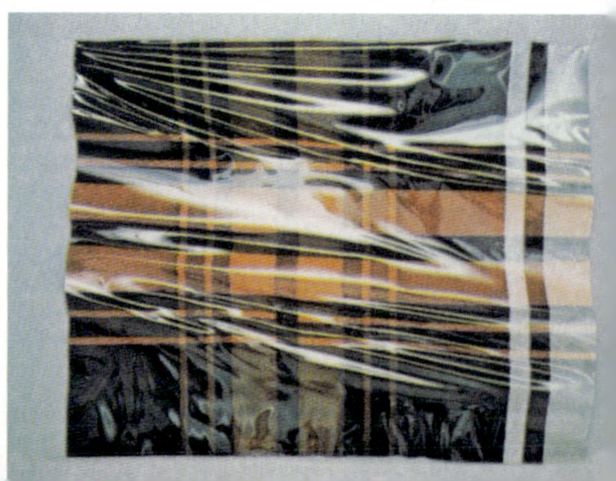

92
Plaid No. 7
12 July 1970
Polyvinyl chloride
and resin
46½″ x 47″ x 1½″

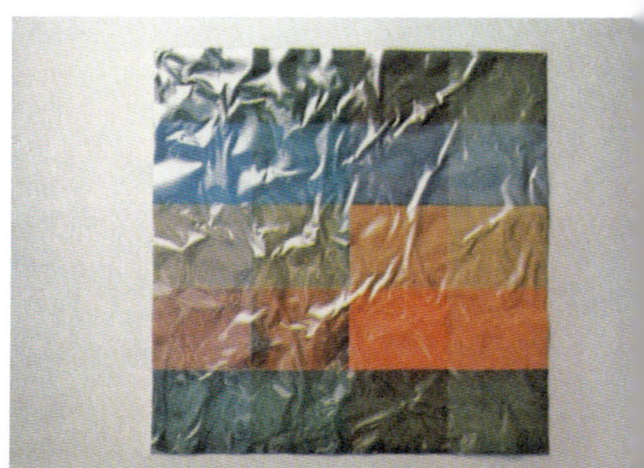

91
Dead of Night
12 July 1970
Polyvinyl chloride
and night light
6½″x 3″x 4″

90
Yellow Scoot
12 July 1970
Mixed media
Size varies with
installation

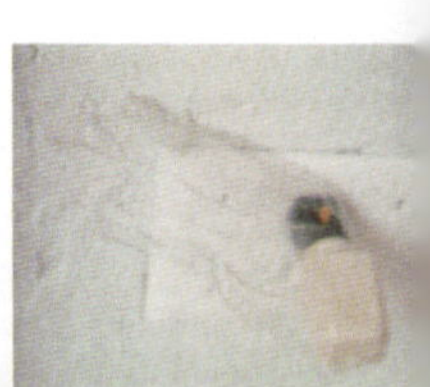

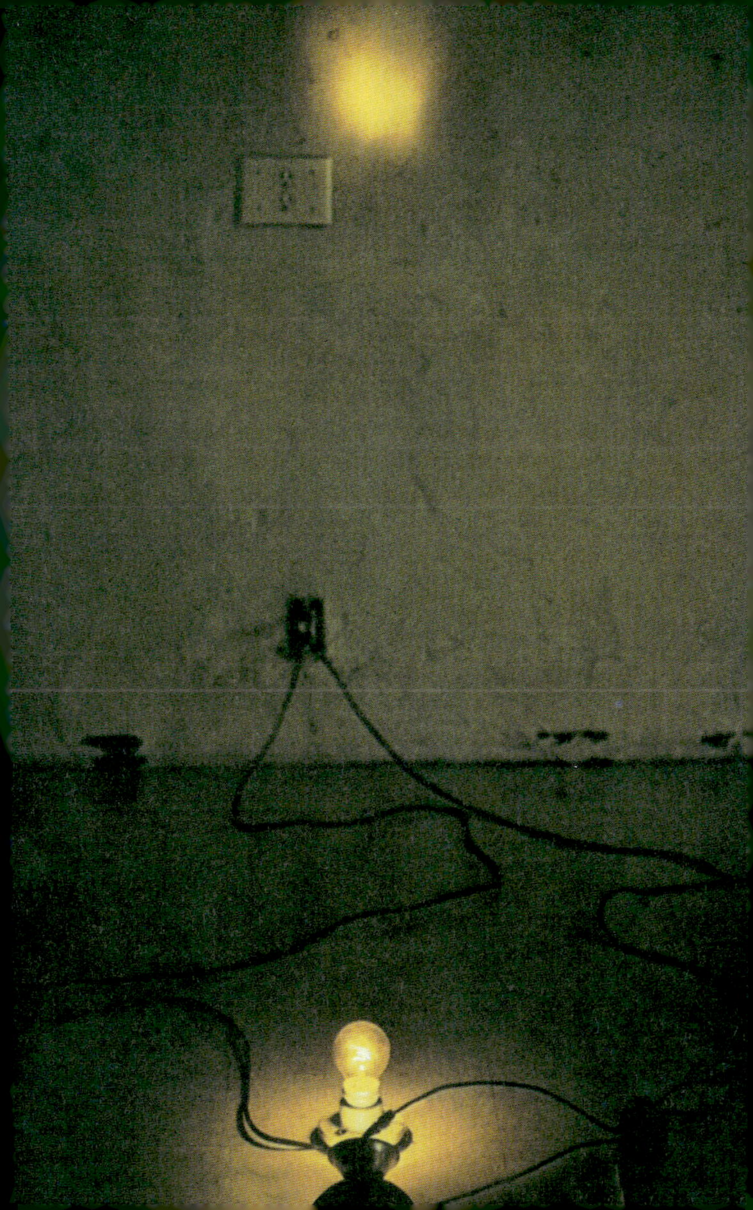

89
Arnoldi's Shine
12 July 1970
Mixed media
Size varies with
installation

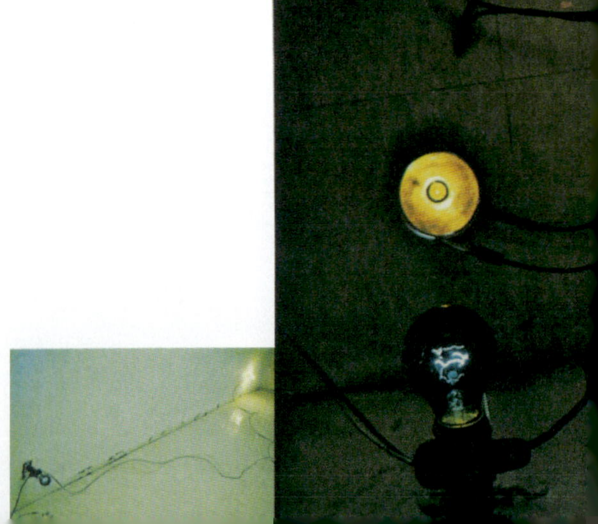

88
Flower
12 July 1970
Polyvinyl chloride,
glass and resin
4″x 19″x 2½″

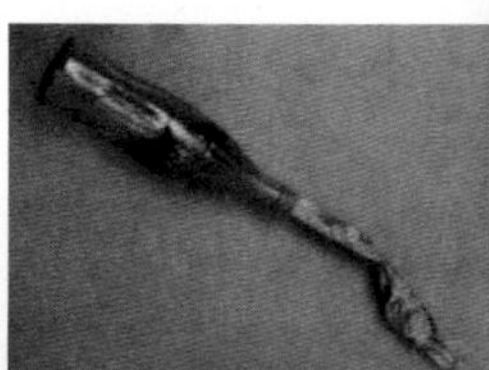

87
Plaid No. 9
12 July 1970
Polyvinyl chloride
and resin
63″x 63″x 3½″

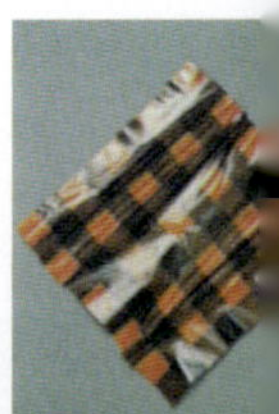

86
Plaid No. 6
11 July 1970
Polyvinyl chloride
and resin
61¼″ x 47¼″

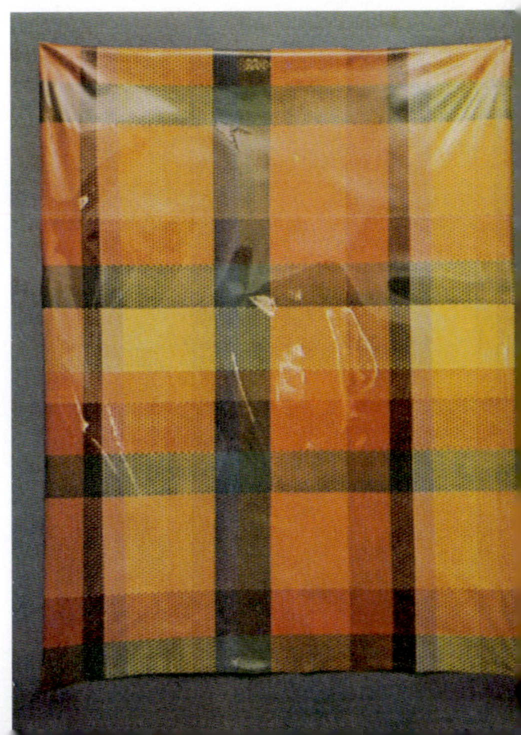

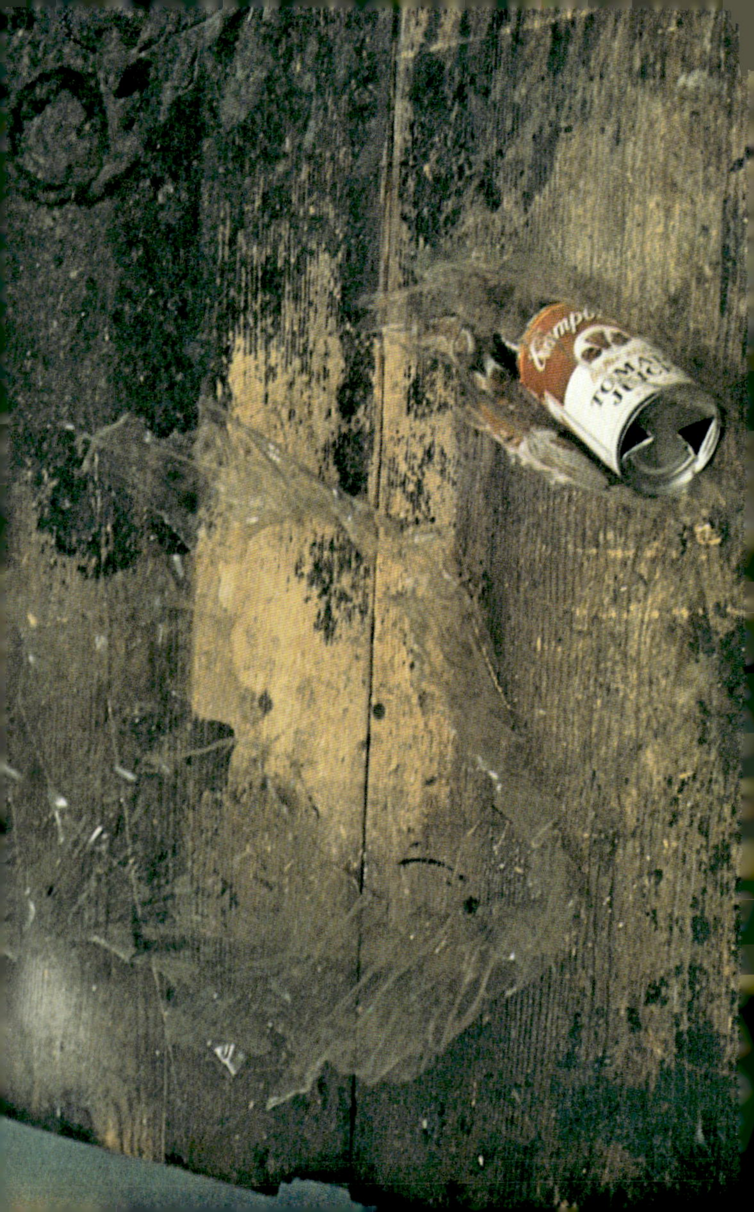

83
Lizard Soup No. 1
11 July 1970
Polyvinyl chloride
and tin can
7″ x 18″ x 24″ approx.

84
Test for Red Stretch No. 2
10 July 1970
Polyvinyl chloride
50″ x 60″ x 3½″
Destroyed Nov. 1972

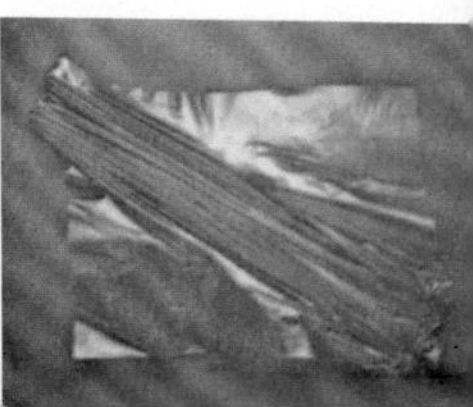

83
Wet Yellow Stretch
9 July 1970
Polyvinyl chloride
and resin
46″x 57½″x 6″

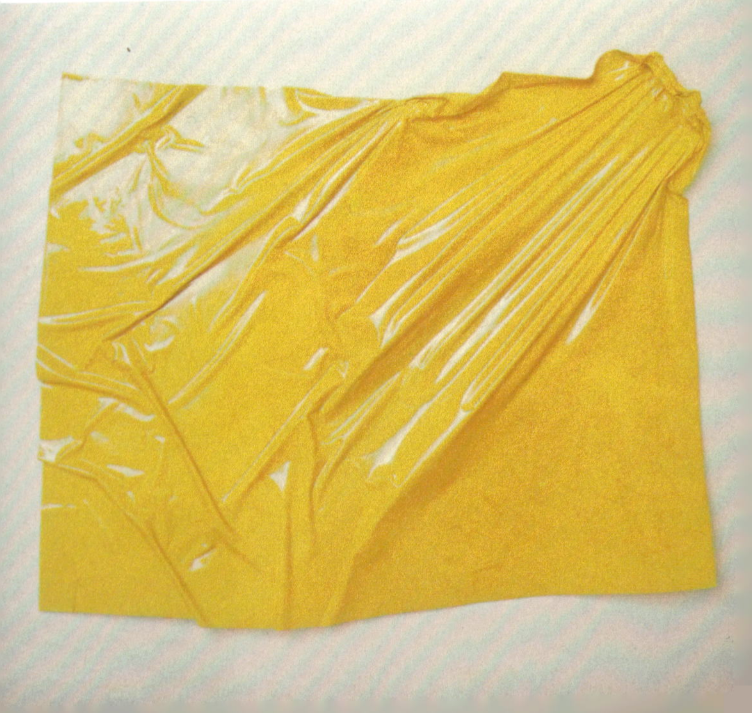

32
Tan and Blue Stretch
8 July 1970
Polyvinyl chloride
and resin
40½″ x 61″ x 3″

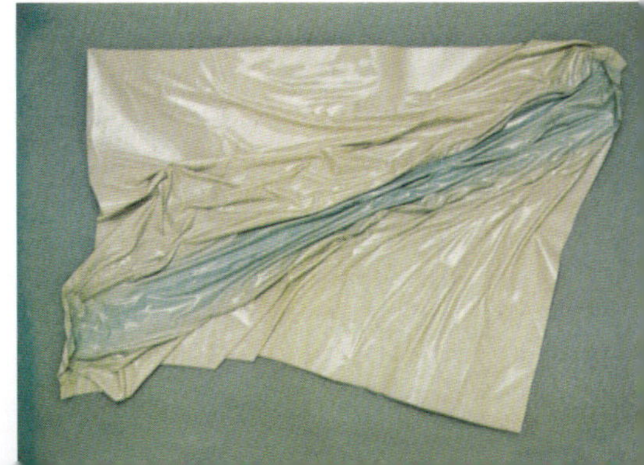

81
Wet Tan Stretch
8 July 1970
Polyvinyl chloride
and resin
44″x 63″x 2½″

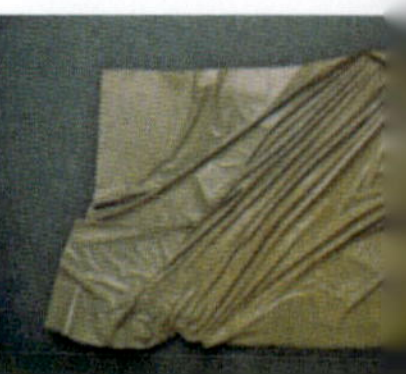

30
Blue Stretch No. 1
8 July 1970
Polyvinyl chloride
and resin
58″ x 49″ x 4¾″

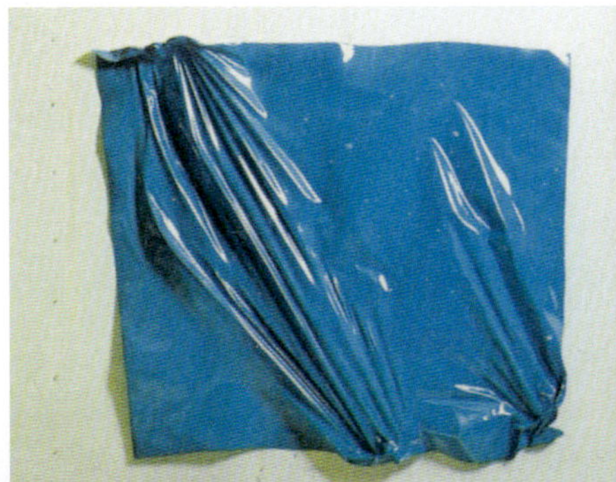

79
Dark Event
7 July 1970
Polyvinyl chloride
and resin
59"x 37"x 3"

78
Dark Event test No. 2
7 July 1970
Polyvinyl chloride
45"x 60"x 3"

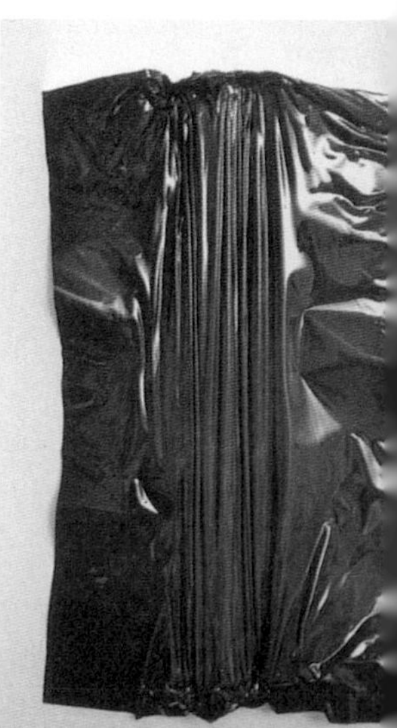

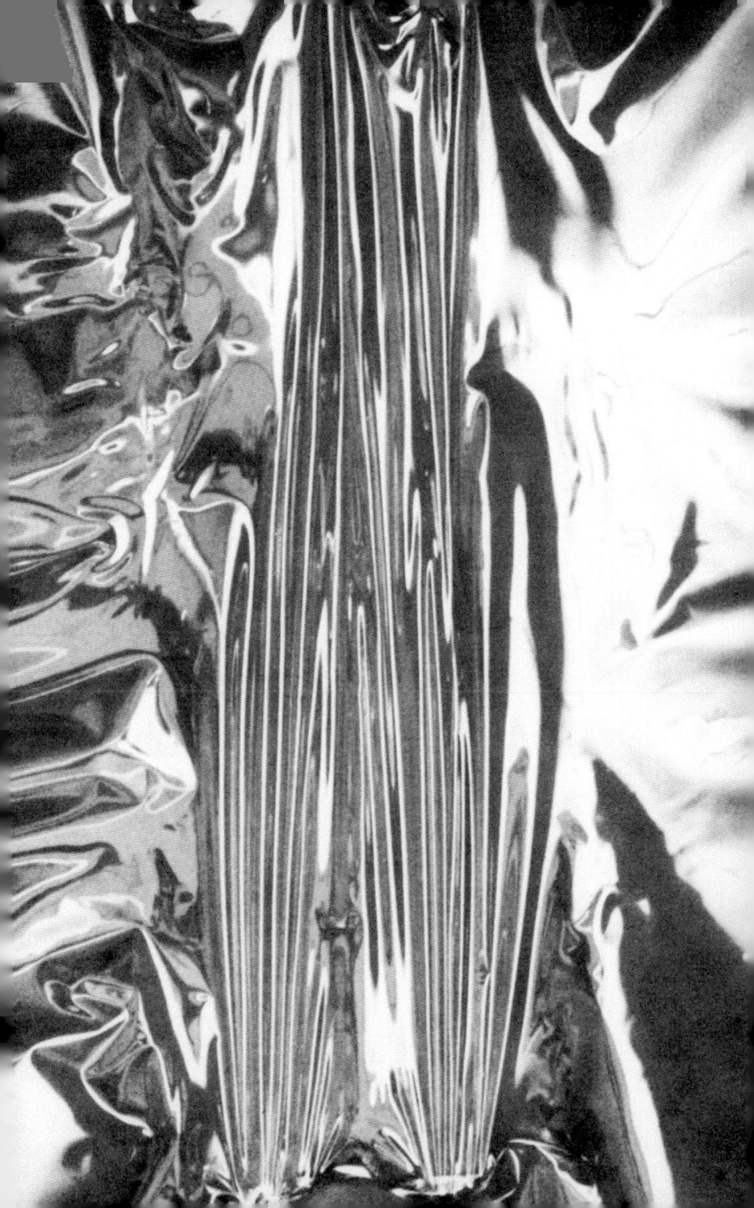

77
Red Stretch No. 1
7 July 1970
Polyvinyl chloride
and resin
45″x 58″x 4″

76
Magnetic Stretch
5 July 1970
Polyvinyl chloride
and resin
48″x 60″x 2″

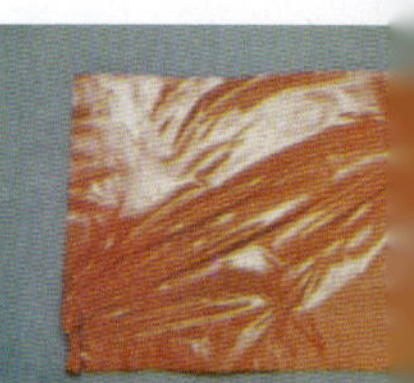

75
Silver Stretch test
1 July 1970
Silver mylar
40"x 29"x 3"

74
Tradition
29 June 1970
Wood and
acrylic lacquer
5½"x 3½"x 3½"
Stolen Jan. 1972

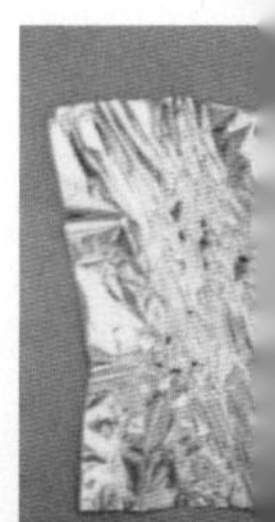

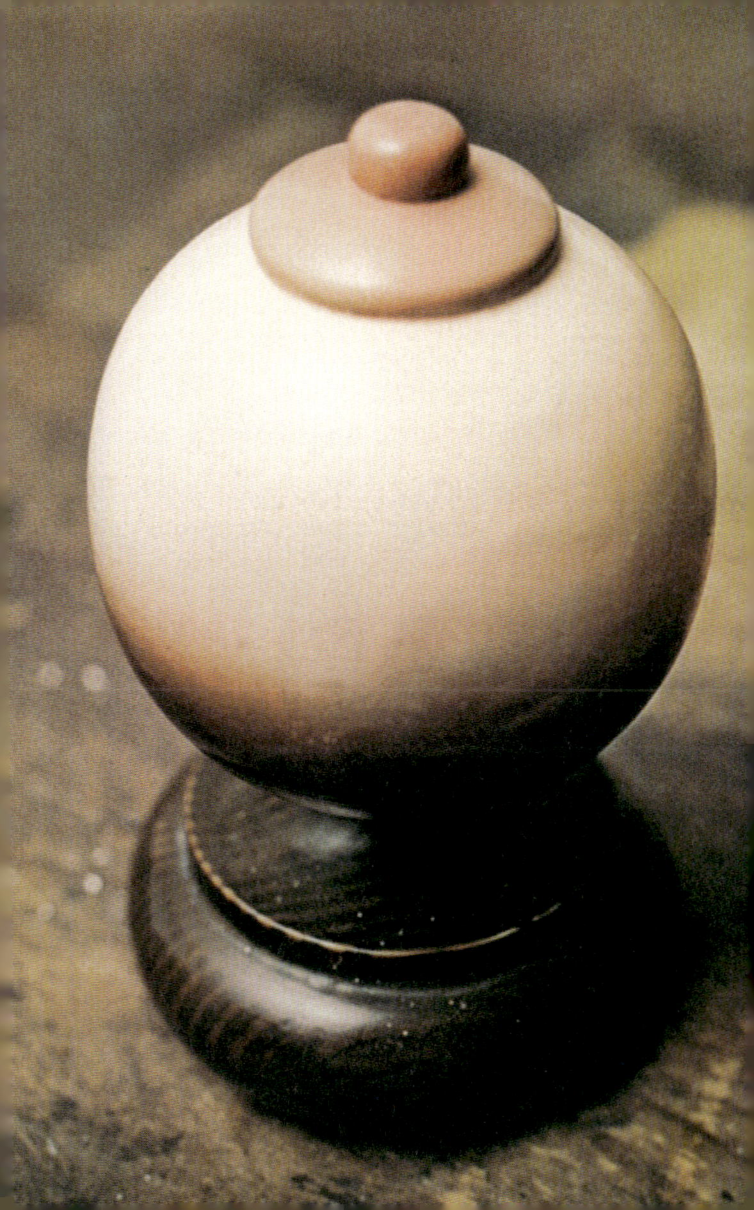

73
"35"
21 June 1970
Polyvinyl chloride
and wood
Overall 48″x 42″x 24″
Destroyed Nov. 1972

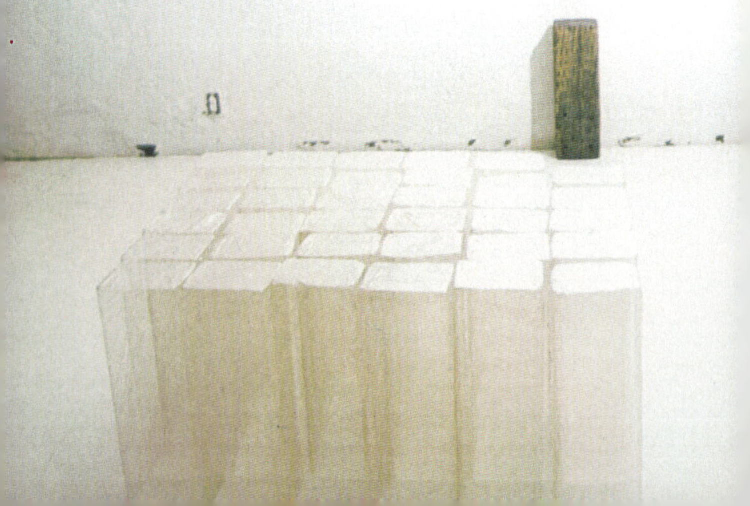

72
Touch Me, A. Klang
14 June 1970
Polyvinyl chloride
and acrylic enamel
31″x 14″x 6″

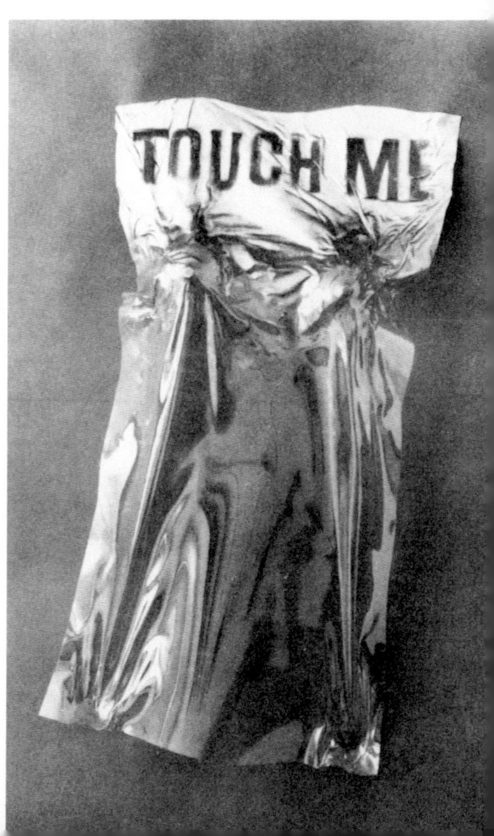

71
Corner moving piece
Polyvinyl chloride
18½″x 12″x 9″

70
About Intent
7 June 1970
Polyvinyl chloride,
wood, metal, string,
and acrylic lacquer
9″x 15″

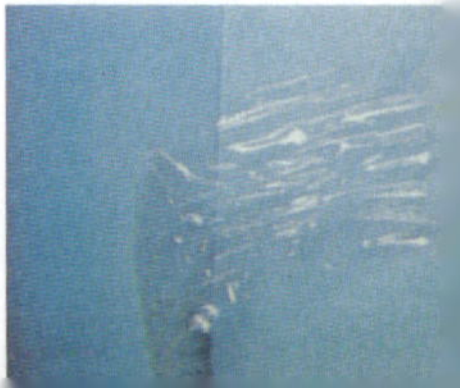

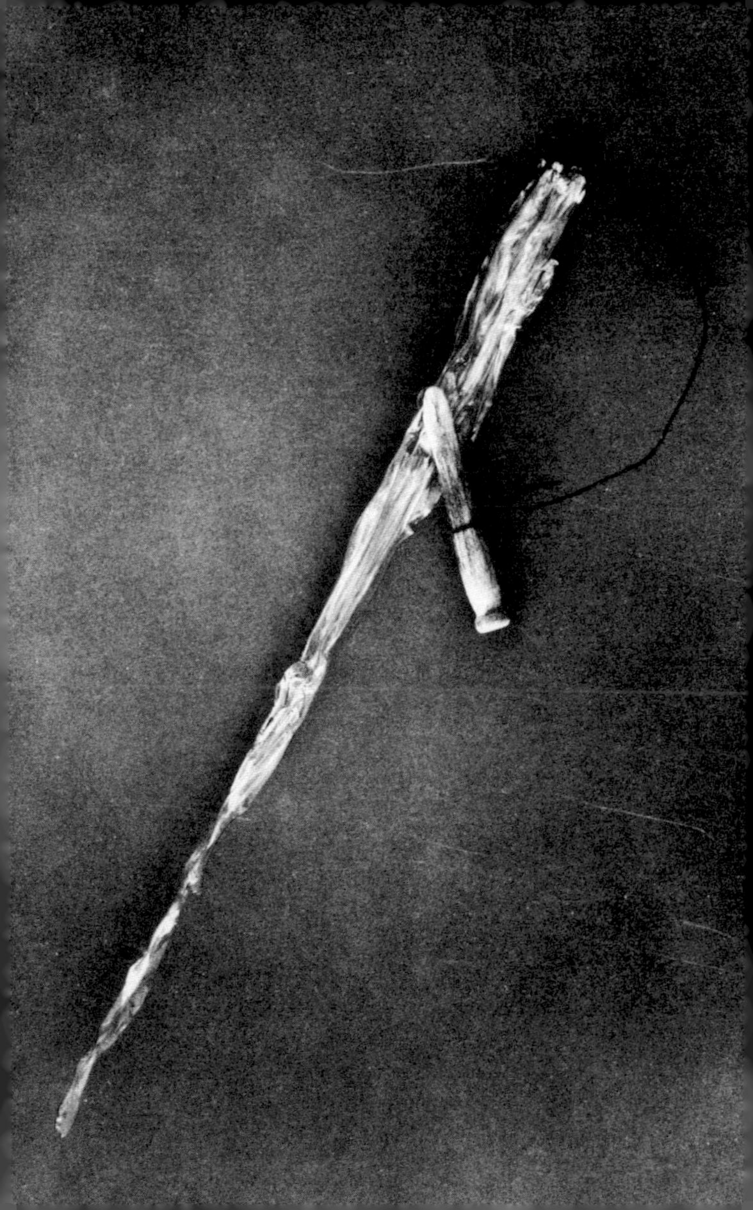

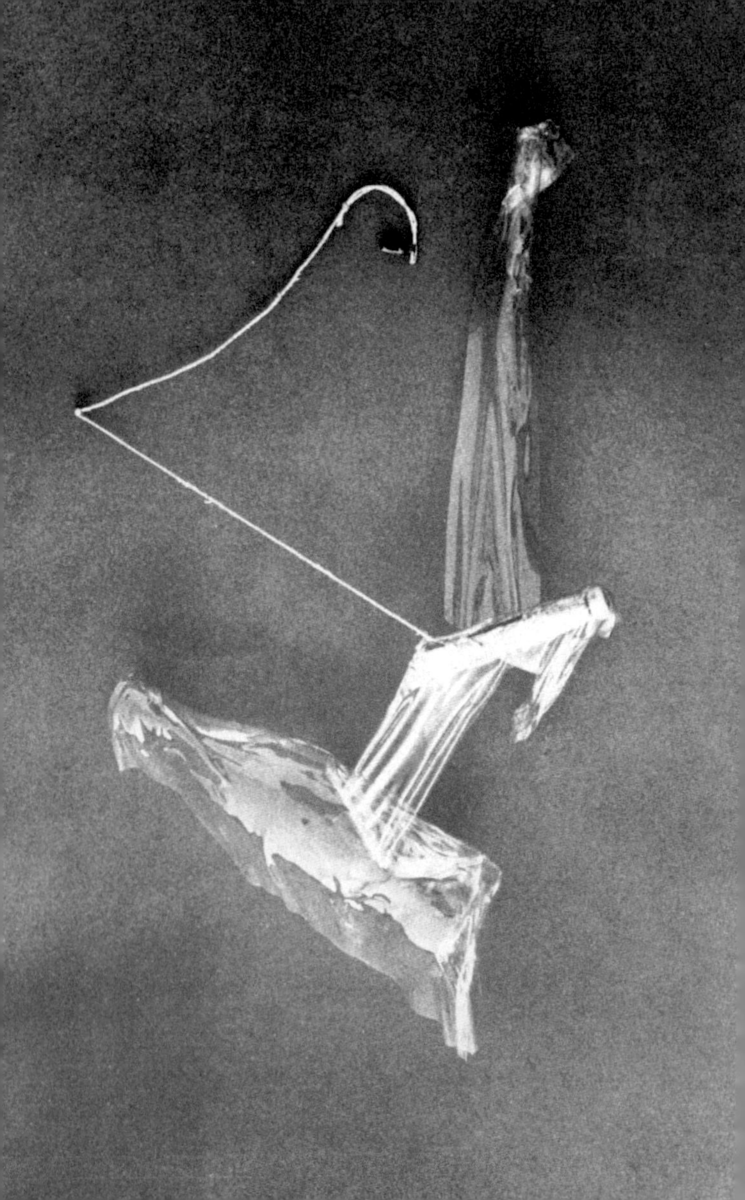

68
Real Time
7 June 1970
Graphite, marker
and ink on paper
11″x 8½″

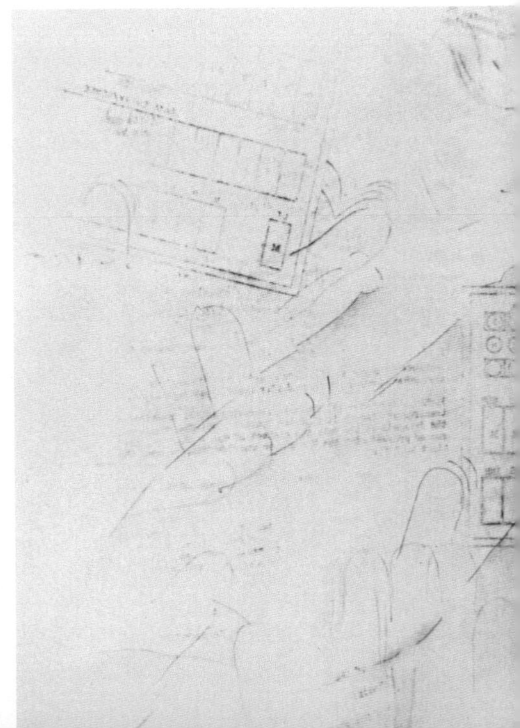

67
Good-by Pin
7 June 1970
Graphite, marker
and ink on paper
11″x 8½″

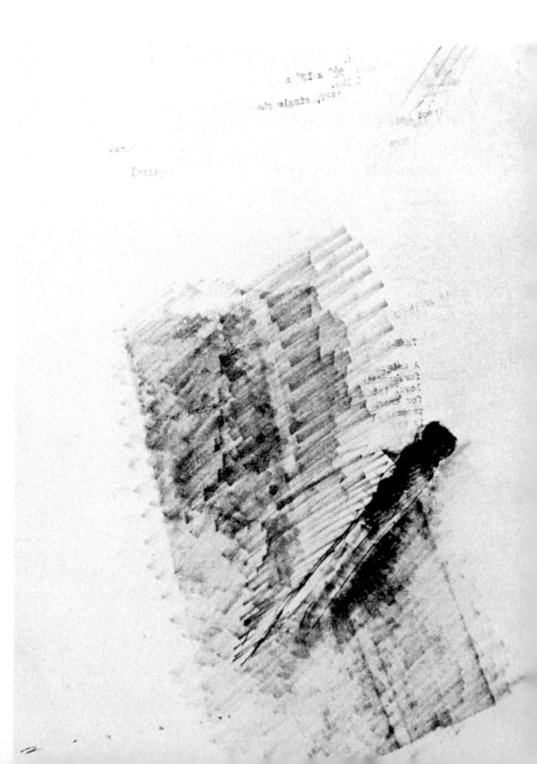

56
The Meaning of Blur
7 June 1970
Graphite, marker
and ink on paper
11" x 8½"

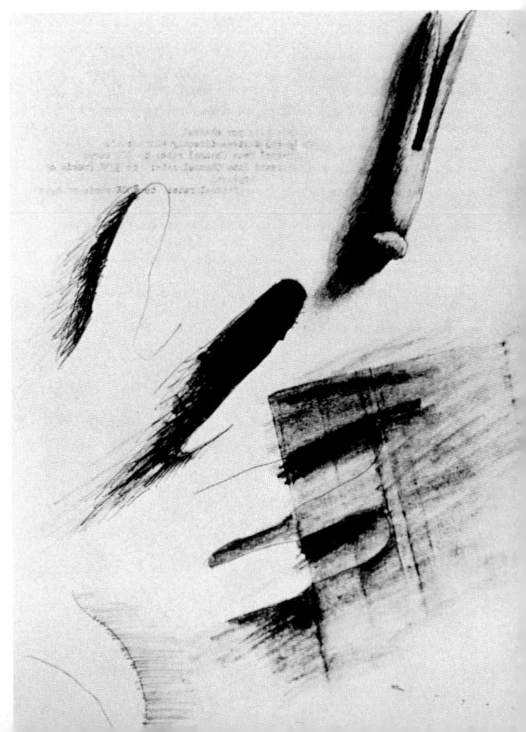

65
Clothes Pin No. 1
7 June 1970
Polyvinyl chloride,
cellophane, wire and wood
35″x 13½″x 3″

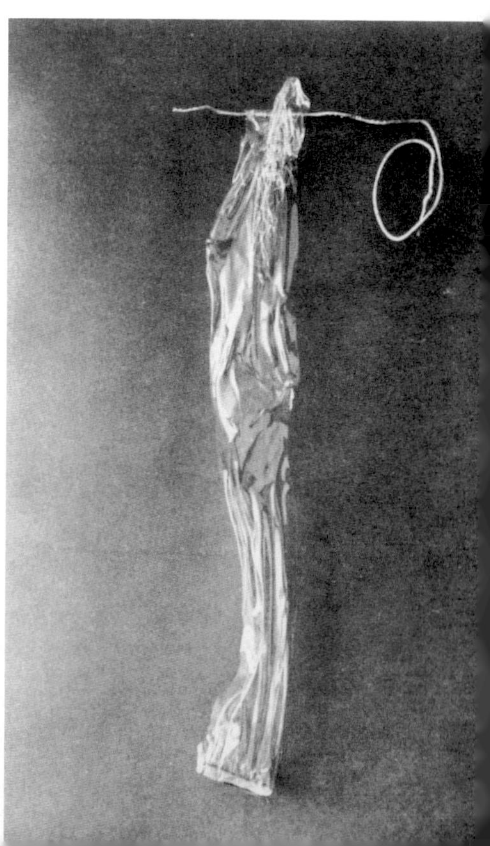

54
About Beginning
June 1970
Polyvinyl chloride, glass
and acrylic lacquer
48″x 12″x 3¼″

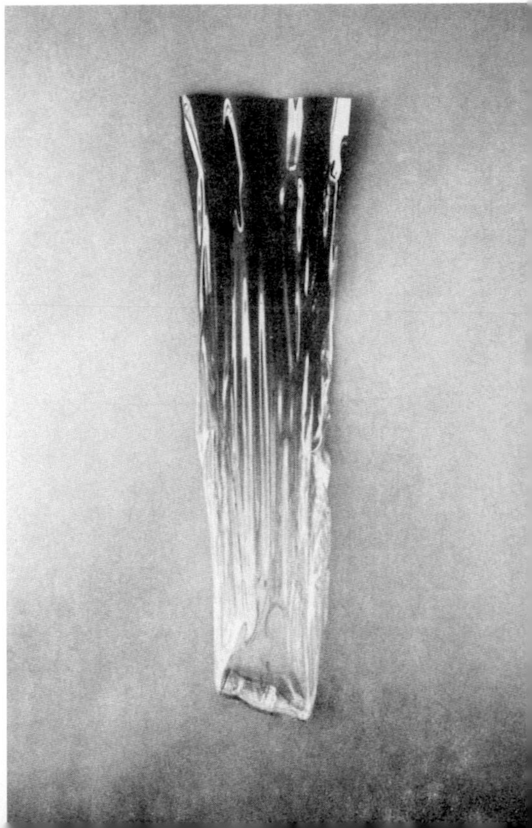

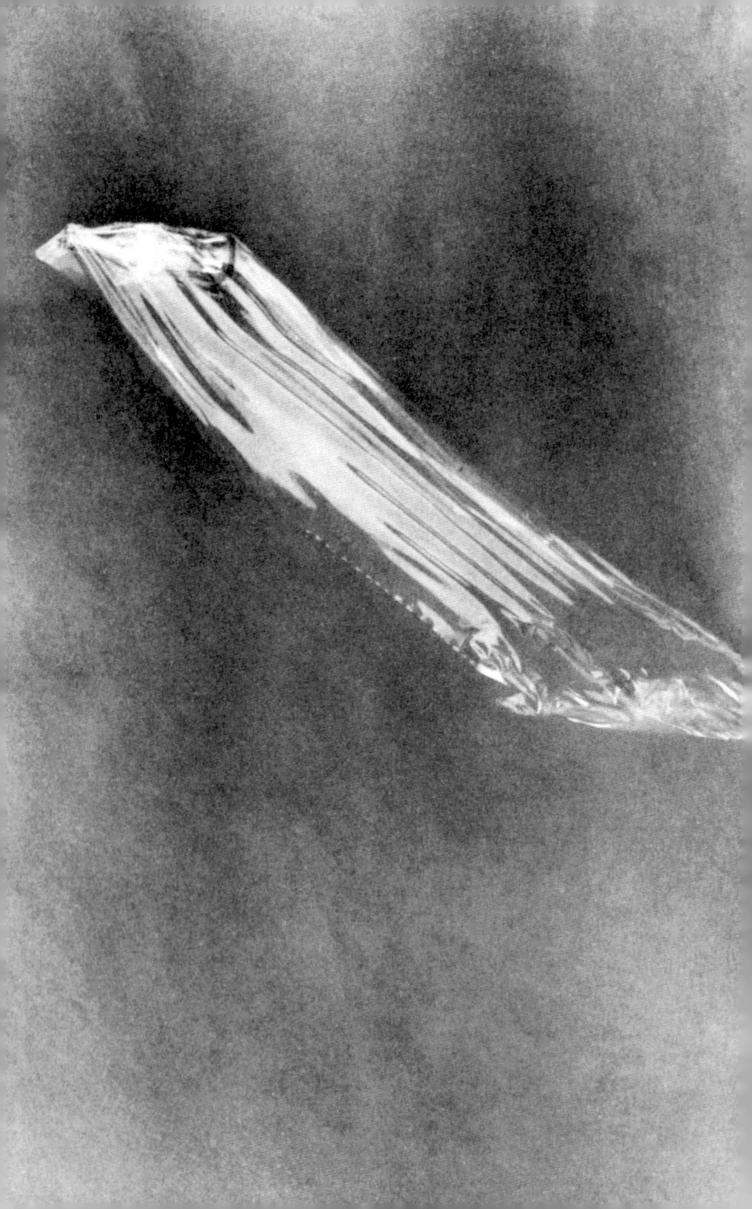

About When
6 June 1970
Polyvinyl chloride
and glass
19½"x 43½"x 3"
Destroyed 1970

62-57
Stretch tests

(62)
Green Lean test
24 May 1970
Polyvinyl chloride
and acrylic lacquer
74"x 16½"x 26"
Destroyed Nov. 1972

(61)
Test No. 3
24 May 1970
Polyvinyl chloride
34"x 23"x 1"
Destroyed Nov. 1972

(60)
Test No. 2
24 May 1970
Polyvinyl chloride
and acrylic lacquer
9½"x 10½"
Destroyed Nov. 1972

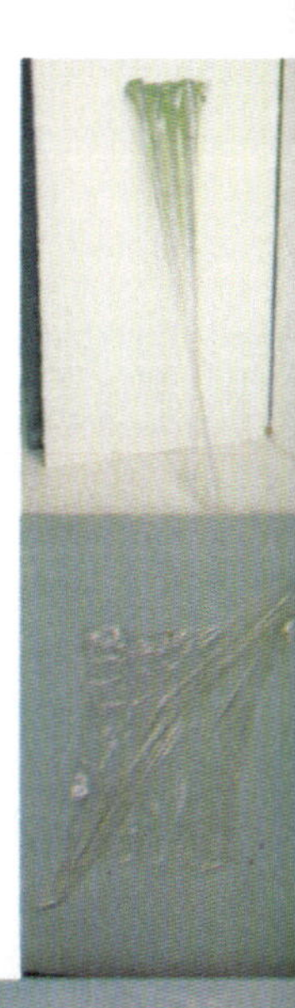

62-57 (continued)
Stretch tests

(59, far right)
Dark Event test
23 May 1970
Polyvinyl chloride
and acrylic lacquer
40¾″x 64½″x 5½″

(58)
Vertical clear with bolus
21 May 1970
Polyvinyl chloride
111″x 16″x 6″
Destroyed 22 Jan. 1971

(57)
Vertical clear
21 May 1970
Polyvinyl chloride
112″x 12″x 5″
Destroyed Nov. 1972

56 (not illustrated)
Five Paul, Jr. sketches
21 May 1970
Graphite on paper
25″x 20″ and 8⅜″x 6¼″
Three destroyed Nov. 1972

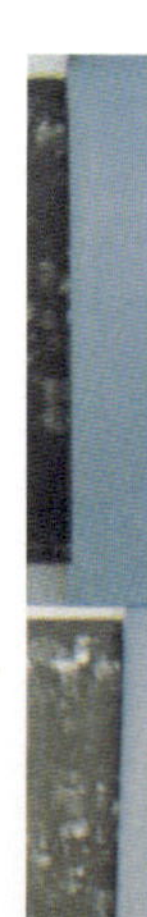

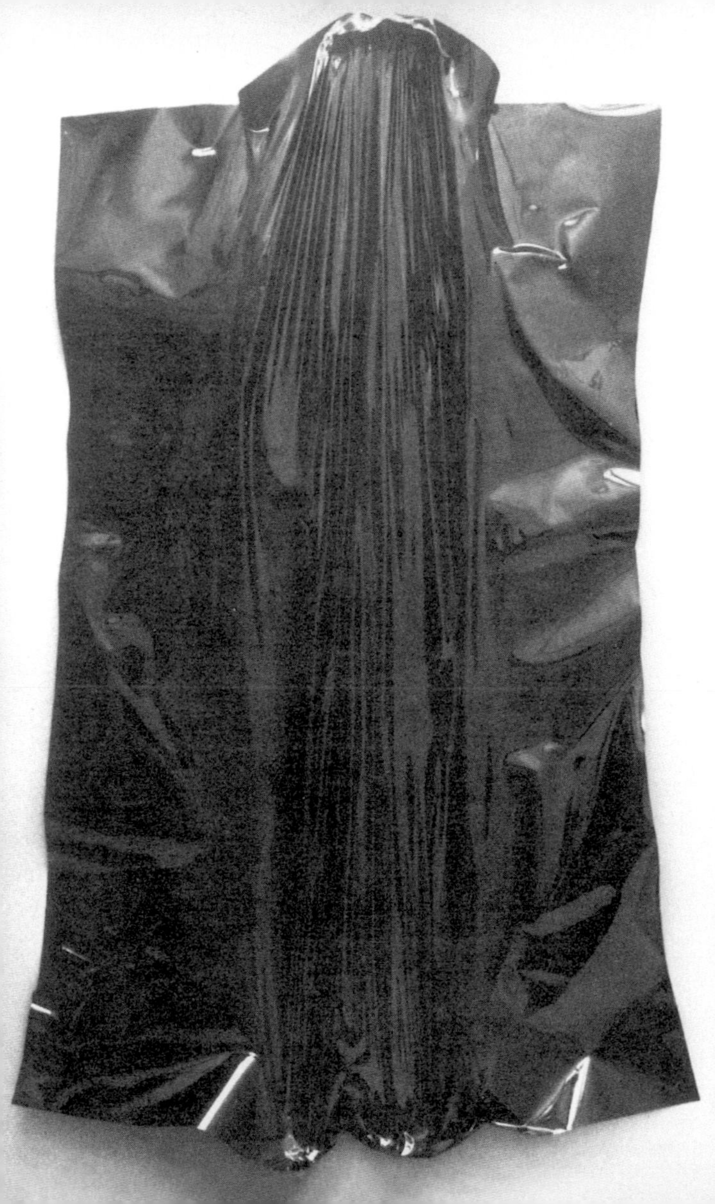

55
Time Was
18 May 1970
Acrylic on board
7½″ x 6″

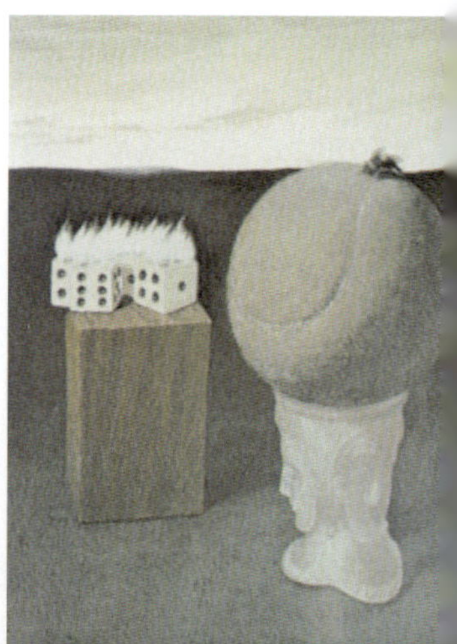

54-49
Various sketches

(54)
Large succulent plants
17 May 1970
Acrylic on paper
26"x 20"

(53)
Succulent plants
17 May 1970
Acrylic on paper
26"x 20"

(52, not illustrated)
Nude
17 May 1970
Acrylic on paper
26"x 20"

(51)
Four soup bowl sketches
16 May 1970
Acrylic on paper
All 26"x 20"

(50)
John Lennon's head
16 May 1970
Acrylic on paper
13"x 13" on 26"x 20"

(49)
Graduation rose
still life
11 May 1970
Acrylic on paper
26"x 20"

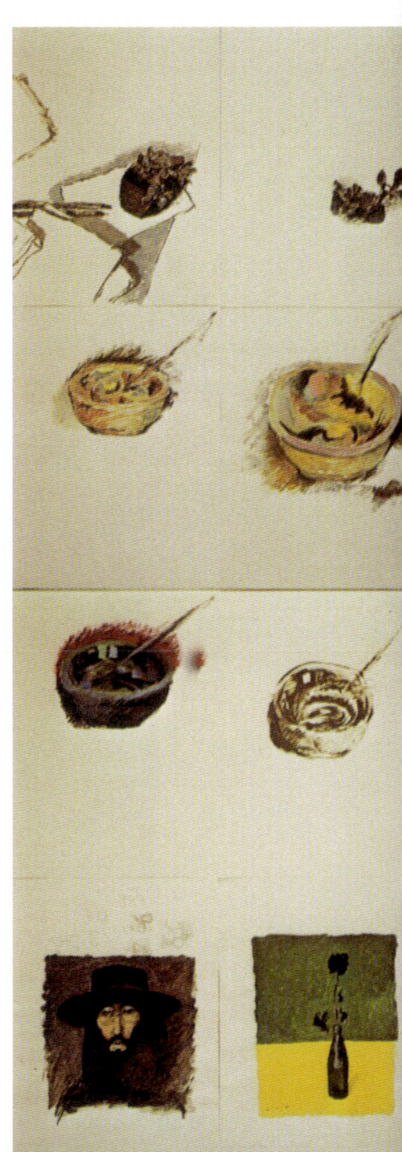

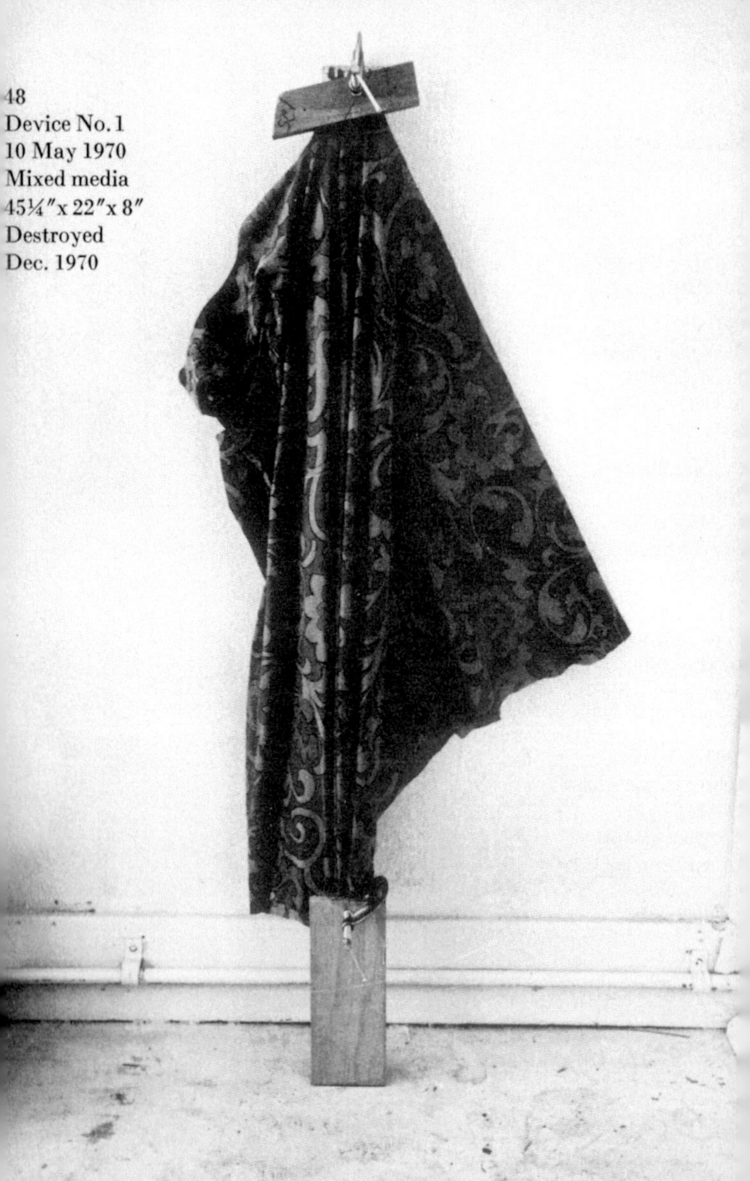

48
Device No.1
10 May 1970
Mixed media
45¼″x 22″x 8″
Destroyed
Dec. 1970

47-41
Various sketches, etc.

(47, not illustrated)
Avocado still life
26 April 1970
Acrylic on foam core board
8½″x 11″
Destroyed Nov. 1972

(46, not illustrated)
Sky Clouds and Sky Stretch
6 April 1970
Acrylic on canvas
18″x 36″ and 53¾″x 60″
Destroyed Aug. 1970

(45)
Lithographix poster
c. April 1970
Offset lithograph
29¼″x 23¼″

(44)
Two Colonel Chicken sketches
5 April 1970
Graphite on paper
Both 20″x 26″
One destroyed Nov. 1970

(43, not illustrated)
Two stretch drawings,
one with can
5 April 1970
Graphite on paper
Both 26″x 20″
Can destroyed Nov. 1972

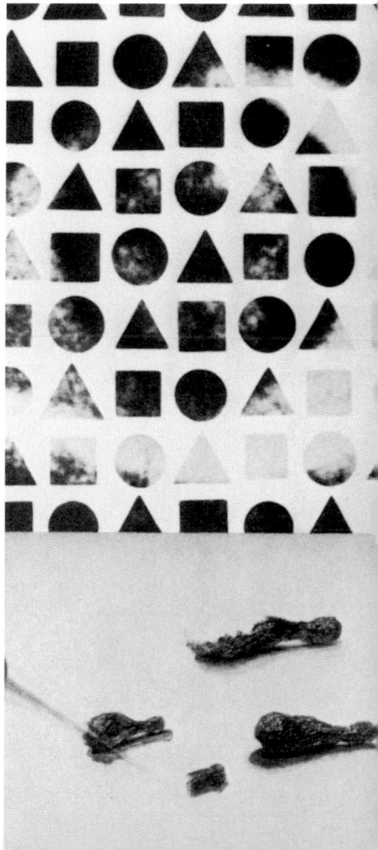

47-41 (continued)
Various sketches, etc.

(42, two illustrated)
Four stretch drawings
30 March and
3 April 1970
Graphite on paper
20″ x 26″

(41)
Jonquil I through XII
28 February 1970
Ink on paper
26″ x 20″
No. VIII, 26″ x 19″

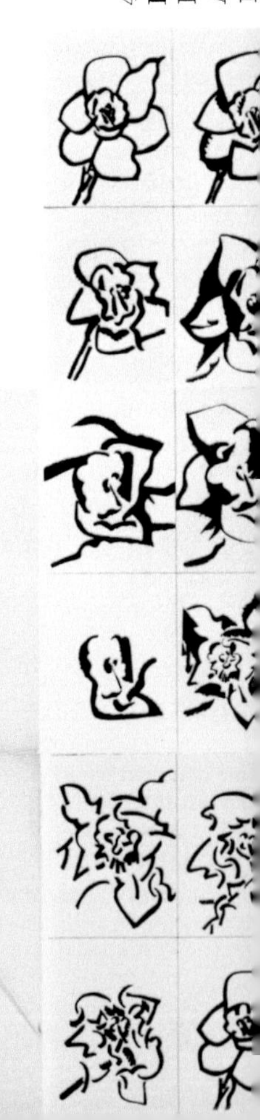

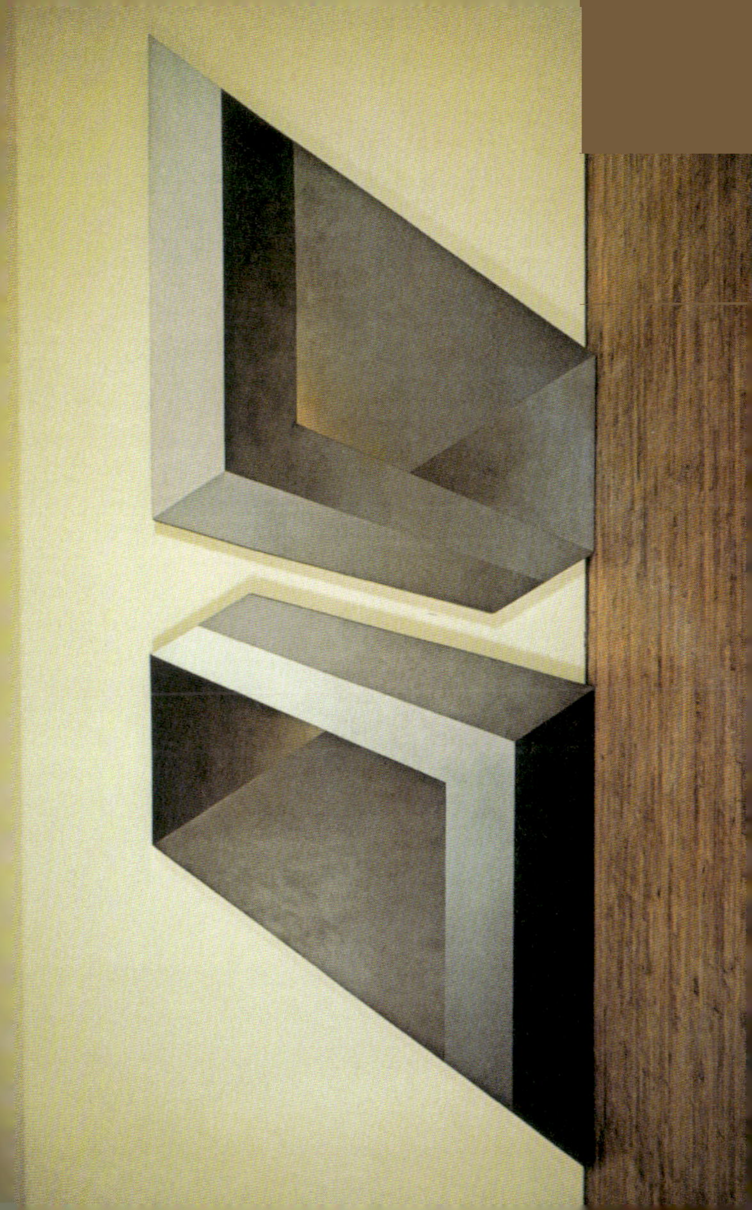

39
Cubist Sink
December 1969
Acrylic on canvas
96″ x 139½″

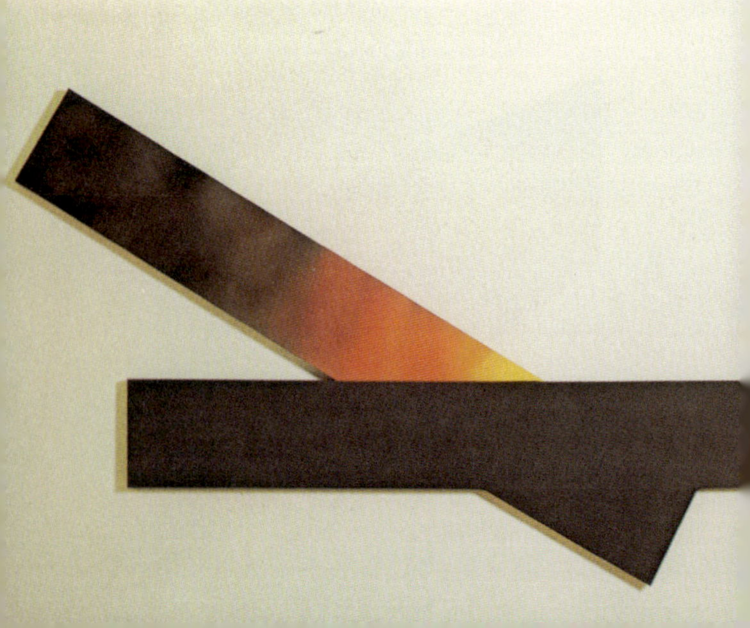

Football
December 1969
Acrylic on canvas
72″ x 73½″

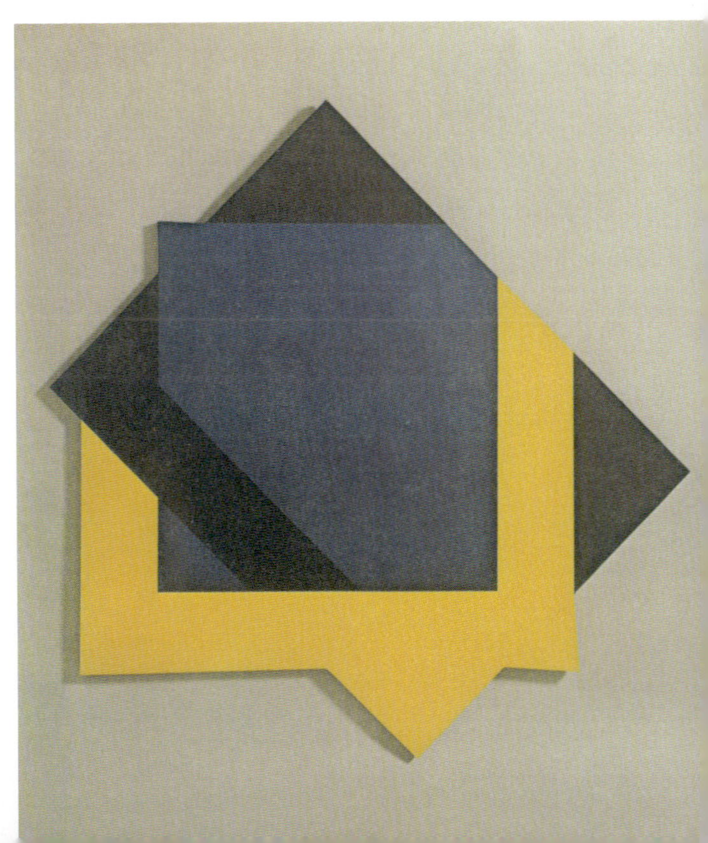

37
Hot Roll
December 1969
Acrylic on canvas
51¾″ x 72″

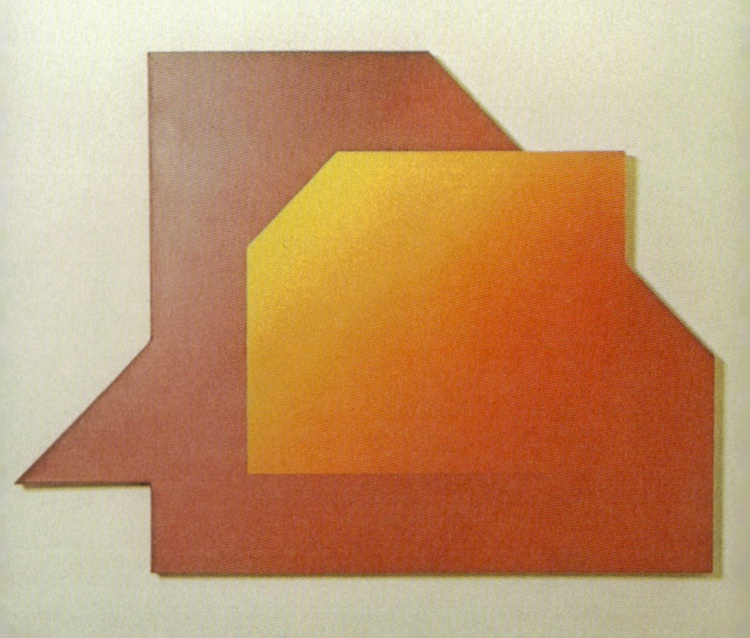

6
Right Turn Only (RTO)
December 1969
Acrylic on canvas
83″ x 74½″

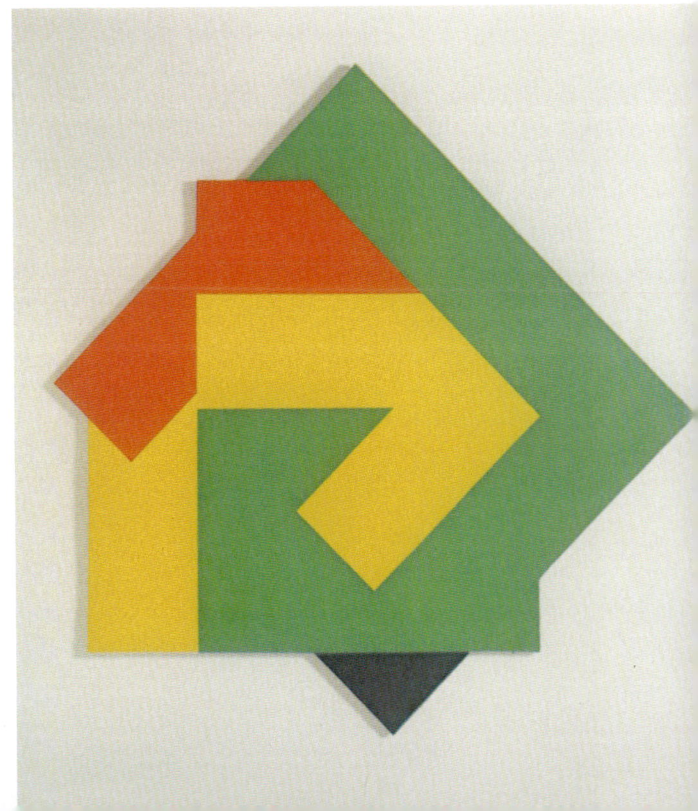

35
Blue Sink
December 1969
Acrylic on canvas
67½″ x 62½″

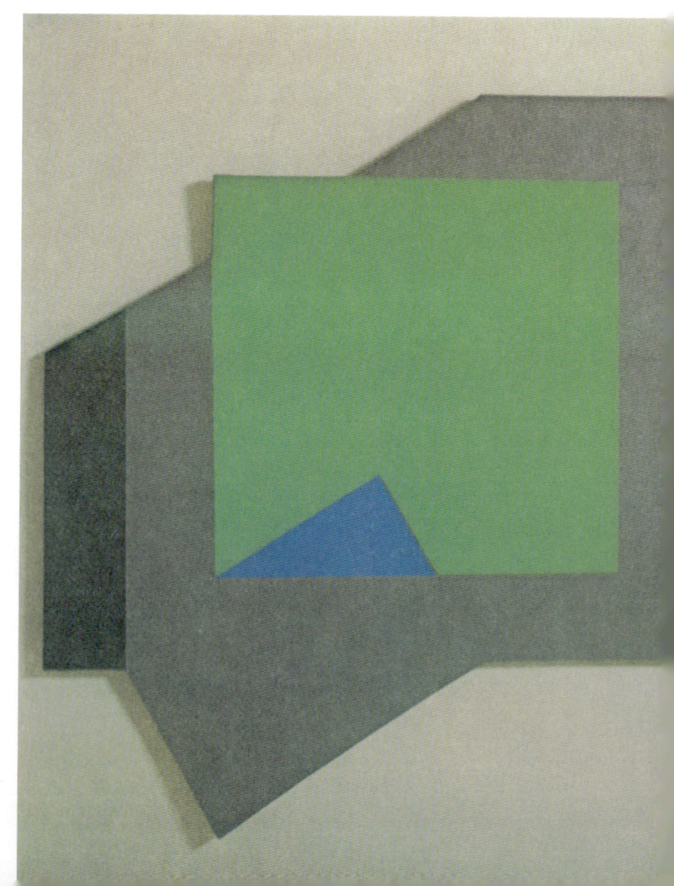

4
Football Fog
5 December 1969
Collage series of 3
6″x 20″

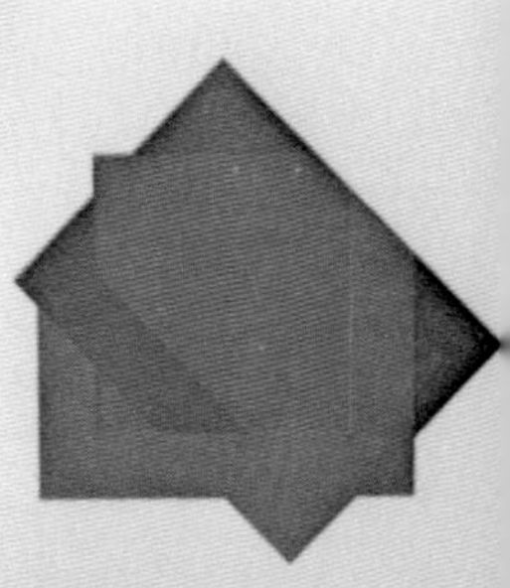

33
Hot Roll Sketch
December 1969
Serigraph
26"x 20"
Issue of 4

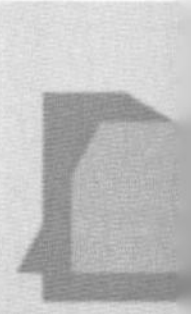

2
Blue Lou
December 1969
serigraph
6″ x 20″
issue of 9

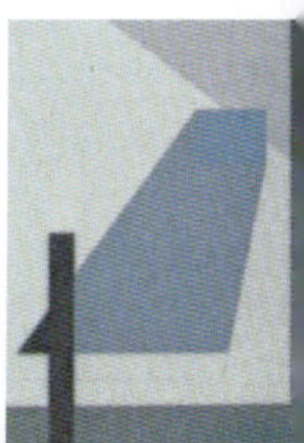

31
Dove Peace Poster
December 1969
Serigraph
26″x 20″
Issue of 10

30
Fe^2 grey, red, yellow, and yellow/blue
September to December 1969
Serigraphs, 17½"x 17½"
Issue 10 each of red and yellow,
7 each of yellow/blue and grey

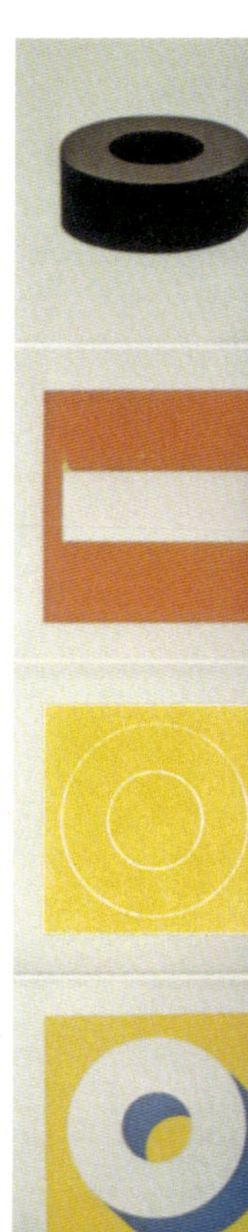

29
The Film and Modern Art poster
October 1969
Offset lithograph
23½″x 18″

28
Ecology 1 and 2
October 1969
Serigraphs on
plexiglass construction
17″x 18″

Ecology 2 study
(not illustrated)
September 1969
Serigraph, 26″x 20″
Issue of 2

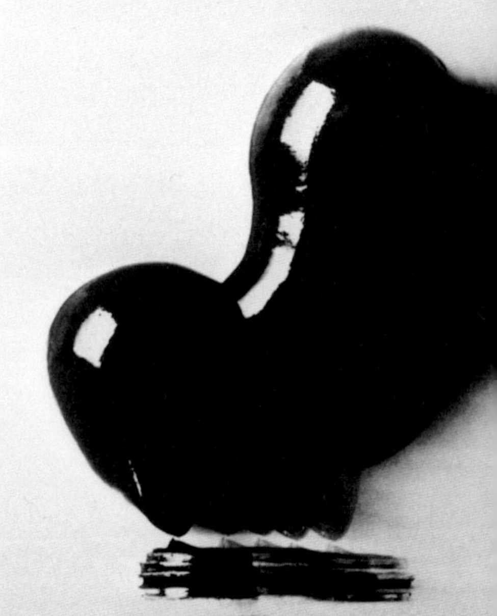

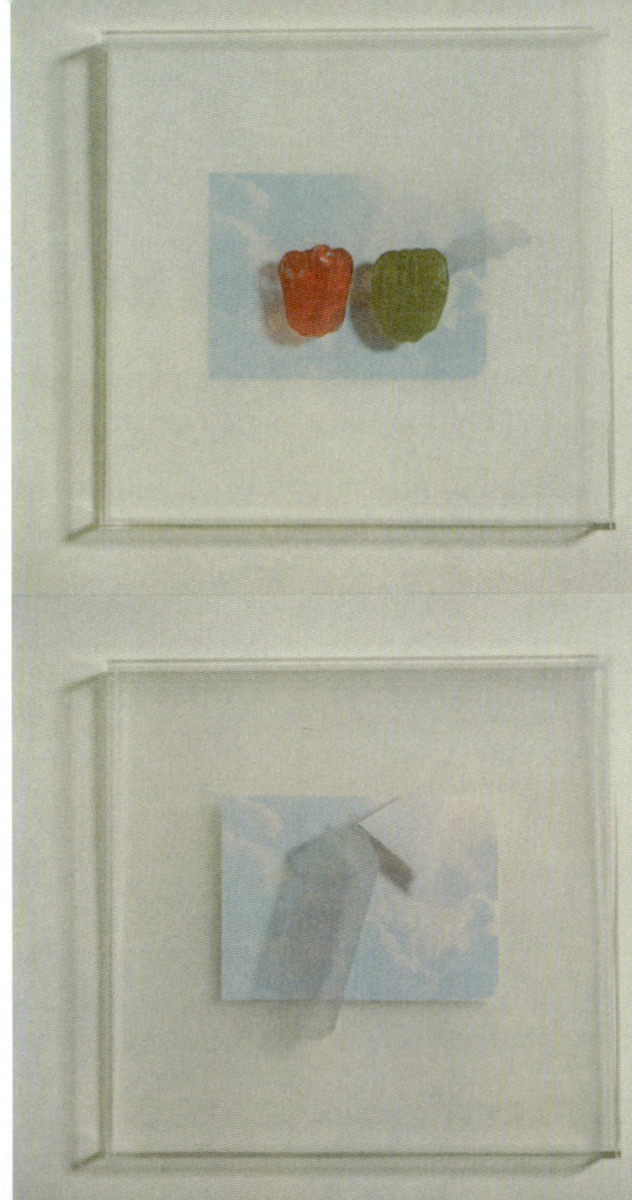

27
Adhesium
October 1969
Serigraph
20″ x 17½″
Issue of 18

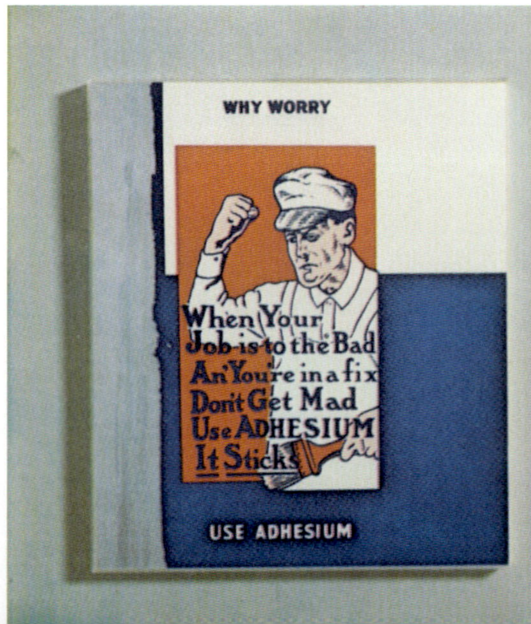

26
White Power
September 1969
Serigraph
26″x 20″
Issue of 4

25
Fe^2, 2a, 2b, 2c
September 1969
Serigraphs
17½″ x 17½″
Issue 6 each of 4

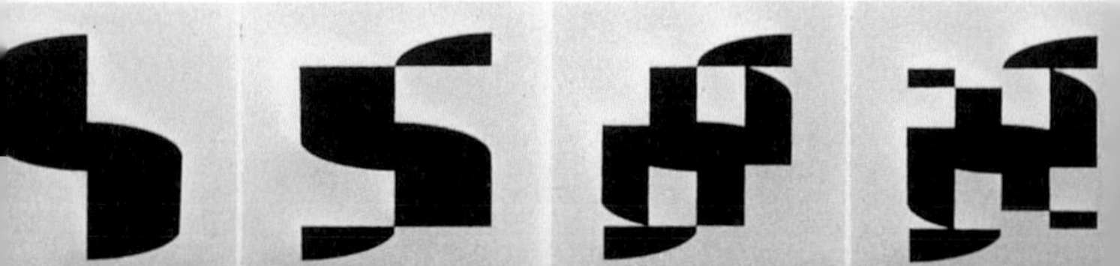

24
Great American Pepper
September 1969
Serigraph
26″x 20″ and 23⅝″x 17¼″
Issue of 10 in various
color combinations

23
Blue Oblique
September 1969
Serigraph
26″x 20″
Issue of 9

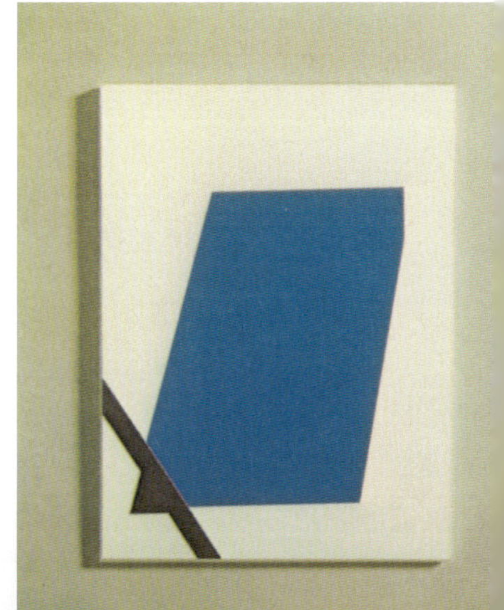

22
Yellow Twist
September 1969
Serigraph
20″ x 26″
Issue of 9

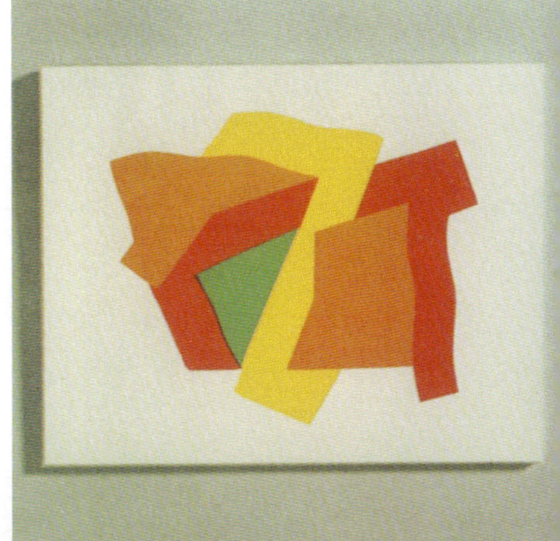

21
Green, Grey, Blue
(study for Blue Sink)
September 1969
Serigraph, 26"x 20"
Issue of 9

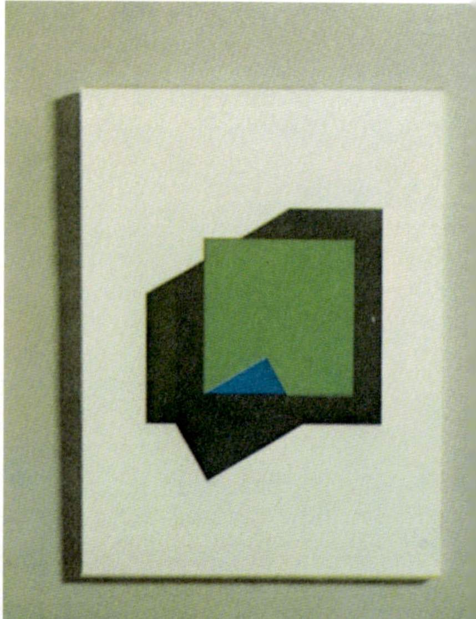

0
Five
September 1969
Serigraph and collage
44½″ x 35¼″
Five Components
in regular and
exploded views
(not illustrated)
September 1969
Serigraph
Both 13″ x 13″

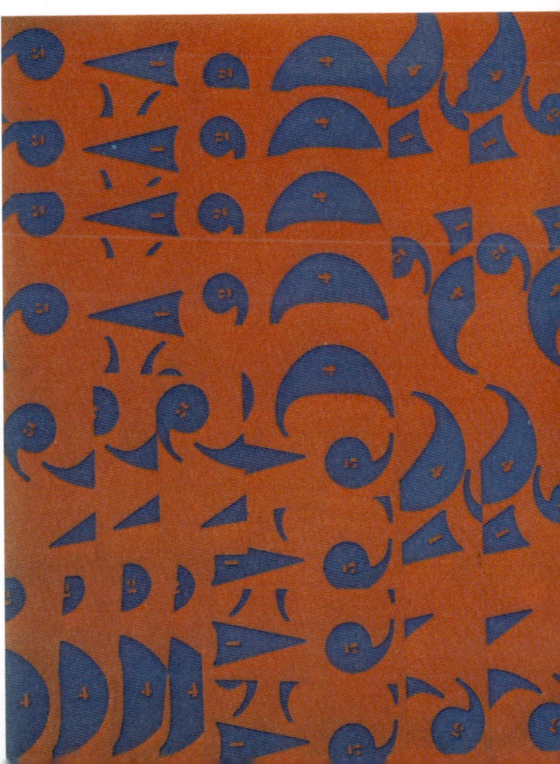

19
Chair drawings
August 1969
Graphite on paper
Both 19″x14¼″
Chair with Smoke
Chair with Clouds

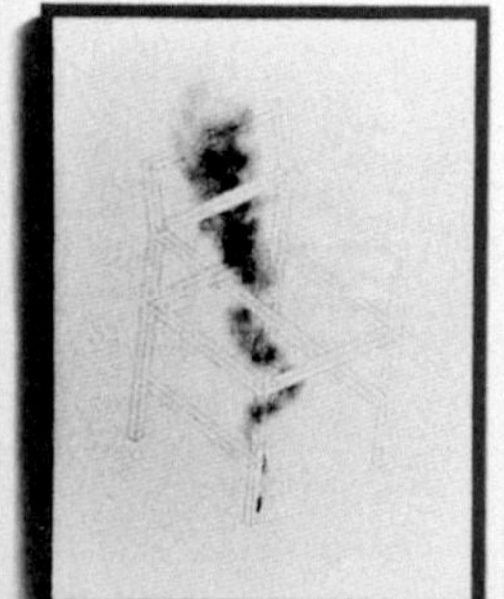

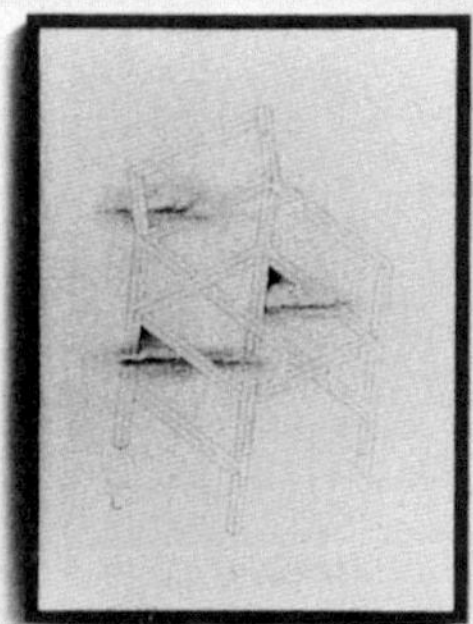

8
And Then There Was Pepper
August 1969
Acrylic on canvas
36" x 36"

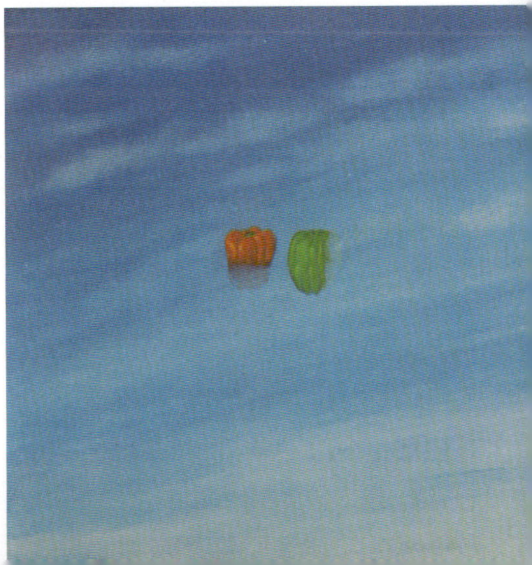

17
Spray Pepper
August 1969
Acrylic on canvas
18″x 22½″

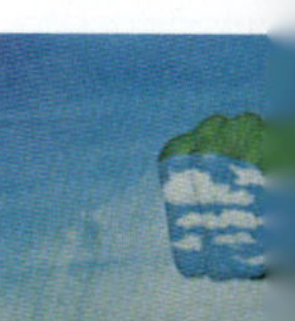

6
ilver
ugust 1969
erigraph
0″x 26″
ssue of 9

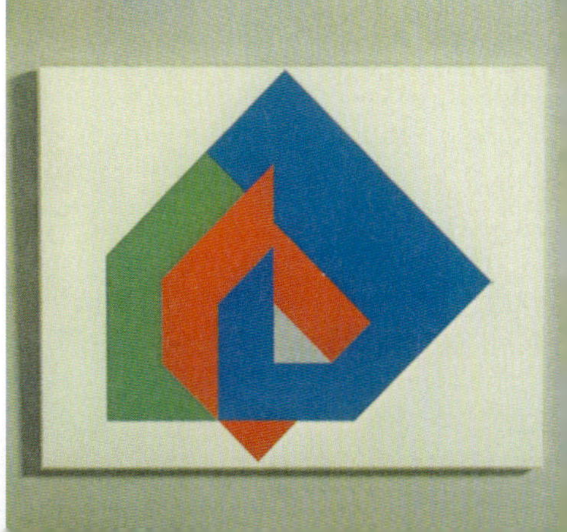

15
Space No. 9
(study for RTO)
August 1969
Serigraph
26″x 20″
Issue of 9

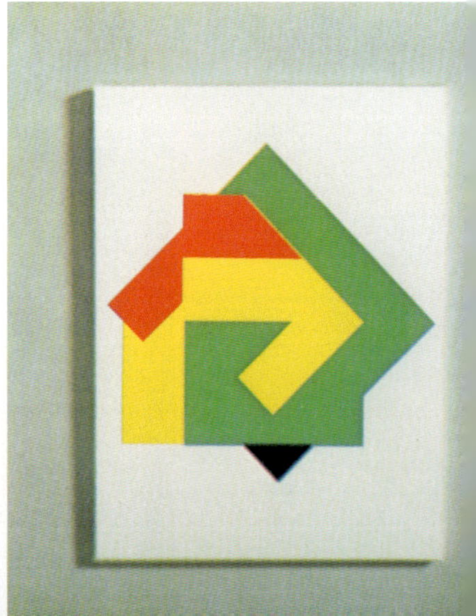

14
Space No. 8
August 1969
Acrylic on canvas
22½″ x 22½″

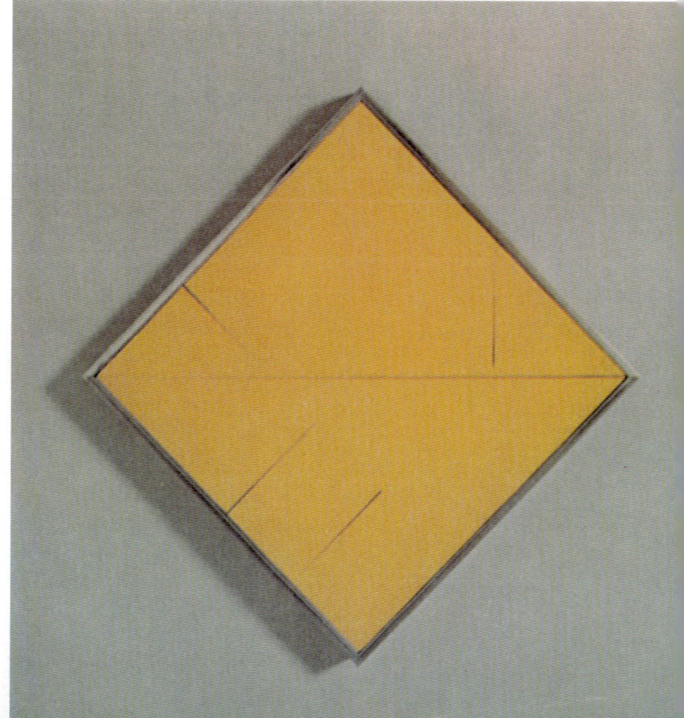

13
Space No. 7
August 1969
Acrylic on canvas
59"x 34"

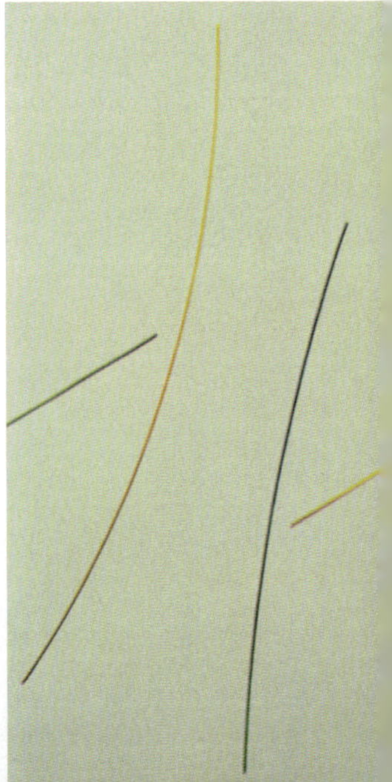

12
Klein's Tree
August 1969
Acrylic on canvas
36"x 36"

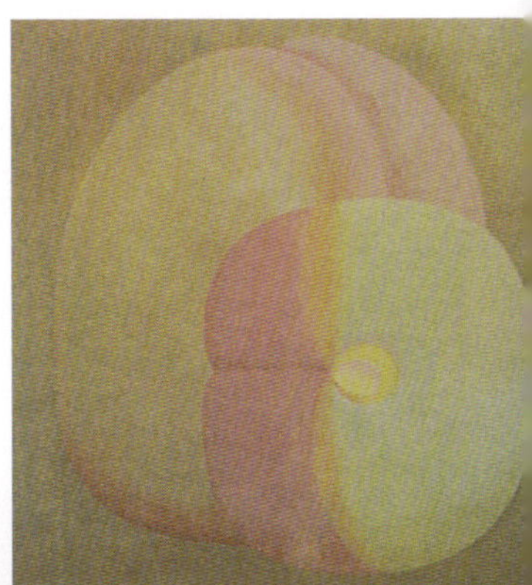

11
Pete's Pepper
August 1969
Acrylic on canvas
36"x 36"

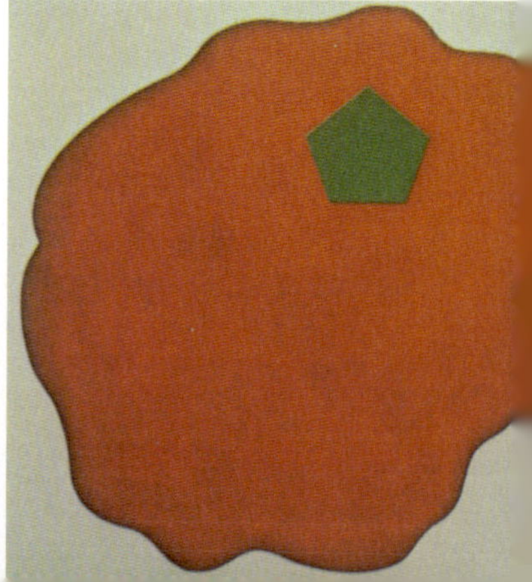

10
N
August 1969
Acrylic on canvas
48″x 48″

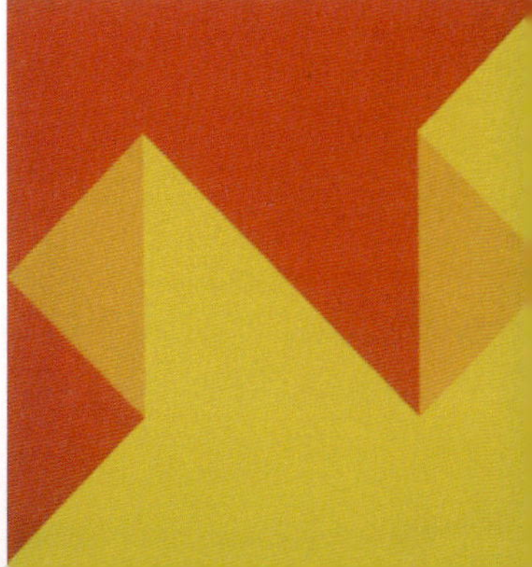

9
California Fruit Pack
August 1969
Acrylic on canvas
48″x 48″

8
Space No. 6
August 1969
Acrylic on canvas
48″x 48″

7
Space No. 5
August 1969
Acrylic on canvas
48″x 48″

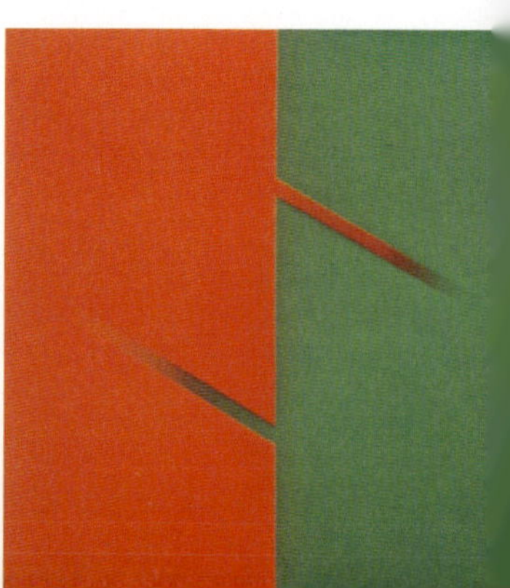

Giant Natural Protruding Rock
July 1969
Acrylic on canvas
48″ x 48″

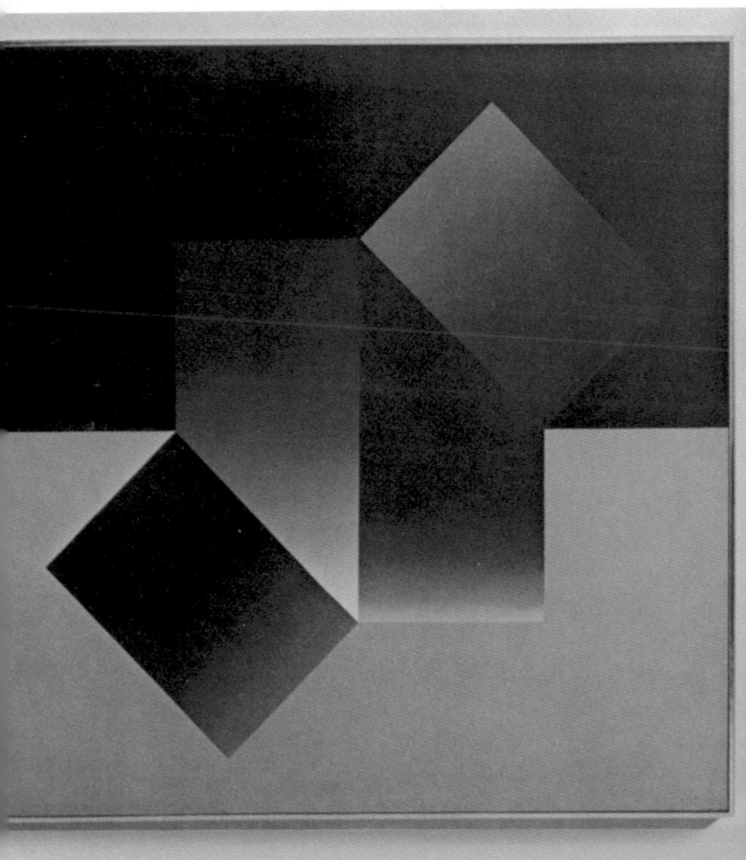

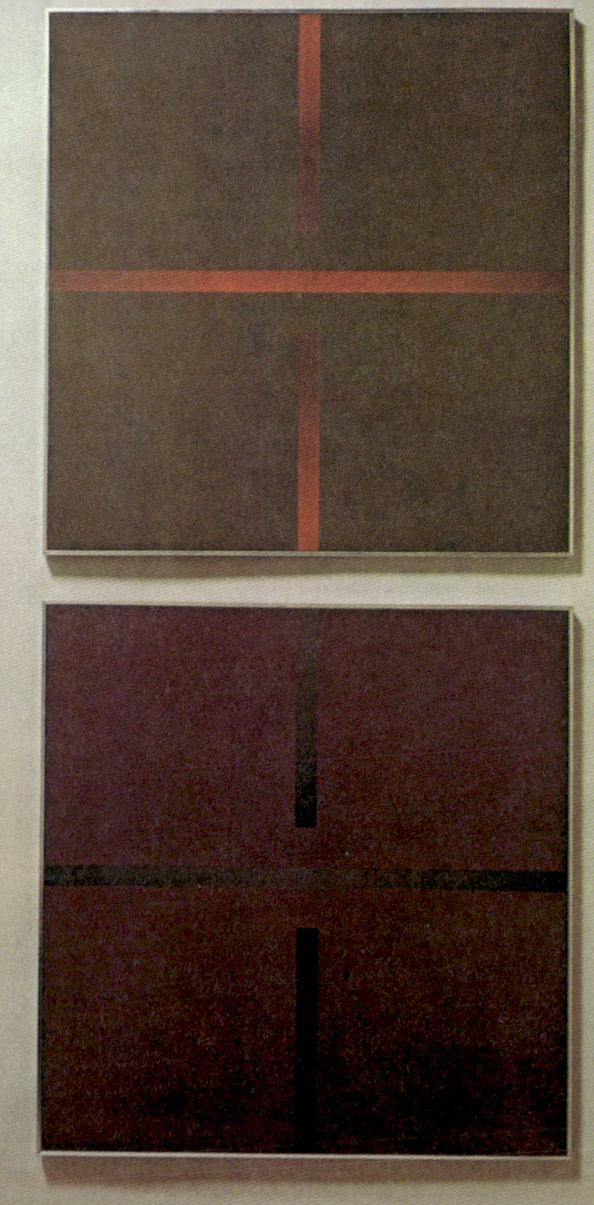

3 (right)
Space No. 4
July 1969
Acrylic on canvas
48"x 48"

4
Space No. 3
July 1969
Acrylic on canvas
48"x 48"

3
Space No. 2
July 1969
Acrylic on canvas
48″x 48″

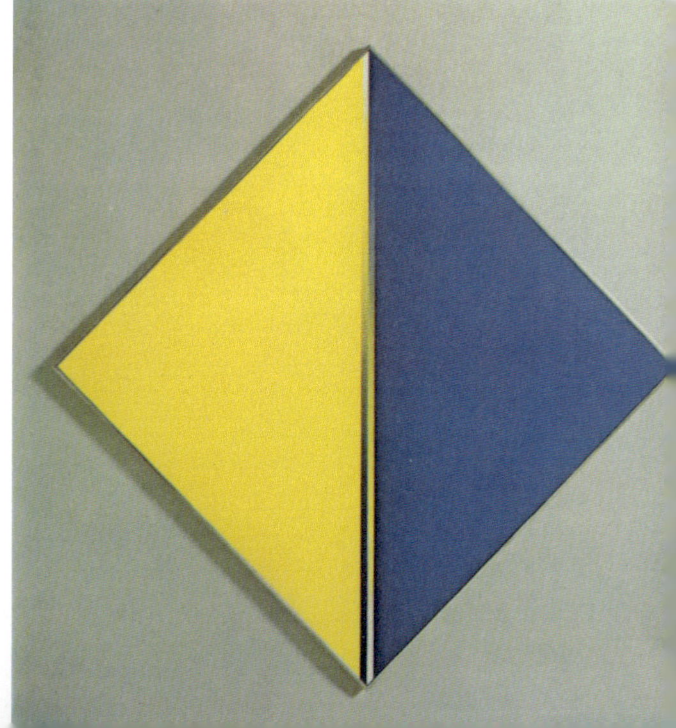

Hello Joe, Howdy Ed
July 1969
Acrylic on canvas
8″ x 48″

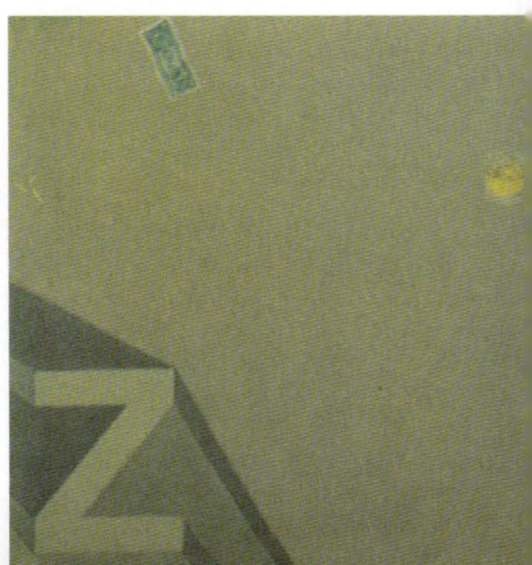

1
Space No. 1
July 1969
Acrylic on canvas
48″x 48″

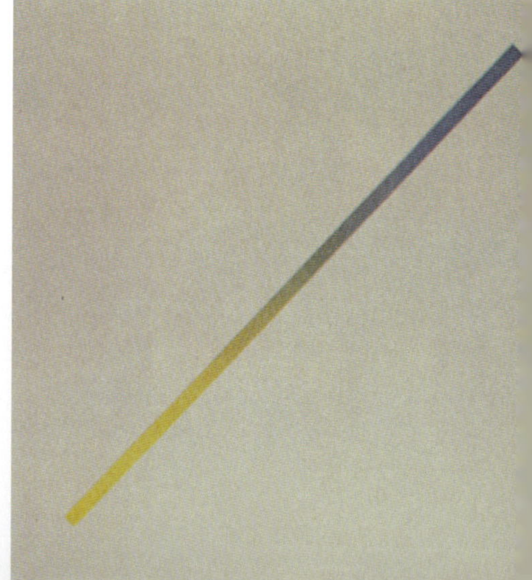